AMERICAN BIBLE SOCIETY

THE AMAZING BIBLE FACTBOOK for kids

D0113430

The Amazing Bible Factbook for Kids
Published in association with The Livingstone Corporation and The American Bible Society

American Bible Society
Nida Institute for Biblical Scholarship
Project Editor: Eric Yost
Contributing Editors: Barbara Bernstengel, Steve Berneking, Charles Houser

Time Inc. Home Entertainment
Publisher: Richard Fraiman
General Manager: Steven Sandonato
Executive Director, Marketing Services: Carol Pittard
Director, Retail & Special Sales: Tom Mifsud
Director, New Product Development: Peter Harper
Assistant Director, Brand Marketing: Laura Adam
Associate Counsel: Helen Wan
Senior Brand Manager, TWRS/M: Holly Oakes
Brand & Licensing Manager: Alexandra Bliss
Design & Prepress Manager: Anne-Michelle Gallero
Book Production Manager: Susan Chodakiewicz
Special Thanks: Glenn Buonocore, Margaret Hess, Suzanne Janso, Robert Marasco, Brooke Reger, Mary Sarro-Waite, Ilene Schreider, Adriana Tierno, Alex Voznesenskiy

The Livingstone Corporation
Visit our Web site at www.livingstonecorp.com.
Editors: Betsy Schmitt and Linda Washington
Support Staff: Lois Jackson, Will Reaves
Contributors: Erika Allen, Geoff Allen, Andrew Apel, Mary Horner Collins, Jeanette Dall, Katy Duffield, Betsy Elliott, Christine Erickson, Linda DeVries Frey, Heidi Krumenauer, Wendy Lanier, Sherry Lenhart, Linda MacKillop, Mark Nesbitt, Carrie Pyykkonen, Betsy Schmitt, Pamela Venneman, Linda Washington, Colleen Yang, Eric Yost

Designed by Larry Taylor, Diane Bay, Lindsay Galvin, Mark Helmke, Russ Peterson, Becky Sells, Mark Wainwright, John Wollinka

Cover designed by Larry Taylor, The Livingstone Corporation

The Mission of the American Bible Society is to make the Bible available to every person in a language and format each can understand and afford, so all people may experience its life-changing message.

The American Bible Society's Eugene A. Nida Institute for Biblical Scholarship is committed to exploring innovative ways of bringing biblical, cultural, anthropological, and linguistic scholarship to the practice of translating and understanding the Bible. The Nida Institute partners internationally with churches and organizations to communicate the relevance of the Scriptures to contemporary society. Visit our Web site at: www.nidainstitute.org.

ISBN 13: 978-1-60320-778-2
ISBN 10: 1-60320-778-3

We welcome your comments and suggestions about *The Amazing Bible Factbook for Kids.*
Please write to us at:
The Amazing Bible Factbook for Kids
Attention: Book Editors
PO Box 11016
Des Moines, IA 50336-1016

If you would like to order any of our hardcover Collector's Edition books, please call us at 1-800-327-6388.
(Monday through Friday, 7:00 a.m. – 8:00 p.m. or Saturday, 7:00 a.m. – 6:00 p.m. Central Time).

CONTENTS

What Are Angels?

You can find out a lot about angels in the Bible. Angels are powerful, super-smart spirits that obey God's every command in an instant and live to praise God (Psalm 103:20-21; Psalm 148:2; Matthew 26:53). There are different kinds of angels: cherubim, guardian angels, and archangels. Daniel 4:13 calls them "watchers." Scriptures like Psalm 91:11 and Matthew 18:10-11 mention that people have guardian angels. Some angels know all the world's languages (Revelation 14:6-7). The angels we see most often in the Bible are messengers.

Types of Angels

Cherubim

Four cherubim (plural for *cherub*) are described as "winged creatures" in Ezekiel 10:1. A cherub and a sword of fire kept Adam and Eve out of Eden in Genesis 3:24. If you think a cherub is scary, check out that fiery sword: it was waving itself around! The curtain of the sacred tent (or tabernacle— Exodus 26:1) and the sacred chest (or ark of the covenant —Exodus 25:18-20) were decorated with cherubim.

iStock.com

How to Spot a Cherub

• Huge crossed wheels covered in eyes surround a cherub, whirling inside each other (Ezekiel 10:12-13).
• A cherub has four faces (one like a man, one like a lion, one like an eagle and one like an ox) (Ezekiel 1:5-6, 10-12).
• A cherub has four wings— two touch the other cherubs and two hang down covering its human hands (Ezekiel 1:5-6).
• A cherub has straight legs that sparkle like bronze and has hooves like a calf (Ezekiel 1:7).
• A cherub "shines like chyrsolite" (a greenish stone) (Ezekiel 1:16).

Note about Cherubim

C.S. Lewis, the author of the *Chronicles of Narnia*, wrote in his book *The Screwtape Letters* that in the Bible an angel almost always has to say "Fear Not!" when it meets a person. He said the pictures we mostly see of angels make them look like they want to say "There, there." Angels are not fat little babies. Take a look at Ezekiel chapter 1 for a scary sight of God's heavenly servants. These powerful angels are the cherubim! The sound of their strong steely wings was like an army and a flood of water. It was so loud it could be heard blocks away.

iStock.com

Seraphim

A seraph is a fiery burning angel (Isaiah 6:6). The name *seraph* comes from a Hebrew word, *saraph*, that means "burning." When you see the word seraphim (plural for *seraph*) in the Bible, it means "burning ones." When Isaiah says he has unclean lips, a seraph touches his lips with a holy burning coal to clean him (Isaiah 6:7). Seraphim shout so loud in Isaiah 6:4 that they shake the temple.

HOW TO SPOT A SERAPH

The seraphim have six wings— two to cover their faces, two to cover their feet, and two to fly with (Isaiah 6:2).

Saraph (Seraph) is the name that the Israeli Air Force calls its Boeing AH-64D Apache Longbow attack helicopters.

Archangels

Ever heard of an "archenemy"? That means your biggest enemy. The prefix *arch* can mean "prince," "highest," or "chief." There is only one angel in the Bible named as an archangel— Michael (Jude 9). (The prefix arch in this word is pronounced ark-angel.) Some people believe that Gabriel is an archangel as well, because Michael comes to help him fight an evil angel, the Prince of Persia, in Daniel 10:13. In that chapter Gabriel tells Daniel that Michael is the "chief prince."

When Jesus returns, there will be a trumpet blast and a loud shout, the voice of the archangel (1 Thessalonians 4:16).

HOW TO SPOT AN ARCHANGEL

Stock Exchange

Messenger Angels

Angels are God's messengers. The word angel comes from a Greek word: *angelos*. Angels can deliver their messages in person or in a dream like the one Jacob had in Genesis 28:10-15, or the one Mary's husband Joseph had, in which the angel told him to name Mary's son Jesus (Matthew 1:20-21).

We first see the angel Gabriel in a vision that Daniel has in Daniel 8:16. Gabriel is most famous for telling Mary that she would be the mother of Jesus in Luke 1:26-38. The angels told the shepherds in Bethlehem that Jesus had been born, and then the angels said praises to God (Luke 2:8-14).

Bigstock.com

5

Other Descriptions of Angels in the Bible

God's Stars

Angels are also called "stars" in Revelation 1:20. Stars are a symbol of the burning brightness of messenger angels. Stars guide travelers and are messengers of changing seasons. Stars give light. God used a star in the east to give the three wise men a message that Jesus was born (Matthew 2:1-2).

The Annunciation (central panel from the Mérode Altarpiece), Robert Campin (1425-1428)

Angel of the LORD

In the Old Testament many people saw the "angel of the LORD" (or the "angel of God"). You can tell the difference in the Old Testament between an ordinary angel and the angel of the LORD. The angel of God speaks and acts directly for God.

Many of those who saw the angel of the LORD said that they had seen God. Others fell down to worship him. People are not allowed to worship angels, and an angel from heaven will always tell a human not to worship him, but to worship God.

Warrior Angels

Angels are the original superheroes. They are warriors sent by God to carry out his judgment.

✻ Revelation 8:1-2 tells us there are seven angels who stand before God. These angels later pour out God's judgment at the end of time (and it's no fun for anybody when they do it).

✻ In 2 Kings 19:35 the proud Assyrian king, Sennacherib, surrounded Israel with his army. An angel from God killed one hundred eighty-five thousand of them. The Assyrians left quickly!

✻ Michael is the highest of the archangels and is called a chief prince of the heavenly army (Daniel 10:13). His name means "who is like God."

PEOPLE WHO MET THE ANGEL OF THE LORD

Genesis 18:1-10; 22:11-16	**Abraham**
Numbers 22:22-35	**Balaam**
Judges 6:11-24	**Gideon**
Genesis 16:7-12	**Hagar**
Judges 2:1-5	**The Israelites**
Genesis 31:11; 32:24-30; Hosea 12:4	**Jacob**
Joshua 5:13-15	**Joshua**
Exodus 3:2	**Moses**
Daniel 3:23-28	**Shadrach, Meshach, Abednego, and Babylon's King Nebuchadnezzar**

Hosts of Heaven

With angels, the word host can mean either an army of angels or a very large number of them. In Genesis 28:11-12 Jacob had a dream from God where he saw angels going up and down on a ladder between heaven and earth. Another place we see the "heavenly host" is when they appear to shepherds to announce Jesus' birth (Luke 2:13-14). Jesus said he would return with a host of angels to judge the earth (Matthew 25:31).

The Songs of Angels

In heaven there are millions of angels who stand by God's throne and sing his praises at all times. Here are a few places you can find what they said in praise.

Reference	Song
Isaiah 6:3	"Holy, holy, holy, LORD All-Powerful! The earth is filled with your glory."
Luke 2:13-14	"Praise God in heaven! Peace on earth to everyone who pleases God."
Revelation 4:8	"Holy, holy, holy is the Lord, the all-powerful God, who was and is and is coming!"
Revelation 5:12	"The Lamb who was killed is worthy to receive power, riches, wisdom, strength, honor, glory, and praise."
Revelation 7:11-12	"Amen! Praise, glory, wisdom, thanks, honor, power, and strength belong to our God forever and ever! Amen!"

Stock Exchange

More Angel Appearances

The Annunciation, Henry Ossawa Tanner (1898)

Exodus 14:19-20	The angel of God is a pillar of cloud by day and a pillar of fire by night to protect and guide the Israelites after leaving Egypt.
Judges 13:2-20	The angel of the LORD tells Samson's parents about their son, a future judge of Israel.
1 Kings 19:5-8	An angel brings food to the prophet Elijah.
Matthew 4:11	Angels help Jesus after he is tempted.
Matthew 28:1-8	An angel appears at the tomb of Jesus to announce his resurrection.
Luke 1:11-20	Gabriel announces the upcoming birth of John the Baptist to Zechariah.
Acts 1:11	Angels tell Jesus' disciples that Jesus has returned to heaven.
Acts 8:26	The angel of the Lord gives the apostle Philip direction.
Acts 10:1-7	An angel tells Cornelius, a captain of soldiers and a religious man, about Peter.
Acts 12:6-11	The angel of the Lord frees the apostle Peter from prison.
Acts 12:20-23	The angel of the Lord strikes down King Herod of Judea.

ANIMALS

Wild Mammals

ANTELOPE

You've probably seen antelopes running free on nature documentaries and in animated movies like *The Lion King*. Antelopes were mentioned in Deuteronomy 14:4-5 in a list of the animals the Israelites were allowed to eat according to the Law of Moses.

BEAR

Though the bears that were found in the ancient Near East in biblical times were not as large as the grizzly and polar bears you've probably seen in the zoo, they were still greatly feared by all who encountered them. Read 2 Kings 2:23-25 to find out what two bears did to some boys who made fun of God's prophet, Elisha.

Bigstock.com

FOX

Nehemiah, a personal servant of the Persian King Artaxerxes, was given permission to rebuild the walls of Jerusalem. During the rebuilding, Nehemiah's enemies gave him a hard time—they said the wall was so flimsy, even a little old fox could knock it down (Nehemiah 4:3). But Nehemiah and his workers didn't flinch. They trusted in God, and fifty-two days later the wall was complete (Nehemiah 6:15).

HARE

The hare is a member of the rabbit family. Like other animals without divided hoofs, hares were considered unclean and not to be eaten (Leviticus 11:6).

iStock.com

HIPPOPOTAMUS

In the wild, hippos eat an average of almost ninety pounds of grass each night. Talk about your giant lawnmower! In some Bible versions, the hippo was known as a Behemoth (Job 40:15-24).

Bigstock.com

LEOPARD

Did you know the markings on leopards' backs are called rosettes? In the book of Jeremiah, God used the leopard as an object lesson to talk about whether it's possible for people to change and do what's right. What do you think? *Can* a leopard change its spots (Jeremiah 13:23)?

LION

A group of jealous men got God's faithful follower Daniel thrown into a pit filled with ferocious lions. The pit's opening was covered with a stone, and these evil men expected Daniel to be the lions' lunch. But no! God saved Daniel from the lions. Read more in Daniel 6.

MONKEY

You could say King Solomon of Israel had it all—the finest jewels, harps, gold, 1,400 chariots, 12,000 horses, and much, much more. Every three years, Solomon sent out his ships to bring back even more treasures—and these interesting treasures included monkeys and peacocks (1 Kings 10:22)!

RAM

To test his chosen follower Abraham's faith, God told him to sacrifice his own son. Just before the sacrifice was carried out, an angel stopped Abraham; then he sacrificed a ram caught in the bushes by its horns instead (Genesis 22:13).

WOLF

Many books and movies today have tried to correct the bad reputation wolves have had over the centuries. But in the Bible, wolves were used as word pictures of human predators. False prophets (those who claimed to speak for God, but who led people away from truth) were described by Jesus as "wolves" who prey on the sheep, the people of God (Matthew 7:15). Maybe that's why the apostle Paul warned believers to be on the lookout for "fierce wolves" (Acts 20:29).

iStock.com

BIRDS

iStock.com

Chicken

When Nehemiah was governor of Judah, instead of charging people for their food, he kept them well fed. He needed his people to be strong while they worked to rebuild the walls of Jerusalem. Think they ate chicken? Find out in Nehemiah 5:17-19.

Goose

In ancient times, Egyptians considered the goose a sacred creature. They thought the spirit of a god lived in the animals. Honk! Honk! Geese are mentioned in 1 Kings 4:23 as a mark of the wealth of Solomon's kingdom.

Dove

Noah used a dove to help him find out if the waters from the flood had receded. Find out how the dove helped him—read Genesis 8:8-12.

Hawk

Red-tailed hawk babies learn to swoop down and catch food in midair when their parents drop it for them. In Isaiah 46:11, Israel's enemies are described as attacking them "like a hawk swooping down."

Quail

When the Israelites roamed the wilderness after leaving Egypt, they grumbled and complained that they had no meat to eat—only manna (a special food God provided for them). So God helped out in a BIG way by sending them so many quail that the birds were stacked up three feet high (Numbers 11:31)!

Eagle

The eagle is mentioned several times in the Bible as a word picture of renewed strength (Isaiah 40:31) or of God's protection (Exodus 19:4; Deuteronomy 32:11-12). The eagles mentioned in the Bible might have been imperial eagles, golden eagles, or spotted eagles.

Ostrich

God often talked to Job, a good man who respected God, by asking him questions and making Job think. In Job 39, God compares Job's foolishness to that of an ostrich's (Job 39:13-18).

9

DOMESTIC MAMMALS

CAMEL

You've probably seen camels in the zoo or in a living nativity performance. Camels were the largest animal in Palestine and are mentioned in many places in the Bible. Because camels carried goods over long distances, they were known as "ships of the desert." One of the most quoted verses about camels is Mark 10:25: "It's easier for a camel to go through the eye of a needle than for a rich person to get into God's kingdom." When the Queen of Sheba visited Solomon, king of Israel, she packed up her camels with all sorts of gifts. To see what she took, read 1 Kings 10:2. (Read more about these amazing pack animals in Transportation, p. 222).

iStock.com

CATTLE

In the Bible, cattle were mentioned as signs of wealth or blessing. We're told about the "cattle on a thousand hills" that belong to God (Psalm 50:10). In a dream that the Pharaoh of Egypt during Joseph's time had, he saw seven "fat, healthy cows" followed by seven "ugly, skinny cows" (Genesis 41:1-4). This dream meant that Egypt would have seven years of good harvests and healthy livestock followed by seven years of famine.

Bigstock.com

DOG

God told the judge Gideon and leader of the Israelites to take his soldiers to a creek and to separate them into two groups—those who lapped up water like dogs and those who drank water from their hand. Which soldiers do you think God told Gideon to send home? Why? (Judges 7:4-7)

Bigstock.com

GOAT

Do you know where the word "scapegoat" comes from? In Old Testament times, the high priest would lay his hand on the head of a live goat and confess the sins of the people. Then the goat would be led into the desert so all the sins would be taken away (Leviticus 16:20-22).

DONKEY

In biblical times, people often rode donkeys or used them to carry their packs. In Jesus' parable (a story with an important meaning), the "Good Samaritan" used his donkey to help the man who was injured by thieves (Luke 10:34). Jesus rode into Jerusalem on a donkey (Mark 11:1-11).

LAMB

God told Moses that the people of Israel should celebrate Passover with a meal of lamb (Exodus 12:3). John the Baptist called Jesus the "Lamb of God" because sadly, he knew that Jesus would be led to his death just like a little defenseless lamb. But as heartbreaking as that was—there was a happy ending. John knew the amazing truth about what that Lamb could do for us (John 1:29)!

HORSE

Talk about your horses of a different color! The book of Revelation tells us about four horses—a white one symbolizing victory, a fiery red one symbolizing war, a black horse symbolizing famine, and a pale green one symbolizing death (Revelation 6:1-8).

MULE

During Old Testament times, royalty often rode mules, while horses were most often ridden in war. When Solomon rode his father's (King David) mule into Jerusalem, he got a great surprise: he was named king (1 Kings 1:44-46)!

PIG

Possessed pigs? Jesus cast out demons from a man and sent them into a herd of pigs. Read the story in Luke 8:26-39.

SHEEP

A man who owned many sheep during biblical times was considered very rich. After Job, a good man who respected God, suffered by losing everything he owned, God blessed him greatly by giving him 14,000 sheep (Job 42:12). That's a lot of lamb chops!

cold blooded things

Crocodile

How would you like to be compared to a giant crocodile with sharp choppers? Would that be a good thing? It wasn't so good for the king of Egypt—find out why by reading Ezekiel 29:2-6.

Frog

Another plague (disaster) God sent to the people of Egypt was an overabundance of frogs. Frogs were everywhere! Even in the bread dough! For the whole story, read Exodus 8.

Worm

Beware! This isn't for the squeamish. When God struck down Herod, king of Judea, for taking his honor, Herod died a hideous death—he was eaten by worms (Acts 12:23). Eeeeuuuw!

Fish

One of Jesus' greatest miracles can be found in John 6:1-15. Jesus fed thousands of people with only five loaves of bread and two fish. (See Miracles, p. 162, to discover more of Jesus' works.)

Snake

Perhaps the most well-known creature in the Bible is the snake that tempted Eve into eating from the forbidden tree in the Garden of Eden (Genesis 3).

bugs

ANT

When you think of ants, what words come to your mind? Hard working? Busy? Movies like *A Bug's Life* showcase these qualities. In passages of the Bible like Proverbs 6:6 and 30:24-25, ants have the reputation of being hard working and wise. Lazy people were advised to check out the ants' example.

Bigstock.com

BEE

We all know bees make honey, a fact described in the Bible. Maybe you've heard of the story of the Bible strongman Samson, who after killing a lion with his bare hands, later found honey the bees made in the skeleton of the lion. Check out Judges 14:5-9.

CRICKET

You can hear crickets chirping on a summer's night. Do you think crickets were on the "clean" or "unclean" list of things to eat? Read Leviticus 11:20-23 to find out.

GRASSHOPPER

Because John the Baptist lived in the wilderness, he sometimes ate "grasshoppers and wild honey" (Mark 1:6). How's that for an interesting snack?

SPIDER

One of Job's friends encouraged him to hang in there through his suffering and trust that God would be there for him, instead of trusting in something "as frail as a spider's web" (Job 8:13-14).

MORE AMAZING TALES OF BIBLE ANIMALS

Other not-so-usual creatures roamed the pages of the Bible. Let's take a look.

BEHEMOTH

This oversized beast was believed to have been a hippopotamus (Job 40:15)

UNICORN

Did unicorns exist in biblical times? No one knows for certain. In some Bible versions, the unicorn is mentioned by name (Numbers 23:22 and Deuteronomy 33:17, *King James Version*), but in other versions the words "wild ox" or "bull" are used instead.

Bigstock.com

DRAGON

Revelation tells of a "huge red dragon with seven heads and ten horns" (Revelation 12:3). Find out who won the battle between the dragon and Michael and his angels in Revelation 12:7-9.

Bigstock.com

SEA MONSTERS

The creature Leviathan (Psalms 74:13-14; 104:26), with its supernatural powers, its "blazing breath" (Job 41:21), and a body that was "harder than iron" (Job 41:23). can be found throughout the Bible. Read more about these sea beasts in Job 41.

Sacrificial Animals

Although today it may seem difficult to understand, in Old Testament times making sacrifices was an important part of worship. Ordinary people gave animals and other items for sacrifices that were carried out by the priests. A portion of all that was sacrificed was to be saved and eaten by the priest and their families. (The priests came from the Levite tribe, and this tribe was not given any land to farm or raise animals. So they needed to be supported by the people from other tribes who did have land and animals.) The laws that God gave to Moses and his people included several different kinds of sacrifices. (Read more in Leviticus 1–7).

SACRIFICE TYPE	ITEM TO BE SACRIFICED	WHY THE SACRIFICE
Sacrifices to ask forgiveness (sin offering)	A young bull, goat, lamb, dove, pigeon, ram, or flour	To ask for God's forgiveness
Sacrifices to please the LORD (whole burnt offering)	Perfectly healthy male sheep or goat, or a dove or pigeon for the poor	To worship God or to ask his forgiveness
Sacrifices to ask the LORD's blessing (well-being offering)	Fat or inner organs of a bull, male sheep, or goat; bread made without yeast	To worship God and to ask for his blessing
Sacrifices to make things right (guilt offering)	A blemish-free ram or the price of a ram plus the money to pay for what was stolen or destroyed	To make up for stealing or damaging another person's property or for cheating God
Sacrifices to give thanks to the LORD (grain offering)	Wheat flour, olive oil, incense, yeast-free bread, and honey loaves	To worship God and to thank him for providing for his people

Other Animal Uses

Many animals that lived during biblical times provided useful everyday objects. Take a look.

ANIMAL PART	USED FOR	CHECK IT OUT
Animal skins	Leather goods and tents	Acts 18:1-3
Ram horns	Trumpets; containers to hold oil	Joshua 6:4-6
Goat skins	Wine container	1 Samuel 16:20
Goat or camel hair	Sackcloth—a type of clothing worn during times of sorrow	2 Samuel 3:31
Jawbone of a donkey	Weapon used by Samson	Judges 15:15
Wool from sheep and goats	Weaving cloth	1 Chronicles 4:21-22
Camel hair	Clothing	Mark 1:6

Art Inspired by the Bible

The Bible has influenced art for many centuries. In fact, until the early 1400s (during the Renaissance period) nearly all art in Europe depicted the Bible in some way—through paintings, sculptures, stained glass, and mosaics.

Early Christian Art

No, it's not the handiwork of artists who like to get up at sunrise. *Early* means the first few centuries after Jesus lived on Earth. Wall drawings have been found in the underground catacombs of ancient Rome. Here are three more examples:

The Annunciation, Ohrid (c. 1259)

❖ DURA-EUROPAS—Digging in this ancient town in Syria in the 1920s and 1930s, archeologists found a synagogue with many wall paintings, including *Pharaoh's Daughter Finding the Infant Moses*. Wall paintings in a nearby house-church included the oldest known representation of *Jesus, The Healing of the Paralytic*. The year of all the artwork? About A.D. 232.

❖ BYZANTINE—In A.D. 330 the Roman emperor, Constantine, moved the capital to Byzantium and renamed it Constantinople, which is Istanbul, Turkey today. Art was dominated by wall mosaics, ornate metalwork, detailed sculptures, and icons (paintings of Jesus, saints, or angels). The Metropolitan Museum of Art, New York City, has an amazing collection—check it out in person or online (www.metmuseum.org/explore/Byzantium/byzhome.html).

❖ MOZARABIC—Christians living in Spain in the eighth to fifteen centuries were ruled by Muslims. Art from this time and place shows an Islamic influence in its geometric shapes, illuminated manuscripts, calligraphy (artistic handwriting), and miniature paintings. The architecture features horseshoe-shaped arches and ribbed domes.

Art From the Floor...

Mosaic tile art was often put on walls. Beautiful examples, dated before A.D. 547, are in the Church of San Vitale, Ravenna, Italy. In a town near Amman, Jordan, however, large floor mosaics were uncovered in sixth-century buildings. The mosaics included Christian prayers, a map of ancient Jerusalem, and the paradise described in Isaiah 65:17-25.

In November 2007, archeologists from the Hebrew University of Jerusalem discovered a synagogue in Galilee 1,600 to 1,800 years old. On the floor was a colorful mosaic picturing several woodworkers building a large structure that scholars think is either Noah's ark, the tower of Babel, or the temple at Jerusalem.

iStock.com

Vatican City is in Rome, Italy. It's where the head of the Roman Catholic Church, the Pope, makes his home and leads the church. One of the most famous parts of Vatican City is the Sistine Chapel, built in 1473.

Many excellent paintings already hung on its walls. Yet in 1508, Pope Julius II decided that the plain ceiling was boring. He hired artist Michelangelo di Lodovico Buonarroti Simoni (1475–1564) for the "small" project. The result: one of the greatest masterpieces of all time. The work was completed in less than four years. It shows scenes from the book of Genesis (three large scenes each of the Creation, Adam and Eve, and Noah), as well as smaller views of the generations between Abraham to Christ.

Although the Sistine Chapel fresco is Michelangelo's best-known work, he was also known for his sculptures. Some of his most famous are those showing people from the Bible: *Moses, David, St. Matthew*, and *the Pietà* (Jesus and his mother). The movie *The Agony and the Ecstasy* (1965), starring Charlton Heston as Michelangelo, tells the story of his work.

DID YOU KNOW?

The famous ceiling of the Sistine Chapel is a fresco. The artist works in small areas at a time and applies paint onto damp, fresh lime plaster. This method of painting became popular again in the twentieth century through the work of muralists such as José Clemente Orozco of Mexico.

iStock.com

Famous Paintings of Bible Stories

Christ Driving the Moneychangers from the Temple by El Greco, 1571-1576 (based on Matthew 21:12-13)

Daniel in the Lion's Den by Henry Ossawa Tanner, 1895 (based on Daniel 6:12-23)

Jacob Blesses Manasseh and Ephraim by Rembrandt Harmenszoon van Rijn, 1656 (based on Genesis 48:1-22)

Losing Paradise by He Qi, 2004 (based on Genesis 3)

The Good Samaritan by Vincent van Gogh, 1890 (based on Luke 10:25-37)

The Last Supper by Leonard da Vinci, 1495-98 (based on Matthew 26:17-30)

The Mocking of Christ by Édouard Manet, 1865 (based on Matthew 27:27-30; Mark 15:16-21)

The Nativity by Sawai Chinnawong, 2004 (based on Luke 2:1-7)

The Peaceable Kingdom by Edward Hicks, about 1845 (based on Isaiah 65:25)

The Raising of Lazarus by Rembrandt, about 1630 (based on John 11:1-44)

The Sermon on the Mount (fresco) by Fra Angelico, 1436-1443 (based on Matthew 5—7)

ILLUMINATED MANUSCRIPTS

What do you call it when the Bible itself becomes art? Johannes Gutenberg invented the movable-type printing press and first printed the Bible in 1455. Until then books were hand copied, usually by monks. Pages in Bibles and hymnbooks often had decorative type and scenes from Scripture. This kind of artwork is called "illuminated manuscripts." Some well-known illustrated manuscripts are:

Deborah and Barak Attack Sisera and His Chariot Drivers (Judges 4–5), from an illuminated manuscript around 1250 in France

Temptation of Christ (Luke 4:1-8), from a fifteenth-century Flemish illuminated *Book of Hours* by the Limbourg brothers

The Burning of Babylon (Revelation 18), from an illuminated manuscript from the eleventh century

DID YOU KNOW?

In 1997, an art gallery opened in the New York City headquarters of the American Bible Society. Eight years later it had moved to a larger space and was renamed the Museum of Biblical Art (MOBIA). It's the nation's first scholarly museum devoted to art and the Bible.

Losing Paradise, He Qi (2004)

LIGHT AND COLOR

For centuries, stained glass has been used in many churches and cathedrals.

Great Rose Window (John 14:6), Charles Connick, 1932, stained glass window in Cathedral Church of St. John the Divine, New York City

Hannah Presents Samuel to the LORD (1 Samuel 1:1—2:11, 18-21), late twelfth century, stained glass window in Canterbury Cathedral, England

Jesus Knocking (Revelation 3:20) by Louis Comfort Tiffany (1848–1933), stained glass window in St. Paul's Episcopal Church, Franklin, Tennessee

Joshua and the Amorites (Joshua 10:12-13), seventeenth century, stained glass in Wragny Church, Switzerland

Saint Timothy (1 Timothy 1:2; 3:6), twelfth century, stained glass window from the Abbey of Neuwiller, Alsace, France

Wheat and Grapes (Hosea 2:21-24; 1 Corinthians 11:23-26), artist unknown, 1930s, stained glass window in the United States

Jesus Knocking, stained glass window

ARTISTS' TOP PICKS

Over the millennia artists really have liked these Bible stories for all forms of artwork.

Creation (Genesis 1)

Garden of Eden (Genesis 2—3)

The Golden Calf (Exodus 32:1-10)

Jesus' Birth (Matthew 1:18—2:12; Luke 2:1-7)

The Good Shepherd (John 10:7-21)

Jesus Feeds Five Thousand (Mark 6:30-44)

Parable of the Prodigal Son (Luke 15:11-32)

The Last Supper (Matthew 26:17-30)

Jesus' Arrest, Trial, and Crucifixion (Matthew 27; Mark 15; Luke 23; John 19)

Jesus' Resurrection (Matthew 28; Mark 16; Luke 24; John 20)

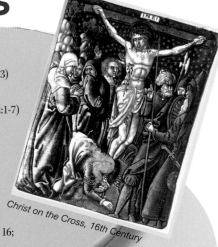

Christ on the Cross, 16th Century

Besides the frescoes of the Sistine Chapel, here are some of the paintings that show these stories:

Apostles at Christ's Tomb, Francisco Ribalta (1590s)

Christ with the Crown of Thorns, artist unknown, African wood carving

The Multiplication of the Loaves, Pablo Mayorga (1982)

The Prodigal Son, Marc Chagall (1975)

The Bible

Word Up!

The word Bible comes from the Greek word *biblia*, which translates in English as "books." The Bible is indeed one book that is many books. In the Bible read by most Protestant traditions, there are sixty-six different books; other traditions have additional books.
(See the chart on page 25.)

Translation or Paraphrase

Not all versions of the Bible are the same. A translation goes back to the original Hebrew or Greek source and writes it in another language. The writer of a paraphrase takes a translation and puts it in his or her own words. Examples of paraphrases are The Living Bible (1971) and The Message (2002).

Today there are dozens of English Bible versions and many Spanish versions as well. Why so many? One reason is that languages constantly change. New words are always being added and others take on different meanings. Another reason is that Bible scholars are always learning new things about ancient Israel and the world of ancient Greece and Rome to help us better understand those times and people. No matter what Bible translation is used, however, the main purpose is to make the Bible reliable and understandable to those who want to read its message

Who Wrote It?

One name for the Bible is "the Word of God." It includes the truths, laws, stories, prayers, songs, and wise sayings that tell us about God, our lives, and our world. For a long time the Scriptures were only passed on by word of mouth. This is called the "oral tradition."

The books in the Jewish Scriptures (Old Testament) were not all written down at once. It took centuries. Scholars don't know exactly when all the books of the Jewish Scriptures were finally collected. Some of the writings may go back as far as 1300 B.C., but the process of bringing the books together may not have begun until around 400 B.C.

The final list of Hebrew Scriptures— what Christians call the "Old Testament"— was made official by rabbis about A.D. 100 (also called C.E. for "Common Era"; see Calendar and Holidays, p. 32). In A.D. 367 church leaders said "Yes!" to the New Testament list of Saint Athanasius.

The Old Testament was first written in Hebrew (and a bit of Aramaic). The New Testament was written in Greek. Today the whole Bible has been translated into hundreds of ancient and modern languages.

DID YOU KNOW?

In 1525 the New Testament was first translated from original Greek sources into English by William Tyndale. Almost nobody had a Bible at home and only heard the Latin version read in churches. Five years later, he published the first five books of the Old Testament in English. Back then, translating the Bible into English was a crime. Threatened by Tyndale's forward-looking and popular work, church officials accused him of heresy (dangerous beliefs). Tyndale was caught and burned at the stake in 1536.

ShutterStock

In many Bibles, Psalms is in the exact middle, making it easy to find a cool collection of songs and prayers.

Both the book of Genesis and the Gospel of John begin with "In the beginning. . ."

What You'll Find

Imagine the Bible as a small library with groups of books placed on different shelves:

☛ **LAW**—The first five books of the Bible (Genesis through Deuteronomy) describe all the laws, commandments, and rules God gave his people. These are also called the Pentateuch (like a pentagon has five sides). In Hebrew, they are known as the Torah, which means "instruction."

☛ **HISTORY**—Joshua through Esther in the Old Testament (OT), plus Acts in the New Testament (NT), are books that read like history books.

☛ **WISDOM AND POETRY**—The books of Job, Psalms, Proverbs, Ecclesiastes, and Song of Songs are in this group.

☛ **PROPHECY**—A "prophet" is one who speaks for God, sometimes in the form of visions and sometimes saying hard truths about the present. Isaiah through Malachi in the OT and Revelation in the NT are prophetic books.

☛ **GOSPELS**—The word *gospel* means "good news." The first four NT books—Matthew, Mark, Luke, and John— tell the good news about Jesus and his ministry.

☛ **LETTERS**—The apostle Paul wrote thirteen letters (also called "epistles") in the NT, some to churches and others to one person. Hebrews through Jude were written by others.

Where To Find Important Stuff

The Creation	Genesis 1:1—2:4	Water into wine	John 2:1-12
Garden of Eden	Genesis 2:4—3:24	Boy raised from dead	Luke 7:11-17
Noah's ark	Genesis 6:1—9:17	Jesus walks on water	Matthew 14:34-36
Isaac's near-death	Genesis 22:1-18	Lord's Prayer	Matthew 6:9-13
Joseph's cool coat	Genesis 37	Parable of the	
Parting of Red Sea	Exodus 14:15-30	Good Samaritan	Luke 10:25-37
Ten Commandments	Exodus 20	The Last Supper	Mark 14:17-26
Deborah wins!	Judges 4:4-17	Jesus dies but	Matthew 27–28; Mark 14–16;
David and Goliath	1 Samuel 17:1-54	lives again!	Luke 22–24; John 13–21
Daniel in the lion's den	Daniel 6	Saul becomes Paul	Acts 9:1-30
Jonah in a fish	Jonah 1–2		
Jesus is born!	Matthew 1:18—2:12; Luke 2:1-21		

Title of Book   **Key Points**

Genesis ("beginning")
The story of the creation of the world and of God's people. It also tells how God made a special promise with Abraham to bless him and his descendants.

Exodus ("going out" or "departure")
The story of how God used Moses to lead the Hebrew people out of a life of slavery in Egypt; the start of the nation of Israel.

Leviticus ("The priests' manual")
Handbook for priests; a guidebook for holy living. The priests of the Israelite religion were to come from the tribe of Levi, the same tribe Moses was from.

Numbers ("counting")
This book gets its name from the two censuses that were taken as the people wandered in the desert for forty years before entering the land God had promised to their ancestor Abraham.

Deuteronomy ("copy of law" or "second law")
Before he died, Moses gave three farewell speeches. In them he reviewed the laws God had given the Israelites. The book gets its name for that review, or "second law."

Joshua (new leader for the nation of Israel)
Before Moses died, Joshua was chosen to lead the Israelites into the promised land. This book describes the history of Israel's military campaign to take over Canaan.

Judges (special leaders to deliver the Israelites)
After Joshua's death, the people disobeyed God and worshiped false gods and fell into enemies' hands. God sent twelve judges to help deliver the people.

Ruth (young Moabite widow)
The story of the love and dedication between Ruth and Naomi, her Israelite mother-in-law. Because of her faithfulness, Ruth found a new husband and had a son, whose grandson became Israel's greatest king, King David.

1 Samuel (last judge and prophet)
Originally one book with 2 Samuel, the first book tells the stories of Samuel and Israel's first king, Saul. God was not happy with Saul and chose a shepherd boy named David to be the next king.

2 Samuel (last judge)
The story of King David and his struggles to keep control of his kingdom and his family. Much of David's troubles are a direct result of his own sin with a beautiful woman named Bathsheba.

1 & 2 Kings (history of Israel)
The history of Israel is continued. The first book tells about King Solomon, and after his death, the split of Israel into two kingdoms. The second book details the eventual fall of both kingdoms and the Israelites being taken into captivity.

1 & 2 Chronicles (royal court records)

These books tell much the same history covered in the books of Samuel and Kings, but from a different viewpoint.

Ezra (scribe and priest)

This book and the following book of Nehemiah were originally one. They tell the story after captivity when the Israelites were allowed to return to Israel. Ezra helped reestablish obedience to the Law of Moses.

Nehemiah (former official in Persian court)

Nehemiah was appointed governor of Judah and helped the people rebuild the wall around Jerusalem so that the people would be safe.

Esther (Jewish woman who became queen of Persia)

This young Jewish woman won a beauty contest and became queen of Persia. She used her position to help expose a plot to destroy the Jewish people. The annual celebration of this victory is the Jewish festival of Purim.

Job (wealthy man who lost everything)

This book, through a series of poetic speeches, deals with the problem of suffering.

Psalms ("songs")

This book consists of 150 prayers and psalms that were used by the Hebrew people as part of their public and private worship. Some date back to the time of King David, who may have written many.

Proverbs ("wise sayings")

This book is a collection of wisdom and teachings for daily life. One of the main teachings is that all wisdom is a gift from God.

Ecclesiastes ("teachings")

This book contains the thoughts of a very wise person known as the "Preacher." It explores the nature of human life, God's mercy and justice, and many other topics that appeal to people today.

Song of Songs

A collection of poems that celebrate the love between a man and woman. It also is understood as a picture of God's love for Israel and Jesus' love for the church.

Isaiah (prophet)

This book contains warnings about God's judgment on the people of Judah for their disobedience. It also has messages of hope for a future king descended from King David who would bring comfort to all nations—Jesus.

Jeremiah (prophet)

Before Babylon destroyed Judah, Jeremiah was sent by God to warn the king, priests, and people of the coming judgment. Jeremiah also pointed to a time when God would make a new covenant with his people.

Lamentations ("sad songs or poems")

Five poems that depict the sorrow about the destruction of Jerusalem by the Babylonians in 586 B.C. While the tone is sad, it also includes an inspiring message of God's unfailing love.

Old Testament

Title of Book	Key Points
Ezekiel (prophet and priest)	Ezekiel lived in Babylon after the fall of Jerusalem, and he shared many insights from visions he received with the Jewish exiles and those still living in Jerusalem.
Daniel (Jewish official)	Daniel served in the courts of Babylonian and Persian kings. The book tells of his faithfulness to God. It also has Daniel's prophetic visions about the downfall of pagan nations and the ultimate victory for God's people.
Hosea ("salvation")	Hosea's message warned the people of Israel and Judah that they were treating God the way an unfaithful wife acts toward her husband. Yet, he also assured them of God's love and forgiveness.
Joel (prophet)	This short book portrays Israel's enemies as a plague of locusts invading and destroying the land. Joel also describes a day when Israel's enemies will be judged.
Amos (sheep farmer)	This sheep farmer from Judah preached judgment against the rich rulers of Israel's northern kingdom.
Obadiah (prophet)	Obadiah prophesied judgment against Edom, one of Israel's neighbors, because they would not help Israel when it was being invaded.
Jonah (prophet)	This short story is about a man who ran from God because he didn't want to deliver God's warning to the people of Nineveh. God used a great fish and a vine to teach this reluctant prophet about God's mercy for all.
Micah (prophet)	This book has harsh words for the rich of Israel and Judah who took advantage of the poor. It also looks forward to a day when justice would be restored under the leadership of a new king.
Nahum (prophet)	This short book tells of the fall of Nineveh, the capital of one of Israel's cruelest oppressors.
Habakkuk (prophet)	This book features a dialogue between Habakkuk and God about suffering and justice.
Zephaniah (prophet)	Zephaniah announced "the day of the Lord," a day when God would bring judgment on Judah and other nations for disobedience.

Haggai
(prophet)

This message was given to the people who had returned to Jerusalem and who were busy rebuilding their own homes. Haggai told them to put God first and rebuild the temple; then they would be richly blessed.

Zechariah
(prophet)

Zechariah also urged the people to rebuild the temple in Jerusalem. Zechariah also had visions that God would provide the people with a king and establish peace among the nations.

Malachi
(prophet)

The last book of the OT, Malachi had strong warnings for the people to be obedient to the law and instructions that Moses had given to them at Mount Sinai.

New Testament

Matthew
(one of Jesus' first twelve followers)

One of four Gospels, this book starts with Jesus' birth and ends with his death and resurrection. The importance of "doing what is right" and obedience to God are important themes.

Mark
(a member of Paul's first mission team)

The shortest Gospel, Mark provides a good overview of Jesus' ministry. This action-packed book is full of miracles—the most powerful of which is Jesus' suffering, death, and resurrection.

Luke
(a member of Paul's team)

Luke's Gospel emphasizes God's care for the poor and that the Holy Spirit is God's great gift for anyone who asks. Luke's book contains the parables of the Good Samaritan and of the Lost Son, which are not in any other Gospel.

John
(one of Jesus' first twelve followers)

John's Gospel stands apart from the other three. It is organized around seven signs (miracles) that point to Jesus as the Son of God. It also has long conversations Jesus had with others about his identity and his mission.

Acts
("actions" of the Apostles)

Written by Luke, it tells the story of the early church. The apostle Peter is a major figure at the beginning of the book; Paul, a Pharisee who persecuted early believers, is a key figure in the second part of the book.

Romans
(church at Rome)

Paul's letters to the church at Rome is his longest, and perhaps his best effort, to explain how people are made acceptable to God because of Jesus' sacrifice for their sins on the cross.

1 & 2 Corinthians
(church at Corinth)

Paul helped found the church in Corinth and he cared deeply for the believers there. These letters were written to resolve a number of disputes, encourage unity among believers, and give warnings against false teachers.

Galatians
(churches in Galatia)

In this letter, Paul asserts that he is a true apostle of Christ. He discusses the importance of faith and the wonderful freedom people receive when they put their faith in Christ.

Ephesians
(church at Ephesus)

This short book summarizes many of Paul's teachings. A strong emphasis is placed on unity that Jesus' followers have and the new life God's Spirit gives them.

Philippians
(church at Philippi)

Paul wrote this letter from prison, encouraging believers to remain faithful to Christ and to rejoice in God, no matter what the circumstances.

Colossians
(church at Colosse)

This letter challenged the church to avoid false teachings, and rather, to set their hearts on Christ who is enthroned in heaven.

1 & 2 Thessalonians
(church at Thessalonica)

Possibly the oldest document in the NT, Paul gives advice to the church about Christ's return and encourages them to make themselves ready.

1 & 2 Timothy
(young leader)

These two letters and the letter to Titus have been called the "Pastoral Letters," because they give advice about what local church leaders should do to look after the spiritual needs of the people in their care.

Titus
(member of Paul's team)

Letter to advise Greek church leader about how to care for the church.

Philemon
(member of Colossian church)

In this letter, Paul urges a wealthy church leader to forgive his runaway slave, Onesimus, who had become a believer and a friend to Paul.

Hebrews
(Jewish Christians)

Written in the form of a letter, this book is about the superiority of Christ. He is superior to angels, Moses, and the sacrifices made in the temple. Jesus is described as both the high priest and the sacrifice that takes away the sins of many.

James
(leader in Jerusalem church)

This short book is a collection of teachings on practical topics, such as learning to control our speech, avoiding favoritism, caring for the sick and needy, and putting faith into action.

1 & 2 Peter
(named after one of Jesus' earliest followers)

These two letters were written to encourage Christians who were being persecuted for their faith and to warn them against false prophets.

1, 2, & 3 John
(named after one of Jesus' earliest followers)

First John affirms Jesus as the Christ and explains basic truths about the Christian faith, with a special emphasis on the command to love one another. The second letter warns of false teachers, and the third letter encourages believers to help other followers spread the truth.

Jude
(believed to be James's brother, Jesus' half-brother)

This letter warns against the influence of ungodly and immoral people who claim to have spiritual authority based on visions they received. Jude encourages readers to keep their faith in God.

Revelation
("vision that explains")

This book was written to encourage persecuted believers by showing God's plan for history and affirming his justice and mercy. Using visions, symbolism, and codes, Revelation proclaims that Christ will ultimately defeat all forces of evil.

Other Scriptures

Certain traditions, particularly the Roman Catholic and Eastern Orthodox churches, have additional books that they include in the Old Testament, called the "Apocrypha" or "Deuterocanonical" books. Some books in this collection, such as *1 & 2 Maccabees, Tobit*, and *Judith*, bear similarities to the Historical Books. Others, like *the Wisdom of Solomon* and *Sirach*, can be seen as expressions of Jewish wisdom traditions. Whether read as sacred literature or as helpful background documents to the time period leading up to the time of Jesus, these books contain much that is interesting, beautiful, and useful.

This chart shows the different books in each tradition.

The Old Testament in Christian Bibles

Protestant	Catholic	Orthodox
Genesis	Genesis	Genesis
Exodus	Exodus	Exodus
Leviticus	Leviticus	Leviticus
Numbers	Numbers	Numbers
Deuteronomy	Deuteronomy	Deuteronomy
Joshua	Joshua	Joshua
Judges	Judges	Judges
Ruth	Ruth	Ruth
1 Samuel	1 Samuel	1 Kingdoms (1 Samuel)
2 Samuel	2 Samuel	2 Kingdoms (2 Samuel)
1 Kings	1 Kings	3 Kingdoms (1 Kings)
2 Kings	2 Kings	4 Kingdoms (2 Kings)
1 Chronicles	1 Chronicles	1 Chronicles
2 Chronicles	2 Chronicles	2 Chronicles
Ezra	Ezra	1 Esdras
Nehemiah	Nehemiah	2 Esdras (Ezra and Nehemiah)
Esther	Tobit	Esther (with additions)
Job	Judith	Judith
Psalms	Esther (with additions)	Tobit
Proverbs	1 Maccabees	1 Maccabees
Ecclesiastes	2 Maccabees	2 Maccabees
Song of Songs	Job	3 Maccabees
Isaiah	Psalms	Psalms (plus Psalm 151)
Jeremiah	Proverbs	Prayers of Manasseh
Lamentations	Ecclesiastes	Job
Ezekiel	Song of Songs	Proverbs
Daniel	Wisdom of Solomon	Ecclesiastes
Hosea	Sirach	Song of Songs
Joel	Isaiah	Wisdom of Solomon
Amos	Jeremiah	Sirach
Obadiah	Lamentations	Hosea
Jonah	Baruch (with letter of Jeremiah)	Joel
Micah		Amos
Nahum	Ezekiel	Obadiah
Habakkuk	Daniel (with additions)	Jonah
Zephaniah	Hosea	Micah
Haggai	Joel	Nahum
Zechariah	Amos	Habakkuk
Malachi	Obadiah	Zephaniah
	Jonah	Haggai
	Micah	Zechariah
	Nahum	Malachi
	Habakkuk	Isaiah
	Zephaniah	Jeremiah
	Haggai	Baruch
	Zechariah	Lamentations
	Malachi	Letter of Jeremiah
		Ezekiel
		Daniel (with additions)
		4 Maccabees

THE SEVEN WONDERS OF THE ANCIENT WORLD

The ancient world of the Bible was full of wonders. Second century B.C. writer Antipater of Sidon is credited with coming up with the first list of ancient wonders. Check them out! Which one is your favorite?

1 The Great Pyramid of Giza (2500 B.C.)

The largest of the great pyramids was built in Egypt for Pharaoh Khufu. The massive monument, with a base that covers a whopping thirteen acres, was constructed of about two million stone blocks. Estimates say the project took well over twenty years and 20,000 to 100,000 men to complete. Now that's a massive project!

While the people of Israel were enslaved in Egypt, they were forced to make bricks. Bricks were used in building cities and to make ramps for constructing pyramids. You can read about that in Exodus 1: 1–14.

2 The Hanging Gardens of Babylon (580 B.C.)

Imagine garden terraces seventy-five feet high, overhanging with all sorts of gorgeous flowers and plants. Now imagine them in the middle of a desert! Some sources say King Nebuchadnezzar II built the gardens for his wife who was homesick for the greenery of her homeland. But how was it possible to keep the gardens in top shape in the hot, dry desert air? To keep the gardens watered, slaves probably used a chain pump that lifted water to the gardens from the Euphrates River. To read more about Nebuchadnezzar, see 2 Kings 24:1-17 and Daniel 1–4.

3 The Statue of Zeus at Olympia (430 B.C.)

Made of ivory and gold, this magnificent statue of Zeus, the Greek god of thunder from mythology, stood as high as a four-story building and overlooked the area where ancient Olympic Games were held. The statue stood so tall its head nearly reached the temple's ceiling. Legend has it that when the statue was complete, the sculptor, Phidias, asked for a sign of approval from the gods. A short time later the temple was struck by lightning! Perhaps the sculptor believed that his work was given a thumbs-up.

4 Temple of Artemis at Ephesus (550 B.C.)

This huge marble temple, located in modern-day Turkey, was built to honor Artemis, the goddess of the hunt and wild animals in Greek mythology. Larger in area than a football field and supported by more than one hundred 60-foot columns, this was the largest temple of ancient times. Elaborate bronze statues decorated the temple's courtyard where people came to buy and sell their goods.

During the first century, the apostle Paul lived in Ephesus for about three years. The temple of Artemis is mentioned in Acts 19:27.

5 The Mausoleum at Halicarnassus (350 B.C.)

The tomb built by Artemisia for her husband, Mausolus, is where the word *mausoleum* originated. This ancient wonder is believed to have been the only one commissioned by a woman. Thanks to the work of architects Pythius and Satyrus, this 135-foot tomb was made even more beautiful by the building of a pyramid roof topped by a sculpture of a four-horse chariot. To learn how God helped the Israelites by disabling Egyptian chariots, read Exodus 14:23-28.

6 The Colossus of Rhodes (292 B.C.)

This 110-foot tall bronze statue of the sun god Helios in mythology was almost the same height as the Statue of Liberty. The immense statue stood watch over the harbor of the Greek island of Rhodes for fifty-six years, until it was destroyed by an earthquake. Even while on the ground, the sight was so impressive, people came from all over to view it. Reports say that the statue's thumb was so large, that very few people could wrap their arms all the way around it. Hundreds of years later, when the statue's scraps were carted away, it took over nine hundred camels to transport the massive amount of debris.

7 The Lighthouse of Alexandria (280 B.C.)

The lighthouse was located on the island of Pharos near Alexandria, Egypt. This stone-block tower, also known as the Pharos, measured about 450 to 600 feet tall, making it one of the tallest buildings of its time. Ptolemy, the ruler of Egypt, commissioned the building. A bright flame led ships at night and a number of shiny bronze mirrors helped them navigate in and out of the harbor during the day. Even today, scuba divers can see underwater remains of the lighthouse near Pharos Island.

The apostle Paul would have seen the Pharos during his missionary travels. To read about Paul's travels on an Alexandrian ship, check out Acts 27.

DID YOU KNOW?
The word Pharos means "lighthouse" in French, Italian, and Spanish.

MORE AMAZING BUILDINGS IN THE BIBLE

▶ SOLOMON'S TEMPLE

For several hundred years, the people of Israel worshiped the God of Israel in a tent called the tabernacle. (See Worship, p. 244, for more information on the tabernacle.) But that changed in a big way when King Solomon came along. Although his father, David, desired to build a great temple for God (see 2 Samuel 7:12-14; 1 Chronicles 17:11-12), Solomon was the one chosen to build it.

The temple had three main areas—an outer room, a main hall, and an inner room called the most holy place. Made of glimmering white sandstone blocks, the temple stood high on a hill in Jerusalem. Think about how noisy this building project was as the workers banged and clanged those chunks of sandstone, beating the blocks into shape. But not a single sound was heard at the work site! How could that be? Solomon didn't want a major racket going on at the holy site, so he had every block cut and shaped at the quarry before it was brought to the construction site (1 Kings 6:7).

▶ SOLOMON'S TEMPLE BY THE NUMBERS

Years to Complete	7
Number of Workers to Cut Logs	30,000
Number of Workers to Cut Stone	80,000
Number of Workers to Carry Stone	70,000
Number of Supervisors	Over 3,000

GO FIGURE

A unit of measurement called cubits was used during Bible times rather than inches or feet. The temple was 60 cubits long, 30 cubits high, and 20 cubits wide. This adds up to 90 feet long, 45 feet high, and 30 feet wide.

iStock.com

In 2007, people from all over the world cast more than 100 million votes to choose the New Seven Wonders of the World. Here are the winners:

LANDMARK	LOCATION	YEAR CONSTRUCTED
THE PYRAMID OF CHICHÉN ITZÁ	YUCATAN PENINSULA, MEXICO	BEFORE A.D. 800
CHRIST REDEEMER STATUE	RIO DE JANEIRO, BRAZIL	1931
THE ROMAN COLOSSEUM	ROME, ITALY	A.D. 70-82
THE TAJ MAHAL	AGRA, INDIA	1630
THE GREAT WALL OF CHINA	CHINA	220 B.C.; 1368–1644
PETRA	PETRA, JORDAN	9 B.C.–A.D. 40
MACHU PICCHU	PERU	1460–1470

HEROD THE BUILDER

The wailing Wall in Jerusalem today

Although the Romans conquered Israel, Herod the Great was the appointed king of the people of Israel around 40–4 B.C. Herod built theaters, palaces, fortresses, and even a gladiator stadium called a hippodrome. Herod's most ambitious project, however, was his expansion of the temple of Jerusalem. Herod wasn't happy with the size of the former temple—he wanted something bigger and better. But there was one problem. In order to build a bigger temple, he had to have a bigger site. Big problem, right? Not for Herod. He instructed those working on the temple to widen the hill upon which the temple stood. Giant retaining walls were added around the outside. Now he had the space he needed.

This temple was 15 stories high and was in use during Jesus' day (see Mark 13:1), until it was destroyed by the Romans in A.D. 70. Today, only the western wall of Herod's temple still stands. Many people visit the site, sometimes called the Wailing Wall, to pray.

FOR MORE INFO...

Visit
http://www.new7wonders.com
to learn more about the recently chosen New Seven Wonders of the World.

Dig This

While many men were busy building structures above ground, King Hezekiah's men were in the dark—literally. They worked underground. Since Hezekiah's people were at war with the Assyrians, Hezekiah worried that people inside the Jerusalem walls would die of thirst if its enemies surrounded the city. So Hezekiah sent one group of men to one side of the city and another group on the other side. They dug and dug in order to channel an underground spring inside the city walls. Lots of backbreaking work and 582 yards later, the two sides met in the middle! Check out 2 Kings 18-21 for more about King Hezekiah of Judah.

iStock.com

The walls of Ninevah

KEEP OUT

Great walls surrounded most cities in Bible times. Walls made of stone, mud bricks, or wood were one of the main defenses against attackers. And these weren't just wimpy piles of stones—they were built with some serious goals in mind. It wasn't uncommon for the thickness of some of the walls to be over 20 feet or more. Walls in Babylon and Nineveh were so wide that six rows of chariots could travel side-by-side down the top of the wall. What a sight that must have been!

THE WALLS OF JERICHO

In the Old Testament, Jericho's walls stood tall and strong. A 15-foot stone wall topped by a 6-foot thick brick wall three or four times as high acted as a great line of defense. But the strength of that wall was no match for the strength of the God of Israel. When the Israelites made ready to move into the promised land of Canaan, God brought Jericho's walls tumbling down. You can read all about it in Joshua 6:1-5.

iStock.com

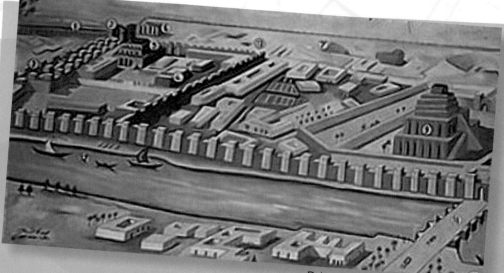

Babylon as it looked in 600 B.C. Wikipedia

▶ THE WALLS OF BABYLON

Babylon's walls were impressive as well. They consisted of a 12-foot wide outer wall and a 21-foot inner wall. The 24-foot space between the walls was filled with dirt. This made a total of 57 feet of solid defense—that's about the length of a whole school bus plus half of another one sitting end to end! And if that's not enough, the outer wall was surrounded by a moat that ranged from 60 to 250 feet wide. Whoa!

THE TOWER OF BABEL

Instead of going out and settling throughout the earth as God had instructed (Genesis 1:28), the descendants of Noah had another idea. Since they all spoke the same language, they decided to settle in one area and build a tower to heaven. This tall tower was known as a ziggurat. Many surviving examples were later found in ancient Mesopotamia.

God was not pleased with the people's decision. To punish them, he confused their language, causing them to "babble," and scattered them all over the earth (Genesis 11:1-9).

The Confusion of Tongues, Gustave Dore, engraving (1865)

31

Marking Time

Perhaps you use your calendar to mark off time until summer vacation. The ancient Israelites used calendars to follow the agricultural seasons (dry, rainy, and cold season) and to keep track of sacred holidays. Their calendar was different from the Gregorian-based calendar used by countries in the western hemisphere.

THE HEBREW CALENDAR

MONTH	HEBREW NAME	EQUAL TO	SEASON
1	NISAN	March–April	Spring barley harvest
2	IYYAR	April–May	Dry season begins
3	SIVAN	May–June	Early figs ripen
4	TAMMUZ	June–July	Grape harvest
5	AB	July–August	Olive harvest
6	ELUL	August–September	Dates and summer figs
7	TISHRI	September–October	Early rains
8	MARCHESVAN	October–November	Ploughing; winter figs
9	CHISLEV	November–December	Sowing
10	TEBETH	December–January	Rains
11	SHEBAT	January–February	Almond blossom
12	ADAR	February–March	Citrus fruit harvest

DID YOU KNOW?

Jewish holidays begin at sundown on the evening of the previous day.

Types of Calendars

- **Solar calendar:** measures time based on the movement of the sun.
- **Lunar calendar:** bases events on the phases of the moon.
- **Gregorian calendar:** a solar calendar named after Pope Gregory VIII in 1582.

1250 B.C.

1000 B.C.

750 B.C.

500 B.C.

250 B.C.

0

250 A.D.

500 A.D.

750 A.D.

1000 A.D.

1250 A.D.

1500 A.D.

Measuring Centuries

DID YOU KNOW?

A vernal equinox is the time in the spring when day and night are equal in length.

B.C. and A.D.

The initials B.C. stand for "Before Christ." The birth of Christ was the marker that separated one era from another. When you see a date like 165 B.C., it refers to an event 165 years before the Christian era. The initials A.D. come from the Latin phrase *anno domini,* or "in the year of our Lord."

Numbering years based on the year of Jesus' birth was actually not used until A.D. 526, when the system was created by a monk named Dionysius Exiguus. Dionysius calculated the year of Jesus' birth using the ancient Roman calendar, but he overestimated Herod's reign by about five years. So Jesus was probably born five years before A.D. officially began!

But two hundred years later, the use of A.D. became common after the Benedictine monk known as the Venerable Bede used B.C. with A.D.

B.C.E. and C.E.

Sometimes B.C.E. and C.E. are used instead of B.C. and A.D. These initials stand for "Before the Common Era" and "Common Era."

DID YOU KNOW?

Two of the oldest forms of ancient time keeping are the water clock and the sundial. A water clock operated by measuring liquid flowing out of one vessel into another. A sundial was marked with the hours of the day. It measured time by the shadow the sun cast along a vertical rod called a gnomon.

Photos.com

Time to Celebrate!

Everyone loves a party! But the holidays or festivals the people of ancient Israel celebrated were special celebrations to show their gratitude to God. Many of these holidays involved sacrifices or offerings in obedience to the law (the first five books of the Bible).

Here are the major festivals and holidays celebrated by the people of Israel. (See also Leviticus 23.)

Festival of Trumpets (Rosh Hashanah)

This festival—the first of the year—is in remembrance of God's agreement with Israel at Mount Sinai (Leviticus 23:23-25; Numbers 29:1-6). Trumpet blasts signal the beginning of this day to rest, worship, and offer sacrifices to God. It takes place on the first day of Tishri.

Great Day of Forgiveness (Atonement or Yom Kippur)

Not all festivals are joyful occasions. This festival, on the tenth day of Tishri, is a time for people to express sorrow for the wrongs they have done by fasting (going without food). In biblical times a priest sacrificed a bull for his sins, a goat for the people's sins, and then sent another goat into the desert to represent the people's wrongs being taken away. The goat was called a *scapegoat*. (See Animals, p. 8.)

Festival of Shelters (Succoth)

This week-long festival, staring on the fifteenth day of Tishri, is a reminder of the Israelites' long, hard journey through the desert after leaving Egypt (Leviticus 23:33-43). *Succoth* means "booths." While Israel wandered in the desert, the people lived in temporary shelters or booths.

Ashkenazi Jews praying in the Synagogue on Yom Kippur, Maurice Gottlieb (1878)

Temple Festival (Hanukkah)

This eight-day festival celebrates a period of history described in a book known as *1 Maccabees*. Judas Maccabeus led a rebellion against Antiochus IV, the ruler of the Seleucid Empire (after Alexander the Great). Judas and his forces defeated Antiochus' army to recapture Jerusalem. The temple was then rededicated in 164 B.C. Hanukkah, also known as the festival of lights, is the celebration of the rededication of the temple. A candle on a menorah is lit for each night of Hanukkah, which begins on the twenty-fifth day of Chislev. The Hanukkah lights are a reminder that during the temple rededication, there was only enough oil to light the menorah in the temple for one day. But that oil miraculously lasted for eight days.

Photos.com

Passover and Festival of Thin Bread

This festival lasts for a week and is a reminder of how God brought the people of Israel out of slavery in Egypt (Exodus 12). The people had to flee Egypt in such a hurry that there was no time for their bread to rise. They had to settle for "thin bread."

Harvest Festival (Shavuoth)

This holiday, beginning on the fifteenth day of Nisan, celebrates the grain harvest and the first fruits. Like other holidays, the people of ancient Israel were to recall how God brought Israel out of Egypt and provided the land in which they could live.

Purim

After Queen Esther of Persia stopped a plot by the king's high official Haman to destroy the Jewish people (Esther 9), a special holiday called Purim was established for the thirteenth day of Adar. A pastry called *hamantaschen* in the shape of Haman's hat is made to remember the story of Esther (see recipe below). (For the full story on Esther, see Heroes, p. 106.)

Shabbat

In addition to yearly festivals, the ancient Israelites and modern Jews celebrate a weekly festival on the seventh day: the Sabbath, or *shabbat* in Hebrew. This is their day to rest, as the word *Sabbath* means rest (Exodus 20:8-11; Exodus 31:12-17). It is a reminder of the creation story in Genesis 2:1-3, in which God "rested from his work" (Genesis 2:3). The command to rest and remember the Sabbath is one of the Ten Commandments (Exodus 20:8-10; Deuteronomy 5:12-15).

DID YOU KNOW?

A Hanukkah menorah has nine candles rather than eight. The extra light is the *shamash,* which also is lit on each night of Hanukkah. The shamash is the candle used to light the other candles.

RECIPE FOR HAMANTASCHEN

To make the dough, you will need:

1 cup shortening

1 ¼ cups sugar

4 egg yolks

5 cups flour

2 tablespoons baking powder

1 tablespoons baking soda

½ cup milk

Cream the shortening and sugar together. Add yolks and beat well. Combine flour, baking powder, and soda. Alternate mixing dry ingredients with milk. Stir together. Chill dough for one hour. Roll out to ¼-inch thickness. Cut into 4-inch circles. Place a teaspoon of jam or prune filling in the center of each circle. Form triangles by folding the sides in towards the middle. Brush with beaten egg. Bake on a lightly greased baking sheet, at 350 degrees Fahrenheit, for thirty minutes or until golden brown.

Christian Church Calendar

(Liturgical Year)

The Christian church also has a calendar of special holidays and seasons, many of which relate to the life, death, and resurrection of Jesus. Certain colors are used as visual reminders of the reason for each season.

Easter Procession in Kursk, Ilya Repin (1880-1883)

Advent: This four-week period before Christmas is the first holiday of the church year. It is a time of preparing for the birth of Christ. (The word advent means "coming.") The time of Advent varies from late November to early December. The colors for Advent are purple, to honor Jesus' royalty, or blue, to signify Mary's faithfulness.

Christmas: The birth of Jesus is celebrated on December 25. White or gold is used to reflect the joy of his birth. Christmas and the days through January 5 are part of a season called Christmastide.

Epiphany: On January 6, many celebrate the magi's visit to the Christ child (Matthew 2:1-12). Since the Day of Epiphany comes at the end of the Christmas season, white or gold is still used. The season of Epiphany lasts until the Tuesday before Ash Wednesday, and the color for the remainder of the season is green.

Ordinary Time: The time after Epiphany and Pentecost are known as Ordinary Time—the time between holidays. During this time, ministers and priests wear green robes.

Lent: This is a forty-day season of fasting and prayer before Easter, observed in February and March. Ash Wednesday is the beginning of Lent. Purple is used as a symbol of penitence, sorrow for wrongdoings.

Maundy Thursday: On the Thursday before Easter, Christians remember the Last Supper of Jesus with his apostles. White is the color for Maundy Thursday.

Good Friday: On this day, many recall the arrest, trial, and crucifixion of Jesus on the Friday before Easter. Many churches strip their altars of all color or use black to symbolize mourning and death.

Easter: Easter celebrates the resurrection of Jesus from the dead. It's called a "moveable feast" because the date isn't fixed. (See Easter, p.70.) White or gold is used to reflect the victory of Jesus' resurrection.

Pentecost: This season is a reminder of the coming of the Holy Spirit (Acts 2:1-13). The Day of Pentecost takes place fifty days after Easter. Red is the color for Pentecost Sunday. The season of Pentecost is the longest season in the church year. In some faith traditions, this period of time is known as Ordinary Time (see above) and lasts until late November or early December, or until Advent and the beginning of a new church year.

test your knowledge

Quiz time! Test your knowledge by taking the following three-quiz challenge.

TRUE OR FALSE

Circle T or F to show whether a statement is true or false. If you need help, refer to the Bible passage or the section in parentheses.

T or F 1. An angel named Gabriel told Mary that she would have a son (Luke 1:26-38; Angels, p. 4).

T or F 2. The curtain of the sacred tent was decorated with archangels (Exodus 26:31; Angels, p. 4).

T or F 3. Samson killed a bear with his bare hands (Judges 14:5-6; Animals, p. 8).

T or F 4. Camels are the "ships of the desert" (Animals, p. 8).

T or F 5. Noah used a dove to see if the flood waters had decreased (Animals, p. 8).

T or F 6. Icons of Jesus and ornate metalwork are an example of Mozarabic art (Art, p. 14).

T or F 7. The New Testament was printed for the first time in 1525 (The Bible, p. 18).

T or F 8. The Statue of Zeus at Olympia is the only one of the Seven Wonders of the World still remaining (Buildings and Landmarks, p. 26).

T or F 9. The Festival of Shelters is the festival to honor Esther's part in saving her people from Haman's evil plot (Esther 9:8-32; Calendar and Holidays, p. 32).

T or F 10. Maundy Thursday is the Thursday before Easter (Calendar and Holidays, p. 32).

Answer Key: 1) T 2) F 3) F 4) T 5) T 6) F 7) F 8) F 9) F 10) T

DID YOU FIND IT?

You won't need a GPS device to find each item below. Just remember what you read! If you need a hint, look at each section in parentheses. You might have to read ahead to find some of the answers. Ready? Where . . .

1. . . . was the first electrically lit Christmas tree displayed (see Christmas, p. 38)?
2. . . . can you find myrrh? (see Clothing and Cosmetics, p. 42)?
3. . . . was Jesus arrested? (see Easter, p. 70).
4. . . . is the exact location of the Garden of Eden (see Geography, p. 84)?
5. . . . is Mount Ararat (today) (see Geography, p. 84)?

Answer Key: 1) New York City 2) Somalia 3) the Garden of Gethsemane 4) No one knows! 5) Turkey

WHO AM I?

See how quickly you can guess the identity of each person below. You only get one clue! If you need help, refer back to the sections included.

1. I'm often called by the plural form of my name—*Elohim*. (See Genesis 2:4, or p. 88)
2. I was the first king of Israel. (Government, p. 94)
3. I was a tax collector before I became one of Jesus' disciples. (Disciples, p. 68)
4. My face was on a denarius that Jesus was given. (Currency, p. 54)
5. I had a strange dream about a sheet with all kinds of animals on it. (Food, p. 80)

Answer Key: 1) God 2) Saul 3) Matthew 4) Caesar Augustus 5) Peter

Christmas

iStock.com

Songs may claim that Christmas is "the most wonderful time of the year" because of all the holiday cheer. But Christmas celebrates the birth of Jesus, and as birthdays go, that certainly makes it "the most wonderful time of the year"! Think you know all about Christmas? Read on.

So It Began

Jesus was born in Bethlehem, in Judea (Luke 2:1-20). Many around the world celebrate this historic event on December 25. But is December 25 Jesus' actual birthday? Some argue that he might have been born in the spring, since shepherds were out at night with their flocks. While no one is sure on what day Jesus was born, December 25 was identified as early as A.D. 221 as his official birthdate.

There are many theories about why December 25 was chosen. Some think it's because December 25 is nine months after the spring equinox (March 25), which was believed to be the day God created the earth. Some think December 25 was chosen to celebrate Jesus' birthday because it's on the ancient Roman winter solstice holiday. On that day, the lengthening of days and the sun's rebirth were celebrated. Since mythological gods like Saturn were celebrated on that day, church leaders decided that celebrating the birth of Christ was a much better idea.

DID YOU KNOW?

Sextus Julius Africanus, a third-century Christian historian who wrote a chronology of the world, believed that Jesus was born on December 25.

LIVING NATIVITY

Some churches and church groups around the world recreate the scene of the nativity using live actors and animals, typically in December. Some living nativities will have multiple scenes that include the events before and after the birth of Jesus, as accounted in the Bible. In Italy, the living nativity is called a *presepi viventi*. In places like Barga in Tuscany and Soriano (near Chia), you can find living nativity scenes at the end of the year up through Epiphany. The living nativity scenes in towns like Abruzzo and Soriano involve hundreds of people. Some living nativities are streamed or posted online, such as on YouTube.

DID YOU KNOW?

St. Francis of Assisi is believed to have been the first person to set up a living nativity scene. Back in the thirteenth century, he used a cave and assembled volunteers to act out the scene of Jesus' birth.

THE TWELVE DAYS OF CHRISTMAS

The Twelve Days of Christmas start on Christmas Day and end on January 5.

EPIPHANY

Epiphany (January 6) is the celebration of the wise men (magi) who visited Jesus and brought him gifts of gold, frankincense, and myrrh. In the Orthodox Catholic Church, the other recorded events of Jesus' life and ministry also are celebrated, including his baptism and the miracle at Cana (changing water into wine at a wedding). Epiphany signifies the end of the Christmas season in many church traditions.

ADVENT: PREPARING FOR CHRISTMAS

The Latin word *advent* literally means "the coming," and it is during these weeks that Christians prepare for the celebration of Jesus' birth. Advent starts on the Sunday closest to November 30.

THE ADVENT CALENDAR

An advent calendar is a way of counting down to Christmas day. Typically advent calendars start on December 1 and have little boxes or windows to open each day. Some advent calendars contain little treats, toys, or Bible verses for children and adults to enjoy as they await the birth of Jesus. The first known practice of counting down the days of advent was in Germany by Lutheran Christians. One method used was drawing marks with chalk on a door each day for twenty-four days. The first printed advent calendars were made in the early 1900s.

THE ADVENT WREATH

The advent wreath has been used in Europe since at least the sixteenth century. Advent wreaths usually are made of evergreens and have four or five candles. A new candle is lit each Sunday while awaiting Christmas, along with any candles lit on prior Sundays. Some light a fifth candle on Christmas day (usually white) to represent the light (or birth) of Jesus Christ. The Catholic Church uses three purple and one rose-colored candle. Other Christian denominations, such as Anglicans and Lutherans, use blue instead of purple in order to save the royalty color (purple) for Lent.

iStock.com

SYMBOLS OF CHRISTMAS

CANDY CANES

Have you ever taken a close look at the popular Christmas confection called a candy cane? It looks like a shepherd's staff (Jesus is called the great shepherd) and if you turn it upside down it is shaped like the letter "J" (which could mean "Jesus"). Legend has it that a choir director in Germany gave candy canes out to children in the 1600s during services to keep them quiet. In the United States, many churches give out candy canes. The colors of the candy cane are said to be symbolic, with the white of the candy representing purity and the red representing the blood Jesus shed for everyone to forgive sin.

iStock.com

CHRISTMAS LIGHTS

In the United States nowadays, even before Thanksgiving is over, Christmas lights begin popping up almost everywhere you go. Christmas lights can be found on trees, houses, wreaths, and light poles. The first electrically lit Christmas tree was displayed in 1882 in New York City by Edward Johnson. In 1917, Albert Saddacca created and started the mass selling of electric Christmas lights for the tree. He wanted to make lights that were safe. Candlelit Christmas trees were considered dangerous due to fires.

iStock.com

FUN FACTS ABOUT CHRISTMAS

CHRISTMAS TREES

Decorating trees with ornaments and lights dates back to sixteenth century Germany. A real or artificial tree is brought into the home or left outside and decorated with items bought, collected, or made. Christmas trees started being sold in the United States in the early 1850s.

The gift-giving tradition, set by the wise men, is still observed by many people today in Europe and Latin America on the day of Epiphany.

CHRISTMAS STAR

Typically people put a star on top of their Christmas tree. (Angels are common also). The star represents the star that the wise men followed when Jesus was born (Matthew 2:1-2). The angel on high represents the angels that the shepherds saw on the night when Jesus was born.

iStock.com

NATIVITY SET

From the big statues in front of the local church to a small re-creation of a manger placed on the coffee table, the story of the nativity is represented in many forms of art. A nativity set is typically statues made of wood, ceramic, or porcelain representing the birth of Jesus. Usually it includes baby Jesus, Mary, Joseph, shepherds, stable animals, and sometimes wise men with their gifts to Jesus.

GIFT GIVING

Many give gifts on Christmas day in remembrance of God's gift to the world, Jesus. Giving gifts is also a practice following the example of the wise men, who gave Jesus gold, frankincense, and myrrh. The yearly practice of gift giving on Christmas Eve or Christmas day did not become popular until the 1700s.

The exchange of Christmas cards began in the mid-1800s.

Christmas was not celebrated as a Christian holiday until at least the fourth century (more than three hundred years after the birth of Jesus).

Saint Nicholas, a bishop from the fourth century, is famous for giving gifts to the poor and needy. He had the Christmas spirit all year round! His feast day is celebrated on December 6.

A manger is a place or a container to put food for animals such as cattle.

Maybe you've seen a Christmas play or a movie based on a Bible story. While we don't have photos of what the people in Bible times wore thousands of years ago, many Scriptures tell us a lot about what they wore.

Common Dress for a Man

Ron Wheeler

◆ **The robe** (inner garment) was a long piece of plain cotton or linen cloth worn as an undergarment for the upper body. It reached to the knees and was usually worn in cool weather. In 1 Samuel 18:4, Jonathan (son of King Saul) gave David one of his robes.

• **The mantle or tunic** (outer garment) was a piece of square cloth wrapped around the body or tied over the shoulders. It was worn over the inner robe in cool weather, or next to the body without the inner robe in warm weather. Jesus had a valuable seamless outer garment that the soldiers gambled over during his crucifixion (John 19:23).

In the Law of Moses, men were told to put tassels on the four corners of their coats to remind them to obey God's laws (Deuteronomy 22:12).

• **The belt** was made of leather or woven cloth, sometimes with a shoulder strap when heavier articles were being carried from it. The Old Testament prophet Daniel had a vision of an angel wearing a gold belt (Daniel 10:5).

• **A cloak or coat** was worn over all of the other clothing as an outer garment for warmth and appearance. In the Sermon on the Mount, Jesus told his listeners to be willing to give up their coat if someone asked for it (Matthew 5:40).

• While most people wore **sandals**, only the wealthy could afford shoes. Shoes were made from soft leather while sandals were made from hard leather and were tied with leather straps. Occasionally, sandals had wooden soles, but usually they were leather. John the Baptist didn't consider himself worthy to even carry Jesus' sandals (Matthew 3:11).

Because of the dust of the roads, feet were often dirty. Slaves washed the feet of guests. Jesus shocked his disciples by washing their dusty feet before the Passover (John 13:3-11).

Common Dress for a Woman

• **The robe** (inner garment) was worn next to the skin, fitting close to the body. It had armholes and sometimes wide and open sleeves. It was usually made of good quality cotton, wool, or linen and was designed to cover the feet.

• **The mantle or tunic** (outer garment) worn by women was their main garment. This full-length garment was usually made of finer quality and enhanced with fine needlework and/or multicolored threads. These were usually worn with a woven belt.

• **The belt** was worn over the outer garment. It was made of colorful silk or wool, sometimes with a fringe from the waist nearly to the ankles.

• **The cloak, cape, or coat** was warm and durable for protection against cool weather, and was usually more intricate than a man's. When Boaz gave Ruth grain (Ruth 3:15), he placed it in her cloak.

• **The sandals** worn by women were made from hard leather or camel hide. Some of the sandals women wore had two straps instead of one.

Footwear Facts

• **Footwear was not worn in any temple or on holy ground. It was always removed when entering a home.**

• **It was customary to remove footwear when mourning a death.**

• **On a long journey through the country, footwear was often removed and carried over the shoulder until arriving in the next town.**

• **Being barefoot in a town was a sign of poverty.**

Photos.com

The Israelites considered their cloaks one of their most prized possessions. They were difficult to craft, so they were expensive. A typical wardrobe rarely consisted of more than one. Cloaks were used as

• A blanket
• A sack to carry things
• Ground covering
• A pledge for a debt
• Protection from cold weather

Cloaks were often used as blankets. The Law of Moses (Exodus 22:26-27) required that any cloak taken as security for a loan had to be returned by sundown.

Weddings: What to Wear?

In biblical times, a bride wore a veil and the kinds of beautiful clothes and jewelry described in passages like Psalm 45:13-14 and Isaiah 49:18. Occasionally, the groom would give the bride a headband of coins.

People attending a wedding dressed in their best clothing. Sometimes the groom or his family provided wedding garments for the guests, as Matthew 22:11-12 mentions.

Photos.com

DID YOU KNOW?

For men and women, hair was important. A woman's hair was often braided. Long hair was considered beautiful (1 Corinthians 11:15).

THEY'VE GOT IT COVERED

A woman's headdress was usually lighter material and finer quality than a man's and more colorful or patterned. With the headdress, veils were often worn as protection from the hot sun. But veils were not always worn. Unmarried women wore them as a sign of modesty. For example, Rebekah did not put on a veil until she was taken to meet her future husband, Isaac (Genesis 24:65).

How Did They Make That?

If you want a new shirt, you can go to the store and expect to find a variety of styles, fabrics, colors, and sizes. Clothing factories didn't exist in biblical times. Neither did stores with large selections. Women were usually responsible for making all the clothing. Look at these processes for making clothes and you will see why it took them so long just to make one item.

DID YOU KNOW?

The first clothing designers were Adam and Eve! After they disobeyed God in the Garden of Eden, they realized they were naked, and tried to cover themselves in fig leaves (Genesis 3:7)—not a look that worked well. But God later made them proper clothing out of animal skins (Genesis 3:21).

DID YOU KNOW?

Long sleeveless external robes of blue or purple fabric were worn by royalty, prophets, and the wealthy. When the soldiers mocked Jesus before his death, they placed a purple robe on his body (Mark 15:17-20).

Spinning

Spinning is the process of creating yarn from various raw fiber materials. Women in Bible times would twist together separate fibers to make them one long, stronger piece of yarn. The quality of the yarn depended on the quality of the fiber and the twist. Skilled women used their hands; others used wooden machines called spinning wheels.

Photos.com

Tanning

The earliest clothing was made from the skins of wild animals. Tanning is the process of turning animal hides and skins into leather by soaking them in lime and the leaves and juices of certain plants. After removing hair from the skins, the tanners would pound dog or pigeon dung into the skins to soften them. Children were often in charge of gathering dung. And you think cleaning your room is an awful job? Tanners, some of the poorest people, lived outside of the city because the smell of the hides and skins was so horrible.

Weaving

Wool from sheep was bleached and spun into thread. The threads were then stretched on looms. Cloth was made when the threads were passed over and under each other repetitiously at perpendicular angles.

DID YOU KNOW?

According to Deuteronomy 22:11, wool and linen were not to be woven together. (For rules on dealing with contaminated fabrics, see Leviticus 13:47-59.)

Types of Fabrics

Fabric	Origin	Who Wore It
Fine linens	Flax plant	Wealthy; royalty; those in high religious positions
Sackcloth	Goat/camel hair	Poor people; worn in times of sadness or mourning
Silk	Silkworms, imported from China	Royalty; wealthy
Cotton	Trees	All social classes
Wool	Sheep	All social classes; often worn for warmth

DID YOU KNOW?

John the Baptist wore clothes made of camel's hair and had a leather strap around his waist (Matthew 3:4). He wanted to distinguish himself from religious leaders who were prideful about their position.

Jewelry

♦ Jewelry often symbolized someone's wealth.

♦ Jewelry was often given as a gift (Numbers 31:50).

♦ Men wore jewels, usually wearing a ring on the finger or on a cord around the neck.

♦ Women wore multiple bracelets on their arms and ankles that jangled when they walked. They also wore earrings. The servant who was sent to select a bride for Abraham's son, Isaac, gave Rebekah a ring and two gold bracelets (Genesis 24:22).

Makeup Anyone?

While statues of Egyptians show that Egyptian women used eye makeup—charcoal and eye shadow in blues and greens—no one can say for sure that the women of Israel wore it. After hundreds of years of slavery in Egypt (Exodus 1), the women of Israel might have been influenced by the Egyptian women.

The wicked Queen Jezebel was known for using eye shadow (2 Kings 9:30). She was a princess from Tyre and Sidon before her marriage to Ahab, king of Israel.

COSMETICS: POPULAR PERFUMES

Nard

Spikenard (or nard) was a very expensive perfume. Nard was produced from a plant that grows in the Himalayas and was very costly to import to the Near East from India. In Mark 14:3-5, a woman anointed Jesus' feet with nard. Her bottle could have been sold for more than three hundred silver coins, which was more than a year's worth of wages.

Frankincense

Frankincense is a resin that comes from the very scraggly but hardy Boswellia tree. Frankincense gives off a slight lemon scent. It is still used in modern perfumery. It is best known as one of the gifts that was presented to Jesus by the wise men upon his birth in Bethlehem (Matthew 2:11).

Myrrh

Myrrh is a valuable, sweet smelling powder, native to Somalia. The aroma of myrrh is slightly pungent; it is bitter to the taste. Like frankincense, myrrh was used in large quantities for the preparation of the perfumed oils used as incense. At his birth, one of the wise men presented Jesus with myrrh (Matthew 2:11). Before Esther was chosen as queen of Persia, she went through a year of beauty treatments (Esther 2:12) that included myrrh and other perfumes.

45

CREATION

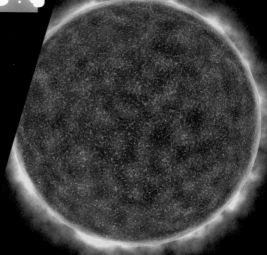

The first thing the Bible tells us about the world is that God made it. The very first words of the Bible are, "In the beginning God created the heavens and the earth" (Genesis 1:1). It's difficult to imagine a beginning to the planet or the universe, isn't it? But the Bible says the earth was without shape and was empty. Above the earth lay a vast quantity of water. The Spirit of God waited above the empty waters. A strong wind from God blew above the empty water. And when God created light, our days began.

DAY 1

God said, "I command light to shine!" (Genesis 1:3). God made light that shone before he made the sun! God made the light shine first because everything else he made needed its energy to grow and live. The word *yom* is a biblical Hebrew word that means "day." Genesis 1:5 says: "Evening came and then morning—that was the first day (*yom*)." *Yom* can also be used to talk about a period of time, a little bit like when older people say "back in my day."

DAY 2

God made the sky to separate the water above from the water below (Genesis 1:6). This is what we call the atmosphere. The blanket or tent of the atmosphere keeps the warmth of the sun in at night and protects us from being blasted by the sun during the day. Without it, all of earth's water would evaporate away into space.

DID YOU KNOW?

There is more to light and energy than what you see! Gamma rays, X-rays, ultraviolet light, visible light, infrared light, microwaves, television waves, and radio waves are all part of the electro-magnetic spectrum. Their light and energy are just a small part of the power of God.

DAY 3

On the third day God separated the oceans from the land. God told the earth to grow all kinds of plants (Genesis 1:9-11).

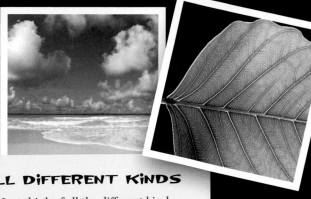

ALL DIFFERENT KINDS

Just think of all the different kinds of life that God created. There are about 350,000 species of plants on this incredible planet!

DAY 4

In Genesis 1:14 we're told that God arranged the lights in the sky to keep regular time—days and nights—and to measure the seasons. Most of the calendars of the world, even in earliest times, have been arranged around the cycles of the sun, moon, and stars. Our solar system includes the sun, the eight planets and their 166 moons, three dwarf planets—Ceres, Pluto, and Eris—and their four known moons, plus other small bodies. While our solar system might seem huge, it is just one speck in our galaxy (the Milky Way), which is in the ballpark of 100,000 light years (625,000 billion miles—how far light travels in a year) across! To give you a better idea: hold a quarter in your hand. If the quarter were the size of the solar system, the galaxy would be the size of North America!

The Terrestrial Inner Planets with Sun in the center

The Asteroid Belt

The Kuiper Belt

The Giant Planet zone

Pluto

Earth (and Moon)

background image by Stock.com

47

DAY 5

In Genesis 1:20-23, we read that "So God made the giant sea monsters and all the living creatures that swim in the ocean. He also made every kind of bird." Some of those "sea monsters" are still around. For example, giant squid are "living fossils"; they can be found fossilized yet still live today. These squishy guys can be as long as forty feet from tentacle tip to tentacle tip.

A coelacanth is another living fossil. Scientists believed it was extinct until a fisherman caught one in his net in 1938.

WHAT A CATCH!

On April 25, 1977, Japanese fishermen on the ship *Zuiyo Maru* dragged what looked like either a dead and rotting plesiosaur or a giant basking shark out of the ocean near New Zealand. The body was about thirty feet long and very smelly! They threw it back after they took pictures and saved some pieces of it.

DAY 6

God told the earth to give life to all animals: wild, tame, and reptile. Even from the beginning, some animals could be tamed and some animals couldn't. God created humans to be like himself and put humans in charge of the earth to care for it. God gave people fruits and grains to eat, and green leafy plants to the animals to eat (Genesis 1:24-31). Did you notice that in the beginning people and animals didn't eat meat? No hamburgers in Eden! At the end of every day that God created things that live, he looked at what he had done and called it "good." Plants are good, fish are good, and birds and animals are good. There was only one day that God said "*VERY* good!" That was the sixth day, when he made people to be, in some way, like him (Genesis 1:27).

DAY 7

On the seventh day, we're told that God rested (Genesis 2:2). The seven days of creation are written as an example to us. God didn't need to rest, but he did it so that we would have a good example to follow. If we worked seven days a week, just think how tired and useless we'd feel!

THE STORY OF ADAM & EVE

[GENESIS 2]

DUST OF THE EARTH Genesis 2:7 says that God made Adam from the dust of the ground. God breathed life into Adam. The breath that God gave to Adam means being alive with a body and being alive with a spirit. We are made alive by the breath of God.

THE FIRST GARDEN God made a garden for Adam full of all sorts of beautiful trees with delicious fruits. In the middle of the garden were two mysterious trees—the tree of life and the tree of the knowledge of good and evil. A river watered the Garden of Eden, and then split into four rivers: the Pishon, Gihon, Tigris, and Euphrates (Genesis 2:8).

Today we only know where the Tigris and Euphrates Rivers are. They begin in Turkey and flow through Iraq. (The Euphrates River also crosses Syria.) They join back together to form the Shatt al-Arab River and pour into the Persian Gulf.

ADAM'S JOB God made the animals and Genesis 2:20 says, "He brought them to the man to see what names he would give each of them. Then the man named the tame animals and the birds and the wild animals. That's how they got their names."

Adam Naming the Animals, Theophenes the Cretan (16th century)

By naming the animals, Adam showed one of the ways that humans are like God. Having the gift of language and being able to name things is a power that people have and God has. Adam's job was to take care of the garden. Some of the animals may have helped him do this, but they could not help in the way a true partner could.

ENTER: EVE Adam probably loved all the animals very much, but he was still lonely because he did not have a partner who was like him. When God created Eve using part of Adam's side, or rib, it showed that men and women can help each other side-by-side in a loving way.

When Adam first saw Eve, what he said is recorded in the Bible in the style of a psalm. A psalm is a Hebrew song. A Hebrew song rhymes meanings instead of rhyming sounds, so we can still understand the rhymes thousands of years later in another language. Adam sings Eve this love song when he sees her:
"Here is someone like me! She is part of my body, my own flesh and bones. She came from me, a man. So I will name her Woman!" (Genesis 2:23)

Crime & Punishment

WHAT WAS CRUCIFIXION?

Throughout history, most civilizations had some form of capital punishment. The Romans often used a gruesome form of execution called crucifixion. Prisoners were beaten with whips and forced to carry their own cross to the place where they would die. They were either tied or nailed to the cross. (The Romans used many kinds of crosses: T-shaped crosses, X-shaped crosses, even the trunks of old trees.) The painful position made it difficult for the condemned person to breathe, and they would eventually die of suffocation. Sometimes people lived for as long as a week before dying. The Romans would often break the prisoner's legs to speed things up.

DID YOU KNOW?

Early Christians probably would have been horrified at the idea of wearing a cross as jewelry or for decoration.

Law and Order—Hebrew Style

God gave the original Hebrew law to Moses on the top of Mount Sinai (Exodus 20–31). As the leader of the people of Israel, Moses served as their judge in cases where God's law had been broken. Later, the people of ancient Israel took their disputes to judges and then to kings. When Israel was ruled by other nations, some cases were heard by government officials of the ruling nation.

The cases brought before a judge were handled much as they are today. Witnesses were called. The accused were allowed to tell their side. These arguments were heard by the judge and a "jury" of local citizens, usually officials of the temple. A guilty verdict might mean simply paying for damages, but it could mean death. Crimes worthy of death included murder, theft, witchcraft, and attacking a parent.

לא תרצח
לא תנאף
לא תנגב
לא תצנה
לא תחמד

אנכי יהוה
לא יהיה
לא תשא את
זכור את יום
כבד את אבן

WHAT IS FLOGGING?

A flogging, or whipping, was a punishment often given to those who committed crimes not worthy of death. The convicted prisoner was stripped naked and tied, hands overhead, to a post. The number of lashes depended on the seriousness of the crime. Under Hebrew law, the prisoner could receive up to forty lashes, but the general practice was to stop at thirty-nine—just in case there had been a miscount.

WHAT IS STONING?

The Martyrdom of St. Stephen, Gustave Doré, engraving (1865)

Stoning may be the oldest form of execution on earth. It was the common form of punishment required for certain crimes by Hebrew law.

The convicted prisoner was thrown into a pit outside the city and then pelted with rocks
until dead. This primitive form of execution is still carried out in some cultures today.

One of the most infamous stonings recorded in the Bible was the stoning of Stephen, one of the leaders of the early church. Read the full story in Acts 6:8—7:60.

WEAPONS FOR FLOGGING

- Rod—or stick
- Whip—usually made of a long piece of braided leather attached to a handle
- Cat of Nine Tails—a whip with several strips of leather bound to one handle
- Whip of Scorpions—a cat of nine tails with bits of glass or metal embedded in the end of each strip

DID YOU KNOW?

In ancient times, you could get the death penalty for cursing your mother or father (Exodus 21:17).

The Flogging of Jesus

Before his crucifixion, Jesus was ordered to be flogged by Pilate. By the time Jesus was led out to Golgotha he was so weak from the beating, he could not carry his own cross (Mark 15:15-22).

The First Punishment

In the beginning Adam and Eve lived in the Garden of Eden. They had everything they needed. There was only one rule: eating fruit from the tree of knowledge in the center of the garden was a big no-no. When the smooth talking serpent came along, Adam and Eve caved in and ate the fruit. For their punishment they were kicked out of the Garden of Eden. On top of that, Eve would have pain in childbirth and Adam would have to work hard to grow food in the very dirt from which he was made. The serpent was doomed to crawl on his belly and eat dust for the rest of his life (Genesis 3:1-19).

Lot and his daughters fleeing Sodom, artist unknown

Don't Look Back

Abraham's nephew, Lot, lived with his family in the city of Sodom. The people of Sodom were wicked. They were so bad God decided to destroy the entire city. God sent two angels to rescue Lot and his family. As the angels herded Lot, his wife, and his two daughters out of the city, Lot's wife looked back. The angel had told them not to, but Lot's wife couldn't help but feel sad about all she was leaving behind. She was going to miss the fine house and the lifestyle they had there. As she turned to look, she immediately became a pillar of salt (Genesis 19:1-26).

Moses Comes Down the Mountain

After spending forty days with God on Mount Sinai receiving the law, Moses came down the mountain to find the people shouting and dancing around a golden calf. He was furious. First he melted the calf and ground it into a powder. The powder was scattered into the water and the people were forced to drink it. Then Moses stood at the gate of the camp and shouted for everyone who was on God's side to join him. As men of the tribe of Levi gathered around Moses, he gave them God's chilling command: strap on your sword and go through the camp killing your relatives, friends, and neighbors because they worshiped an idol. About three thousand men died that day (Exodus 32:19-29).

Moses Showing the Ten Commandments, Gustave Doré, engraving (1865)

Stolen Goods

When the dust from the battle of Jericho had cleared, God said all the spoils of the battle were to be his. But Achan, from the tribe of Judah, couldn't seem to resist. He took some of the things for himself and hid them under his tent. God told Joshua what Achan had done. When Achan confessed, he and his entire family were stoned to death. Their bodies, everything Achan had owned, and the stolen goods were then burned together (Joshua 7:1-26).

Abimelech's Punishment from Above

Abimelech was a son of Gideon (Gideon was one of Israel's judges) by a woman from Shechem. After Gideon's death, Abimelech's ambition was to become king of Israel. To get rid of the competition he killed seventy of Gideon's sons. Only one escaped. God punished Abimelech for killing his brothers by allowing a woman to drop a millstone (a stone used for grinding grain) from the top of a building onto his head. With his head cracked open and bleeding, Abimelech ordered one of his soldiers to run him through with a sword so that no one could say he had been killed by a woman (Judges 9:52-57).

A Lying Servant

Naaman, a commander in the Syrian army, had leprosy. At the prophet Elisha's instructions, Naaman dipped himself seven times in the Jordan River and was healed. Naaman tried to reward Elisha with a gift, but Elisha refused. After Naaman left, Elisha's servant, Gehazi, followed Naaman. He lied to Naaman and told him Elisha had sent him to ask for clothes and silver for two young prophets from the hills of Ephraim. God told Elisha what Gehazi had done. Caught in his lies, Gehazi turned white with leprosy (2 Kings 5).

Ahab and Jezebel: Doomed by Their Own Evil Deeds

Ahab was one bad dude—and not in a good way. The seventh king of Israel, Ahab married Jezebel, daughter of the king of the Sodonians, and began to worship and serve Baal as she did. Ahab did more to make God angry than any king before him had ever done. The last straw came when Ahab decided he wanted a vineyard belonging to another man. When the man wouldn't sell, Ahab and Jezebel plotted to have the man put to death on false charges. As Ahab was taking over his new property, God sent him a message through the prophet Elijah. The message was: "On the very spot where dogs licked up Naboth's blood, they will lick your blood. . . . You and every man and boy in your family will be wiped out. . . . As for Jezebel, dogs will eat her body in Jezreel" (1 Kings 21:17-24). Three years later everything happened just as Elijah had said (1 Kings 22:29-38; 2 Kings 9:30-37).

Elijah confronting King Ahab, chromolithograph (mid-19th century)

A Lie That Led to Death

Ananias and his wife Sapphira owned a piece of land. As members of the early church, they sold the land and donated the money to the apostles. But Ananias must have had second thoughts about his donation. With Sapphira's knowledge, Ananias kept back part of the money and took the rest to the apostles, pretending that it was the entire amount. The Holy Spirit spoke to the apostle Peter, who exposed Ananias's lie. Ananias fell down dead on the spot. A few hours later Sapphira came in search of her husband. When Peter questioned her, she insisted her husband had brought the full amount for the land. Immediately she was struck dead, too (Acts 5:1-11).

53

CURRENCY

The Beginning of Money

Ever trade a game or a favor with someone in exchange for something else? We call that bartering. Long before the birth of Christ, the first financial systems were developed from a barter system, where items that a person owned were exchanged for other items that they needed. Under this system, no money changed hands. In fact, money as we know it today didn't even exist.

The first international trade—trading between countries—started between the rulers. Meanwhile, people began to barter as a way to get the goods they needed. Silver, gold, and other precious jewels were used as money. These items were weighed according to standard scales to make sure cheating did not occur.

Over the years as money began to develop and banks were created, many people continued to use the barter system to acquire their merchandise.

Timeline

10,000 - 7,000 B.C.	3,000 - 2,000 B.C.	2,250 - 2,150 B.C.	about 2,100 B.C.	about 1,750 B.C.
Farmers and herders use livestock and grain as money in a barter system.	Banking begins in Mesopotamia.	Rulers of Cappadocia (Turkey) guarantee the purity and weight of silver bricks.	Ur-Nammu, a Sumerian king, creates a law code that sets monetary fines to punish crimes.	Babylonian king Hammurabi creates laws that set punishments for crimes and govern banking operations.

DID YOU KNOW?

King Solomon's chariot imported from Egypt cost around fifteen pounds (600 shekels) of silver, and a horse cost four pounds of silver (160 shekels) (1 Kings 10:28-29).

Kings Make a Trade

King Solomon needed lumber to build the Jerusalem temple and the royal palace. Hiram, the king of Tyre, had lots of lumber, so they made a deal.

Hiram gave Solomon all the cedar and pine logs he needed. In return, Solomon gave Hiram about 125,000 bushels of wheat and about 1,100 gallons of pure olive oil each year (1 Kings 5:10-11).

John Wollinka

Products of Tyre

In Ezekiel 27, God reminded Ezekiel of the powerful trading city of Tyre before its destruction. This chart, with references to Ezekiel 27, shows the kinds of items traded in ancient times.

Merchants from southern Spain	Silver, iron, tin, lead (27:12)
People of Greece, Tubal, and Meshech	Slaves; things made of bronze (27:13)
People from Beth-Togarmah	Work horses, war horses, mules (27:14)
People from Rhodes, nations along the coast	Ivory, ebony (27:15)
Edom	Emeralds, purple cloth, embroidery, fine linen, coral, rubies (27:16)
Judah and Israel	Wheat, fancy figs, honey, olive oil, spices (27:17)
The people of Damascus	Wine, wool (27:18)
Vedan and Javan	Iron, spices (27:19)
The people of Dedan	Saddle blankets (27:20)
People from Arabia and the rulers of Kedar	Lambs, sheep, goats (27:21)
Merchants from Sheba and Raamah	Spices, precious stones, gold (27:22)
Merchants from Haran, Canneh Eden, Sheba, Asshur, and Chilmad	Clothing, purple and embroidered cloth, rugs, rope (27:23-24)

Coins in the New Testament

COIN	ORIGIN	WORTH	MADE OF	WHAT'S SPECIAL ABOUT IT?
Lepton	Minted by Alexander Jannaeus, king of Judea (103–76 B.C.)	Half a quadran	Bronze	This was the widow's "mite" (Mark 12:41-44).
Quadran	Roman	Low value	Bronze	This was probably the coin referred to by Jesus in the Sermon on the Mount (Matthew 5:26).
Denarius	Roman	One day's wage	Silver	This Roman coin was the most common coin in circulation during the time of Jesus. This was the coin given to Jesus in Luke 20:24.
Drachma	Greek	Equal to a denarius	Silver	This coin could purchase one sheep. The lost coin in Jesus' parable (Luke 15:8) was probably a drachma.
Didrachmon— the double drachma	Greek	Half a shekel	Silver	Jews used it to pay temple taxes (Matthew 17:24-25).

about 640 B.C.	about 600 B.C.	about 538 B.C.	336 - 323 B.C.	323 - 30 B.C.
The first true coins—a natural mixture of silver and gold called *electrum*—are minted in Asia Minor.	Pythius's records, from Asia Minor, are the oldest surviving banking records.	The Persians introduce the coin system to Palestine. One Persian coin is the *daric*.	Alexander the Great uses Persian gold to pay his soldiers, and is the first ruler to put his face on coins.	The first unified banking system is created during the dynasty of Ptolemy of Egypt and his descendants.

Weights and Values

Coins were not used much in Old Testament times before the time of the Persian Empire. Lumps of pure silver or gold were used as payment. Standards were established for acceptable weights.

WEIGHT	How long would it take an average worker to earn this amount?
One shekel = 20 gerahs (about 4/10 oz.) (Ezekiel 45:12)	Four days
One mina = 60 shekels (about 1.25 lbs.) (Ezekiel 45:12)	Three months
Talent = 60 minas (about 75 lbs.) (Ezra 8:26)	Fifteen years

Heads or Tails?

Take a look at some of your loose change. Whose images do you see? U.S. Presidents, right? In New Testament times, the Romans displayed their emperor's image on the coin. This was less about patriotism than about reminding the Roman subjects that the emperor was in charge. In Matthew 22:18-22, Jesus was given a denarius (silver coin) with the image and name of Tiberius Caesar Augustus. (See also Mark 12:15-17; Luke 20:22-26.)

DID YOU KNOW?

A shekel weighs about the same as a U.S. half-dollar (a fifty-cent piece). If you hold forty half-dollars in your hand, that is equal to about one pound of silver.

Images by iStock.com

Common Spices Used as Currency

Many spices were valued for their medicinal benefits, and they were highly sought after. Spices were often used as a form of money. These are a few of the valuable and costly spices:

Aloes *(John 19:39)*

Calamus *(Song of Songs 4:14)*

Cassia *(Exodus 30:23-25)*

Cinnamon *(Exodus 30:23-25)*

Cummin *(Isaiah 28:27; Matthew 23:23)*

Galbanum *(Exodus 30:34-35)*

Henna *(Song of Songs 4:13)*

Nard/Spikenard *(Mark 14:3)*

Onycha *(Exodus 30:34-35)*

Saffron *(Song of Songs 4:14)*

Stacte *(Exodus 30:34-35)*

Perfume

Perfumes were often given as gifts because they were highly desirable. They were considered luxury items. They cost a fortune to make because their ingredients had to be imported from far-off lands! Upon Jesus' birth, wise men from the east gave the infant Jesus frankincense and myrrh, two very sought-after perfumes (Matthew 2:11). Other highly valued perfumes and ingredients included aloes, cinnamon, nard (spikenard), and saffron. Spices to make perfumes were brought into Palestine from India, Arabia, Persia, Mesopotamia, and Egypt. Mixed with other scents, spices, and oils, they were used for:

Preparing sacred incense to be burned during worship (Exodus 30:34-38)

Anointing or dedicating people or items for God's service (Exodus 30:23-26, 30-32)

Personal hygiene for special events like weddings (Psalm 45:8)

Embalming and preparing the dead for burial (John 19:39-40)

John Wollinka

How Much Is Your Brother Worth?

Sometimes we don't get along with our siblings. But could you ever sell your brother for a few dollars? Joseph's brothers (the sons of Jacob) were jealous of him and decided to sell Joseph to passing traders for twenty pieces of silver (Genesis 37:27-28).

Payday

Do you get paid for a job or for responsibilities around your home? How do you like to get paid? With money, most likely. In biblical times, some people usually didn't have a choice how they were paid.

shepherds (Genesis 30:31-32; 31:7-8)	A portion of the flock or herd of animals
farm laborers (Matthew 21:41)	A portion of the harvest
skilled laborers (Matthew 20:2)	One denarius or "the usual amount" for a day's work

DID YOU KNOW?

Judas Iscariot betrayed Jesus for thirty silver coins (Matthew 26:14-16). After Jesus' death, he threw the money at the temple leaders. They used the money to buy a field (Matthew 27:3-8).

Why Did They Do That?

Sometimes we find strange stories in the Bible that make us curious. Why did some men have two or more wives at the same time? Why would anyone wash another person's feet? To understand the Bible better, it's helpful to look at the cultural background of the ancient Near East. In the following pages, we'll look at some of the fascinating and fantastic customs of the world of the Bible.

The Strange, the Surprising, and THE EXTRAORDINARY...

Household Customs:
Home Is Where Your Tent Is!

The first houses of the ancient Israelites were tents (Genesis 18:1). Like their ancestor Abraham (God's chosen follower), God's people were mostly a nomadic (wandering herder) people. They were always moving from place to place. Even when they began to settle in cities, the earliest Israelites still used words to describe their houses that more accurately referred to features of their tents. The tent was divided into two sections: the front, where visitors were welcome, and the back, where the women and children were kept strictly separate.

Illustration by Ron Wheeler

Rules of Hospitality

In Bible times, hospitality was not an option; it was a rule, and often a matter of life and death. Even if you were enemies with someone, you were still expected to overlook the feud temporarily by offering them water, food, and shelter. Hospitality also included giving water to their animals.

Because of the dusty, dirty climate they lived in, any stranger in the desert was to be offered not only water, food, and shelter but also a modest foot washing.

Photos.com

So That's Why . . .

Rebekah, who became Isaac's wife, gave water to a stranger's ten camels. This was not a little sip of water from a cup. She had to climb down a steep stairway and bring up 300 gallons of water! (See Genesis 24:17-20.)

While on the run from the jealous King Saul, David became angry with the rich sheep owner, Nabal, for ignoring the tradition of hospitality. Nabal refused to give food to David and his men after they had watched his flocks. Nabal's foolish behavior earned him a death sentence (1 Samuel 25:2-40).

Photos.com

Jesus washed his disciple's feet (John 13:4-15) as a way of saying, "Anyone who welcomes you welcomes me" (Matthew 10:40).

Did You Know?

Kisses were exchanged when a guest arrived and departed (Genesis 29:9-14). It was a sign of welcome and friendship. If you were really respected, someone might even kiss your feet. Sadly, the disciple Judas used this tradition to let Jesus' enemies know who he was. In greeting Jesus with a kiss, Judas was really betraying him (Matthew 26:48-50).

Ancient Near Eastern Etiquette Guide

Let's just pretend
for a moment that you were suddenly transported back in time three thousand years to ancient Israel, and a guest suddenly showed up at your tent. You wouldn't want to be unprepared. The following guide will help you know what to do:

iStock.com

- ✿ If he is a relative, greet him with a kiss on both cheeks (Exodus 4:27).

- ✿ Offer him water right away because he is probably parched from the desert heat (Genesis 24:14; John 4:6-8).

- ✿ Make sure you water his camels (Genesis 24:19-20). (You might need your servants to help you with this. Camels drink up to twenty-five gallons a day, and the jars used to carry water from the well only held up to three gallons each.)

- ✿ Pick a nice fat calf and take time to prepare it for a meal. This will take hours of hard work so it would be good to start early (Genesis 18:7).

- ✿ In the meantime, bring out water and towels and wash the mud and dust off the guest's feet so he can lounge comfortably in the shade of your tent (Genesis 18:4).

- ✿ Prepare a place for the guest and his animals to sleep (Genesis 24:32).

Livelihood Customs:
Horseless "Cowboys" of the Desert

Many nomads in the ancient Near East were sheepherders and cowherders. They lived off their animals and traveled to spots where their herds could graze. Because of this dependence on their animals, they developed interesting customs of hospitality.

DID YOU KNOW?

There was a belief that if two plain colored sheep mated in front of a streaked and spotted branch, they would produce speckled and spotted offspring.

So THAT'S WHY . . .

Laban (who was Rebekah's brother) and his relative Jacob spent a lot of time trying to trick each other. Jacob was tricked into taking the speckled or spotted sheep as payment, and found out that there were no speckled or spotted sheep. When he tried the old spotted branch trick, Jacob found to his delight that it worked. He was rich with spotted sheep! (See Genesis 30:25-43.)

Mealtime Customs: Mind Your Manners!

Eating and preparing food together was a big part of the life and culture of Israel. Eating food with someone was a way of saying, "You're my friend" or "I want to do business with you."

 ## So That's Why . . .

▶ Queen Esther of Persia organized a formal meal in the form of a banquet to break the news to the king about his official, Haman, who was plotting to kill the Jews. She waited until the second night of feasting to break the news (Esther 5:4-8; 7:1-6).

▶ If someone invited you into his or her house in ancient times, it was automatically assumed that a meal would be served. Because of the strict laws about what Jews could and could not eat, it was difficult for them to be friends with Gentiles (people outside of their culture). Such friendship could mean that they would eat with them and then partake of nonkosher foods such as pork.

Contract-Making Customs:
Break a Promise, Break a Leg or Worse!

When we say, "I swear," the words are used for emphasis. In Bible times, to swear an oath was to seal a binding contract (Numbers 30:2; Matthew 5:33-37). Oaths were not to be made lightly! There were many ways that oaths or contracts were made.

One way to make a contract was to take off your sandal and give it to the person with whom you were making your promise. This was a sign to all that a deal had been made.

Another way of sealing an agreement was cutting an animal in two and walking between the two parts. This may have been a way of saying, "May this, or worse, happen to me if I break this agreement."

So That's Why . . .

▶ After God made a covenant or agreement with Abraham, Abraham took a cow, a goat, and a ram and cut them in two. God, represented by the smoke and fire, passed between the two halves (Genesis 15:9-21).

▶ In the book of Ruth, Boaz, rather than a man who was a closer relative, agreed to buy the property that belonged to Naomi's husband, who had since died. (Naomi was Ruth's mother-in-law.) The relative gave Boaz his sandal. In doing this the relative acknowledged that Boaz now had the right to marry the widow Ruth (Ruth 4:7-8). This comes from the idea that with your shoes you can walk the length of the land, and so the sandal became the "movable title" to that land.

Marriage Customs

There was no such thing as dating in ancient Israel. A girl was under her father's authority and he was the one to make the marriage plans, though she usually could decide if she liked the man or not. Marriage was an agreement between families. Having children was the main purpose of marriage, and sometimes people had more than one wife so that there could be more children.

When a girl or boy turned twelve or thirteen, they were considered adults and could marry, though they usually waited until the age of eighteen.

Since marriage was like a business arrangement, a price had to be paid for a bride. According to Deuteronomy, the minimum or usual price for a bride was at least fifty silver shekels—double the price of a slave. Some girls were bought for exploits in war.

Later, when literacy was more common, a certificate of divorce was given if a wife displeased her husband (Deuteronomy 24:1).

So THAT'S WHY . . .

▶ The older sister often had to be married before the younger one could be married so that she wouldn't be a financial drain on the family. Because of the custom of the bride being veiled at the wedding, Jacob was tricked into marrying Rachel's older sister, Leah, first. Jacob had to work seven more years to pay the bride price for Rachel (Genesis 29:21-27).

▶ Jesus talked about the misuse of the divorce rule (Matthew 19:8-9). He also explained that a man could not divorce his wife just because he didn't like her, but only when he could prove she had been unfaithful to him (Matthew 5:31-32).

Burial and Mourning Customs

In the ancient Near East, there was a public tradition of mourning. When Jacob died, Joseph "had everyone mourn and weep seven days for his father" (Genesis 50:10). This biblical account grounded the Jewish practice of mourning called "sitting shiva" for a deceased relative (*shiva* means "seven"). But the process of mourning could go on for weeks or months.

Unlike the Egyptians, the people of Israel did not practice embalming.

So THAT'S WHY . . .

▶ Joseph, an Israelite who had lived for many years in Egypt, had his father Jacob's body embalmed. The process took forty days. The people of Egypt mourned for Jacob for seventy days (Genesis 50:1-3)!

▶ In some cases professional mourners were hired to wail and moan loudly for the dead person's loss (Mark 5:38).

Ten Ways to Mourn in Ancient Times

1. Cry and wail loudly (Mark 5:38).

2. Throw dirt or ashes on your head (Nehemiah 9:1).

3. Tear your clothes (Ezra 9:3).

4. Shave your head (if you are a man) (Job 1:20).

5. Go barefoot (2 Samuel 15:30).

6. Pound your chest (Luke 18:13).

7. Refrain from washing or eating (2 Samuel 12:16-17, 20).

8. Pull hair from your beard (if you are a man) (Ezra 9:3).

9. Roll in the dust (Micah 1:10).

10. Wear coarse cloth called sackcloth (Genesis 37:34).

The Wedding and Engagement

So what would it look like once the families decided a marriage was acceptable? There were two stages. The first stage was the betrothal or the *kiddushin*, which means to sanctify or set apart. Although it was only the first stage of the marriage, it was as binding as the marriage itself. That's why i-n the New Testament, Joseph, although engaged to Mary, would have had to divorce her in order to break the engagement (Matthew 1:18-20).

The second stage was the *nissu'in*, which means to complete the marriage by making the woman the man's bride in every way.

First Stage: Betrothal (Kiddushin)

The matchmaker or father showed his intent to ask the woman to marry. Abraham's servant asked Rebekah's father, Bethuel, and her brother Laban to give their permission for Isaac to marry Rebekah (Genesis 24:49-51). A bride price was paid, as in Genesis 24:52-53, where Abraham's servant gave silver, gold jewelry, and beautiful clothing to Rebekah.

A contract (called a *ketuvah*) was made. The families had a ceremony with wine, and the bride returned to her own home. The betrothal usually lasted one or two years, but could last even longer than that.

During the time of separation, the bride-to-be learned how to be a virtuous wife, spoken of in Proverbs 31:10-31. The groom built the *chupah* and *chedar*, which were the wedding canopy and chamber.

The bride was then publicly veiled, letting others know she was set apart and "owned" by her husband. Rebekah put on a veil before meeting Isaac (Genesis 24:63-65).

Second Stage: Marriage Ceremony (Nissu'in)

A celebration was held with feasting and dancing (John 2:1-12). Towards evening, the bridegroom, accompanied by people dancing and celebrating, made his way to the wedding canopy and chamber in his house (Matthew 25:1-13).

The bride, veiled and decked out in jewelry, was escorted to the wedding canopy to meet the bridegroom, where a short ceremony was performed, sealing the contract with at least two witnesses. (Psalm 45:10-15).

DISASTERS AND CATASTROPHES

NEWS

You may have noticed that the Bible is full of references to earthquakes, fire, hail, and swarms of bugs. But why are these things mentioned so frequently? Many people in the Bible disobeyed God by ignoring his laws and by following other gods. Sometimes God used disasters and catastrophes to punish disobedience.

The Flood

(Genesis 6-9)

Long after the time of Adam and Eve, people became so evil that God decided to destroy every creature he had created. Only Noah pleased God. Only Noah loved God and kept his commands. God told Noah to build an ark, a huge boat to protect himself and his family from the flood. He also commanded Noah to bring seven pairs of the animals used for sacrifice, seven pairs of every kind of bird, and one pair of every other kind of animal. God did not want the animals on earth to be completely destroyed.

Noah's ark was 450 feet long, 75 feet wide and 45 feet high.

iStock.com

DID YOU KNOW? The Epic of Gilgamesh, an ancient text written by the Sumerians, also contains what is known as a "flood narrative." The story of the flood told in Gilgamesh has some similarities with the flood story of the Bible, but there are very significant differences as well, especially concerning God's love and protective care of Noah, his family, and the animals.

THE PROMISE OF THE RAINBOW

After the flood waters subsided, God promised Noah and his family that he would never again strike down every living thing or destroy the earth with a flood. As a sign of this promise, God placed a beautiful rainbow in the sky (Genesis 8:20—9:17).

THAT'S A LOT OF WATER!

Have you ever wished it would stop raining so that you could go outside rather than be stuck in your house? During the flood, it rained for forty days and forty nights, and the water stayed on the earth for 150 days (Genesis 7:17-24). The water above the sky and the water below the ground came together to create a huge flood. The waters rose so high that the highest mountains were under almost twenty-five feet of water (Genesis 7:19)!

Photos.com

DID YOU KNOW?

When the water went down, Noah's boat came to rest in the Ararat mountains (Genesis 8:4). Although there is a Mount Ararat in modern-day Turkey, no one is certain if this is the exact mountain mentioned in Genesis.

THE LIE THAT LED TO TROUBLE

When food became scarce in their homeland of Canaan, Abram (who would later become Abraham) and Sarai, his wife (later Sarah), went to live in Egypt. Abram was afraid that the king would notice that Sarai was very beautiful and would want to marry her. Because he feared that the king would kill him in order to marry Sarai, Abram told her to tell the king that she was Abram's sister. The king was fooled and brought Sarai into his household. Suddenly everyone in the king's household suffered terrible diseases. When the king discovered the lie, he ordered Abram and Sarai to leave Egypt (Genesis 12:10-20).

DiD YOU KNOW?

Three Egyptian gods were associated with the Nile: one of their most important gods, Osiris (the god of the Nile); their oldest god, Nu (the god of life in the river); and Hapi (the god of the flood). By turning the water of the Nile to blood, God showed that he was greater than Egypt's gods.

Plague	Bible Reference (EXODUS)
the Nile river turns to blood	7:14-24
frogs	7:25—8:15
gnats	8:16-19
flies	8:20-32
death of livestock	9:1-7
sores	9:8-12
hailstones	9:13-35
locusts	10:1-20
darkness	10:21-29
death of the firstborn sons and animals	11:1—12:30

NEWS

The Ten Plagues of Egypt

(Exodus 7–12)

Maybe you've heard the story of the ten plagues of Egypt, which God used to free the people of Israel from slavery.

The purpose of the plagues was to show the Pharaoh—the king of Egypt—and his people that the God of Israel was the one true God—not just of Israel, but of the whole world.

DiD YOU KNOW?

The Egyptians worshiped the god Heka, who was depicted with the head (and sometimes the body) of a frog.

Although the Pharaohs did many good public works projects they were known to be temperamental and very stubborn.

Gnats

The dust in Egypt became gnats during the third plague (Exodus 8:16-17). That's a lot of bugs! The word *kinnim*, which is translated in the Bible as "gnats," means "lice" in modern Hebrew. Since the bugs were on the bodies of men and animals, it is possible that the "gnats" were actually lice or mosquitoes.

Flies

These aren't the flies that annoy you during a picnic. Huge swarms of disease-carrying flies infested the land of Egypt. It is possible that the flies actually brought about the next two plagues. After all, some scholars believe that the disease that killed the Egyptian's livestock was anthrax, which can be spread by the insects. The sores or boils on the people and animals in the sixth plague may well have been caused by the bites of the flies, too.

A River of Blood

The people of Egypt were completely dependent upon the Nile River. They drank its water and used it to water their crops. When the waters of the Nile turned to blood, all the fish died and the river stank. Blood was everywhere in Egypt (Exodus 7:17-24).

frogs

Frogs completely covered the land of Egypt. Just because he was royalty didn't mean Pharaoh escaped the amphibian invasion. The man the Egyptians considered a god ended up with frogs in his bedroom and bed (Exodus 8:2-6)! Not only did the dead fish from the first plague cause the country to smell, when the frogs from this plague died, they polluted the land and caused Egypt to reek.

DiD YOU KNOW?

While Pharaoh's magicians were able to re-create some of the plagues, during the sixth plague the magicians were in such agony from the sores, they were unable to even approach Moses (Exodus 9:11).

Boils

The ancient Egyptians were very interested in medicine and looked to their gods and goddesses for healing from disease. They believed that healing power came from Amun-Re, the king of the Egyptian gods, and Thoth, whom many worshiped as the god of knowledge. The Egyptians also believed that the lion-headed goddess Sekhmet was able to both cause diseases and cure sickness. None of the Egyptians gods, however, could stop the plague of sores and boils.

Darkness

The Egyptians considered Amon-Re, the sun god, to be their most powerful god. But God proved that Amon-Re was no match for him by darkening the sun for three days (Exodus 10:21-23). Not being able to see for that long would scare the wits out of anyone—but especially a people who worshiped the sun.

Photos.com

Cow Catastrophe

Cows and bulls were sacred to the Egyptians. Egyptians worshiped a number of animal-headed gods, such as Apis (a bull), Mnevis (a bull), and Khnum (a ram). Even the queen of the gods, Isis, was sometimes pictured with cow horns on her head. So imagine how the Egyptians felt when their cattle died. But not just cattle—all of their animals died too (Exodus 9:1-6).

Hailstones

Hail is formed when drops of rain fall through alternating warm and cold air currents. You may have seen hail fall from the sky, perhaps before a major thunderstorm. Hail can damage crops and property. The hailstorm that God brought upon Egypt during the seventh plague destroyed everything. It was so severe that it could kill people working in the fields (Exodus 9:19). Only Goshen, the land of the Israelites, remained untouched (Exodus 9:26).

Not Just a Grasshopper

The plague of hail already destroyed most of Egypt's crops, but the plague of locusts ate everything that was left. Locusts are a type of grasshopper traveling in huge, destructive swarms, destroying every plant in their path (Exodus 10:15). The dead bodies of the insects could have led to a number of diseases, such as typhus, which affected people and animals.

iStock.com

DID YOU KNOW?

Locust swarms can contain millions of insects. The book of Joel says that swarms of locusts could be so large that they could literally blot out the sun, making the daytime as dark as night (Joel 2:10). Though the people of Israel were protected during the eighth plague, the Bible teaches that at other times, locusts were sent as a punishment for the Israelites' disobedience and stubbornness (Deuteronomy 28:42; Amos 4:9; 7:1-3).

DID YOU KNOW?

Besides Amon-Re, the Egyptians also worshiped falcon-headed Horus, the god of the sunrise; Aten, the god of the midday sun; and Atum, the god of the sunset. The Egyptians believed that Pharaoh was the son of Amon-Re.

The Death of the Firstborn

Have you ever studied ancient Egypt in school? If so, you probably gathered that the Egyptians were extremely interested in death and the afterlife. One of the primary gods of Egypt was Osiris, who was the god of the Nile and also the god of the dead. Osiris was assisted by Anubis, the god of the underworld, whom the Egyptians believed guided the dead into the afterlife. The tenth and final plague proved that Egypt's gods were completely powerless. Though all of Egypt's firstborn sons were killed (Exodus 12:29-30), not one of the Israelites saw death during this plague.

Photos.com

NEWS

EARTHQUAKES

Have you ever felt an earthquake? Amos 1:1 and Zechariah 14:5 both reference a great earthquake during the reign of King Uzziah of Judah. When a man named Korah rebelled against God and attempted to turn the Israelites against Moses, God used an earthquake to swallow him up, along with his followers and their families (Numbers 16:30-33). There was an earthquake when Jesus died on the cross (Matthew 27:51). First Samuel 14:15, Isaiah 29:6, and Revelation 6:12 show how God can use earthquakes!

NEW

DREAMS ABOUT COWS

Everyone has strange dreams at times, but one pharaoh of Egypt had some really strange ones about cows and scorched heads of grain. Joseph, a Hebrew man, explained that the pharaoh's dreams were a prediction of a famine that would strike Egypt. After seven years of fruitful crops and plenty to eat, Egypt would suffer seven years of famine. Joseph instructed the king to collect one-fifth of all the crops harvested in Egypt for the next seven years, so that when the famine came, the people would be ready (Genesis 41).

DROUGHTS

The word *drought* is used to describe the absence of rain over long periods of time. Droughts often result in famine. In the ancient Near East, droughts often meant that people would not have adequate food or crops.

NO RAIN IN SIGHT

King Ahab of Israel and his family angered God by worshiping Baal, a god of the Canaanites. In response to Ahab's idolatry, Elijah, a prophet of God, told Ahab that no rain would fall until the prophet said so (1 Kings 17:1). The drought lasted three years, and it brought a famine.

FIRE AND BRIMSTONE

Brimstone is an old name for sulfur, a yellowish, acidic, foul-smelling element. Sulfur is highly flammable. When God destroyed Sodom and Gomorrah, he "sent burning sulfur down like rain" on these cities (Genesis 19:24). Fire and brimstone are also mentioned in the book of Revelation as a form of punishment for those who have worshiped the beast (Revelation 14:9-10).

The Disciples

The Bible describes the ministry of Jesus, which took place mostly in the region of Galilee. His ministry lasted between one and three years. During that time, Jesus attracted many followers and he chose twelve of these followers to be key disciples (apostles). The word *disciple* comes from the word for "student" in Latin—not just any student but one getting *discipline* ("instruction, training") from a master teacher.

The story of how Jesus chose his disciples and began their training is in three of the four Gospels (Matthew 10:1-15;

Mark 3:13-19; Luke 6:12-16). They are also called the Twelve.

Jesus called together his twelve disciples. He gave them the power to force out evil spirits and to heal every kind of disease and sickness. (Matthew 10:1)

Jesus at the Last Supper stone carving, based on Leonardo da Vinci's famous painting

Jesus Taught . . . They Learned!

Why Twelve?

The number twelve is important in biblical history, referring back to the twelve tribes of Israel. In Matthew 19:28, Jesus promised his disciples that they would judge the twelve tribes of Israel. Israel is the name that God gave to Jacob. The twelve tribes were named after Jacob's sons— Reuben, Simeon, Levi, Judah, Zebulun, Issachar, Dan, Gad, Asher, Naphtali, Ephraim and Manasseh (the Joseph tribe was divided according to his two sons), and Benjamin. (See Genesis 49:1-28.) For more on the number 12, see Numbers, p. 184.

Apostles

DiD YOU KNOW?

• The twelve disciples were not well-educated men. But the teaching, training, and talents Jesus gave them made them an amazing force for God. They started the early Christian church and spread the gospel throughout their world, recorded in the book of Acts.

• An *apostle* is a follower who takes the teacher's mission and message to others. The Twelve became apostles after Jesus' resurrection. Several years later, so did Paul.

• Peter, James, and John were Jesus' most loyal and trustworthy disciples. They were present when Jesus raised Jairus's daughter from the dead (Mark 5:21-43). Jesus even let these three see him in his divine glory, talking with Moses and Elijah, both of whom had been dead for centuries (Matthew 17:1-8). They also were present with Jesus in the Garden of Gethsemane (Matthew 26:36-46) right before Jesus was arrested.

• At least five of the disciples were fishermen when they met Jesus. So he said, "Follow me! I will teach you how to bring in people instead of fish" (Matthew 4:19).

• Jesus chose his followers without regard to their social class, their politics, or their gender. His followers included Simon (a Zealot), Matthew (a tax collector), Nicodemus (a Pharisee), and many women such as Mary Magdalene, Mary, and Salome (Mark 15:40-41).

Name	Nickname	Former Job	Known For ...	Famous Quote	Key Bible References
Simon (son of John)	Also called *Peter* (in Greek, it is *Petros,* which means "rock," so he could have been called Rocky!)	Fisherman, from Bethsaida (Matthew 4:18)	Denying Jesus three times; becoming a great church leader	"You are the Messiah, the Son of the living God." (Matthew 16:16)	Matthew 16:16-19; Luke 22:31-34; John 21:15-25; Acts 1–5; 10:1–11:18
Andrew (Peter's brother)	None given in Scripture	Fisherman, from Bethsaida (Matthew 4:18)	Leading his brother Peter to Jesus; eager to bring others to Jesus	"We have found the Messiah!" (John 1:41)	Matthew 4:18-20; John 1:35-42; 6:8-9
James (son of Zebedee)	*Boanerges,* which means "sons of thunder" or "thunderbolts"	Fisherman (Matthew 4:21-22)	Wanting fame early, but very faithful; first disciple to be martyred (Acts 12:1-2)	"When you come into your glory, please let one of us sit at your right side and the other at your left." (Mark 10:37)	Mark 10:35-40; Luke 9:51-56; Acts 12:1-2
John (son of Zebedee)	*Boanerges,* which means "sons of thunder" or "thunderbolts"	Fisherman	Healing a lame man; defending the gospel news about Jesus	"Do you think God wants us to obey you or to obey him?" (Acts 4:19)	Mark 10:35-40; Luke 9:51-56; Acts 3:1–4:22
Philip	None given in Scripture	Fisherman, from Bethsaida (John 1:43)	Leading Nathanael to Jesus	"Lord, show us the Father. That is all we need." (John 14:8)	John 1:43-46; 6:2-7; 12:20-22; 14:8-14
Nathanael	*Bartholomew*	Unknown, from Cana (John 1:45)	First doubted, then believed	"Can anything good come from Nazareth?" (John 1:46)	Mark 3:18; John 1:45-51; 21:1-14
Thomas	*Didymus* ("twin")	Unknown	Needed to see proof of risen Jesus for himself	"I must put my hand where the spear went into his side. I won't believe unless I do this!" (John 20:25)	Matthew 10:3; John 14:5; 20:24-29; 21.1-13
Matthew	Also called *Levi*	Tax collector, from Capernaum	Hated for his job; had a dinner for Jesus; said yes to Jesus right away (Matthew 9:9-13)	When questioned why he associated with Matthew, Jesus said, "I didn't come to invite good people to be my followers. I came to invite sinners." (Matthew 9:13)	Matthew 9:9-13; Mark 2:13-17; Luke 5:27-32
James (son of Alphaeus)	None given in Scripture	Unknown	Followed Jesus; sometimes identified with "James the younger" in Mark 15:40	Unknown	Matthew 10:3; Mark 3:18; Luke 6:15
Thaddaeus	Also called *Judas, Jude, Judah*	Unknown	Followed Jesus and asked him about God's unfolding plan.	"Lord, what do you mean by saying that you will show us what you are like, but you will not show the people of this world?" (John 14:22)	John 14:22-31
Simon	The "Eager One," or "the Zealot"	Unknown	Unknown	Unknown	Matthew 10:4; Mark 3:18; Luke 6:15
Judas Iscariot	The "Betrayer"	Unknown, from Kerioth	Betrayed Jesus for money; took his own life	"How much will you give me if I help you arrest Jesus?" (Matthew 26:15)	Matthew 26:14-16; 20-25; John 12:4-8; 13:21-31

iStock.com

69

DID YOU KNOW? The French word for Easter, *Pâcques*, comes from the Greek word for "Passover."

What Is Easter?

Among Christians, Easter is a celebration of the resurrection of Jesus Christ after his death on the cross. In A.D. 325, the Council of Nicea (the first unified council of the Christian churches) decided that Easter should be celebrated on the first Sunday following the first full moon after the vernal equinox. This calculation causes it to fall on a Sunday sometime between March 22 and April 25. For Eastern Orthodox Christians, the date is calculated a little differently, normally leading to a date a week or several weeks later.

The early church celebrated the resurrection of Jesus at about the same time of year, around Passover, because the Gospels state that the events of Jesus' last days took place at that time.

The Main Events

(according to Gospel Traditions) Many events led up to and followed the death and resurrection of Jesus.

An Easter Timeline

Jesus enters the city of Jerusalem riding a donkey to shouts of "Hosanna!" *Matthew 21:1-11; Mark 11:1-11; Luke 19:28-38; John 12:12-19*

Jesus throws the moneychangers out of the temple. *Matthew 21:12-17; Mark 11:15-19; Luke 19:45-48; John 2:13-22*

Religious leaders plot to kill Jesus. *Matthew 26:1-5; Mark 14:1-2; Luke 22:1-2; John 11:45-53*

Judas agrees to betray Jesus. *Matthew 26:14-16; Mark 14:10-11; Luke 22:3-6*

Jesus shares the Passover meal with his disciples. *Matthew 26:20-30; Mark 14:12-21; Luke 22:7-13; John 13:21-30*

Jesus predicts Peter's denial. *Matthew 26:31-35; Mark 14:27-31; Luke 22:31-38; John 13:31-38*

Jesus goes to the Garden of Gethsemane to pray. *Matthew 26:36-46; Mark 14:32-42; Luke 22:39-46*

WARNING: BEING A FOLLOWER OF CHRIST MAY RESULT IN INJURY OR DEATH

Being a part of the early Christian church sometimes meant secret meetings and a life of hiding. Because Christians refused to worship the Roman state or its emperor, they were sometimes considered enemies of the Roman Empire. For this, they could be arrested and beaten or even killed. It is likely that the early Christians did celebrate Christ's resurrection in some way—but quietly. Attracting a lot of attention would not have been a good idea.

Easter: The Cast

Peter—On the night before the crucifixion, Peter denied knowing Jesus three different times (Matthew 26:69-75; Mark 14:66-72; Luke 22:54-65; John 18:25-27). (For more information on Peter, see Disciples, p. 68.)

Pontius Pilate—the Roman prefect (governor) of Judea at the time Jesus was crucified. When Caiaphas and the Jewish council (the Sanhedrin) decided Jesus must die, they handed him over to Pilate to do their dirty work. Pilate tried to release Jesus three times, but agreed to crucify Jesus to keep the peace (Matthew 27:11-26; Mark 15:2-15; Luke 23:1-25; John 18:28—19:16).

Barabbas—a criminal or revolutionary, mentioned in all four gospels. He was imprisoned by the Roman government at the time Jesus was brought before Pilate. It was Pilate's custom to release one prisoner chosen by the people. The crowd wanted Barabbas released instead of Jesus. (See references above.)

Caiaphas—the Jewish high priest in Jerusalem from about A.D. 18–36. He presided over the council that condemned Jesus to death (Matthew 26:57-68; Mark 14:53-65).

Easter: The Cast

Mary—mother of James and Joseph who witnessed Jesus' crucifixion and later went to anoint Jesus' body. She was among the first to see Jesus alive again after his death (Matthew 27:55-56; 28:1; Mark 15:40-41; 16:1; Luke 24:9-10).

Mary Magdalene—a devout follower of Jesus after he delivered her from seven demons. She followed his body to the burial site and was the first person to see and talk with Jesus after his resurrection (Mark 16:9-11; John 20:11-18).

The Other Women—followers of Jesus who witnessed the crucifixion and probably went together to anoint the body on Easter morning. The group may have included Salome (the wife of Zebedee and the mother of James and John), Joanna (the wife of Chuza, Herod's steward), and others. (See references in Mary and Mary Magdalene; also Luke 24:1-12.)

Simon—(called Simon from Cyrene) a man pulled from the crowd and forced to carry the cross of Jesus to Golgotha when Jesus could not carry it (Matthew 27:31-32; Mark: 15:21; Luke 23:26).

Joseph of Arimathea—a secret disciple of Jesus and a member of the Jewish council (the Sanhedrin who had no part in the decision to put Jesus to death. After Jesus' death, Joseph buried Jesus in an unused tomb cut into the rock (Matthew 27:57-60; Mark: 15:42-46; Luke 23:50-54; John 19:38-42).

Photos.com

Jesus' words from the cross, commonly known as "The Seven Last Words," are recorded in the four Gospels (Matthew, Mark, Luke, and John), but none of the Gospels contains all "seven words."

JESUS' SEVEN LAST WORDS

"Father, forgive these people! They don't know what they're doing."—Luke 23: 34

"I promise that today you will be with me in paradise."—Luke 23:43

When Jesus saw his mother and his favorite disciple with her, he said to his mother, "This man is now your son." Then he said to the disciple, "She is now your mother."—John 19:26-27

"Eli, Eli, lema sabachthani?" which means, "My God, my God, why have you deserted me?"— Mathew 27:46 (also Mark 15:34)

"I am thirsty!"—John 19:28

"Everything is done!"—John 19:30

"Father, I put myself in your hands!"—Luke 23:46

DID YOU KNOW?

The word *Hosanna* was part of a traditional Jewish prayer asking God for deliverance.

JESUS APPEARS TO HIS FOLLOWERS

Many people saw Jesus after his resurrection.

Photos.com

Person	Place	Where You Can Read This
Mary Magdalene, Joanna, Mary the mother of James, and others	The Tomb	Luke 24:1-10
Two followers of Jesus, one whom was Cleopas	Road to Emmaus	Luke 24:13-35
Peter	Unknown location in or near Jerusalem	Luke 24:34; 1 Corinthians 15:5
The disciples, minus Thomas	Jerusalem (after Peter's report)	Luke 24:36-43 John 20:19-23
The disciples, specifically Thomas	Jerusalem, a week after Jesus appeared to the disciples	John 20:24-29
The disciples	Sea of Galilee	John 21:1-14
The disciples	A mountain in Galilee	Matthew 28:16-20
The disciples	Near Bethany	Luke 24:50-51
The disciples	Various places over 40 days	Acts 1:1-11
500 followers	Unknown	1 Corinthians 15:6

Passion Plays

A passion play is a play about the life, death, and resurrection of Jesus. Passion plays began in the Middle Ages and have endured in one form or another to modern times. Some of the best known are:

Oberammergau in the Bavarian Alps—an amateur performance given every ten years beginning in 1634. The play is the result of a vow made during a plague. The only interruptions have been because of war.

Iztapalapa near Mexico City—is one of the most famous Easter events in Mexico. After a deadly cholera epidemic in 1833, the survivors put on the play as a way of giving thanks. The play is presented annually with the whole town participating.

EASTER SYMBOLS

THE LAMB

According to the Law of Moses, a blood sacrifice was needed to remove the uncleanliness caused by a person's sins (Hebrews 9:22). John the Baptist identified Jesus as the Lamb of God, whose purpose was to take away the sins of the world (John 1:29). The Gospel writers and early Christians also understood there to be a connection between Jesus the Lamb of God and the lamb sacrificed at the Passover Seder. The lamb, often shown together with a cross, is known as Agnus Dei, which means "Lamb of God" in Latin.

THREE CROSSES ON A HILL

iStock.com

Three crosses on a hill is a common Easter symbol. The three crosses represent the two thieves and Jesus who were crucified at the same time (Luke 23:32; 39-43). For Christians, it is a reminder of the Savior who gave his life on the cross for their sins

EASTER EGGS

Long before Christians began celebrating the resurrection of Jesus, eggs were used as a symbol of rebirth. It was common to exchange eggs as part of springtime celebrations. The eggs were often wrapped in colored paper, gold leaf, dyed, painted, or were decorated in some way. The eggs could also be used in games such as egg hunts and egg rolls where children rolled them down hills.

In Medieval times, eating eggs was forbidden during the Lenten season. The best way to preserve the eggs laid during this time was to boil them. All those boiled eggs became a big part of Easter meals and were prized gifts for children and servants.

EASTER BUNNIES

Photos.com

The first Easter bunnies probably originated in Germany, sometime in the sixteenth or seventeenth centuries, where parents told stories about an "Easter hare" who laid eggs for children to find. The custom was brought to America by German immigrants beginning in the 1700's.

EASTER LILIES

During the Middle Ages (from about A.D. 500–1500), lilies became associated with Mary the mother of Jesus, and were a symbol of purity for Christians. White trumpet lilies, also known as "Easter lilies," were first brought to the United States from Bermuda in about 1900. Because they bloom in the spring, they quickly became a favorite Easter decoration.

Last Days of Christ in Beaumont, Texas—a free-admission event that runs Thursday through Saturday nights before Easter each year. An outdoor interactive play, Last Days of Christ began in 1997 with one scene and eight actors. Today the performance stretches for a city block and involves over 600 actors and volunteers from more than twenty-five churches of various denominations.

Great Passion Play in Eureka Springs, Arkansas—hosts one of the most popular tourist' attractions in America. The Great Passion Play is presented daily, beginning in the spring and running throughout the summer. It is the centerpiece of an entire theme park that includes a Christ of the Ozarks giant statue, Museum of Earth History, Bible Museum, Sacred Arts Center, and a New Holy Land Tour.

France

France—For the French, Easter, or Pâcques, is mostly for the children. Bells and fish play a big part in their celebration. French Easter fish are called Poisson d'Avril. Paper fish are plastered to the backs of as many adults as possible as a sort of April fool's trick on April 1, and chocolate fish are sold in shops.

French Catholic tradition says that on Good Friday all the church bells in France fly to the Vatican in Rome, taking with them all the misery and grief of those who mourn Jesus' crucifixion. The flying bells (cloche Volant) return on Easter morning in time to celebrate Jesus' resurrection, leaving chocolate and eggs in the yards for the children. As part of the tradition, church bells remain silent from Good Friday through Easter Sunday.

Photos.com

Germany

In Germany, Easter is celebrated with Easter fires. Christmas trees are burned to show the end of winter and the beginning of spring. Everyone's house gets a good spring cleaning, and small trees or branches are brought inside to decorate with eggs.

Easter

Israel

Christians and Messianic Jews in Israel celebrate Easter with a sunrise service at the Garden tomb in Jerusalem. Easter mass is celebrated at the ancient Church of the Holy Sepulcher. During this time, many people also participate in processions that travel the route Christ took to Golgotha. The route is called the Fourteen Stations of the Cross, the Way of the Cross, or the Via Crucis (Latin for "Way of the Cross").

Mexico

Many people in Mexico participate in re-creations of the Via Crucis (the "Way of the Cross") on Holy Friday, or Viernes Santo. They attend an evening mass where they light candles at the altar. After the mass, parishioners gather outside to burn papier-mâché figures of Los Judas (the disciple Judas Iscariot, who betrayed Jesus). Each figure is set on fire and blown to pieces to symbolize the triumph of good over evil.

iStock.com

Greece

In Greece, Easter is one of the biggest celebrations of the year for Orthodox Christians. Eggs are boiled and dyed red to represent the blood of Jesus. The eggs are sometimes placed in the center of traditional Easter sweet bread called *tsoureki* before baking.

DID YOU KNOW?

The White House hosts an annual Easter Egg Roll on the grounds, which is attended by thousands. Begun in 1878 by Lucy Hayes, the First Lady of President Rutherford B. Hayes, the family event invites kids of all ages to hunt and race eggs on the White House lawn. (Contact the National Parks Service for tickets and rules.)

Norway

Norwegians take advantage of a public holiday from Holy Thursday through Easter Monday to read detective novels and watch crime dramas. No one is quite sure why, but it may have something to do with Christ's violent death.

Traditions Around the World

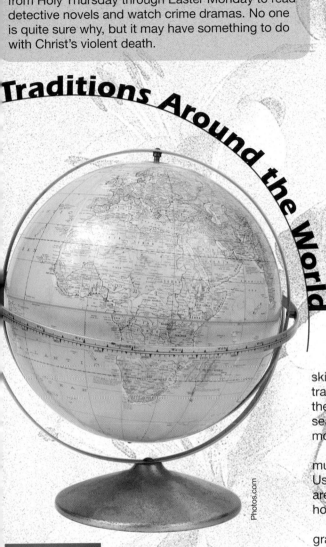

Photos.com

Photos.com

Sweden

People living in the western provinces of Sweden hold competitions to see who can build the biggest bonfire. Many people also shoot off fireworks.

United Kingdom

Until the beginning of World War II, skipping rope was a popular Easter tradition in Cambridge. The turning of the rope was a sign of the changing seasons. Dads turned the rope while moms and children jumped.

Many other English traditions are much like those in the United States. Usually on Good Friday, Easter eggs are decorated and Easter bread and hot cross buns are made.

The Welsh like to decorate the graves of family and friends on the Saturday before Easter with flowers. The colorful spring flowers are a celebration of the hope of resurrection Christians have in Jesus Christ.

Italy

During the week of Easter, people all across Italy fill the streets to participate in re-creations of Christ"s death sentence, suffering, and crucifixion called via cruces, which means "way of the cross." One of the largest is led by the Pope and begins at the Coliseum in Rome.

iStock.com

75

Ever wonder how people in ancient Israel were educated or what they learned? Read on...

PARENTS: The First Homeschoolers

Parents were expected to teach their children about God's laws. Their duties were first explained to them by Moses in one of his sermons:

Memorize [God's] laws and tell them to your children over and over again. Talk about them all the time, whether you're at home or walking along the road or going to bed at night, or getting up in the morning. Write down copies and tie them to your wrists and foreheads to help you obey them. (Deuteronomy 6:6-8)

Since women were not to study the Law of Moses (the first five books of the Bible), fathers were responsible for teaching their sons to read, write, and conduct business. While mothers helped as well, particularly when the children were young, the main responsibility fell to the fathers. However, if a father was away frequently on business, he could also hire a tutor.

Mothers were responsible for training their daughters in household duties, to be good wives, mothers, and useful members of the community.

DID YOU KNOW?

According to Deuteronomy 6:9, the people of ancient Israel were commanded to attach verses of the law to their doorposts to remind them to remember God's law. Jews continue this ancient practice today. The container with Scripture verses is called a *mezuzah*.

LEVITES AND PROPHETS: Spokesmen for God

Under the law given to Moses, the Levites were considered the priests and teachers of the people (Deuteronomy 33:10). In 2 Chronicles 17:7-9, Jehoshaphat, the king of Judah, sent Levites throughout the land to teach the people about the law. Some of these Levites were called prophets because they not only taught the people the law but they also spoke the words they believed God told them to speak. (For more information, see Prophets and Prophecies, p. 212.)

SCRIBES AND RABBIS:
The Scholars or Professors of Ancient Times

The scribes and rabbis were scholars or teachers (*rabbi* means "teacher" in Hebrew) who studied and interpreted the Law of Moses. Scribes sometimes taught in private houses, synagogues, or in the temple courts, and the pupils sat on the ground at their master's feet. They used an oral method of teaching, relying on speaking rather than writing. That means the rabbi or teacher would say something, have the students repeat it, and then test them by asking questions. It was very important that the students be able to repeat exactly from memory what they had learned. The apostle Paul was taught in this way. According to Acts 22:3, his teacher was the first-century rabbi Gamaliel.

Teaching Outside the Synagogue,
Solomon Alexander Hart (1831)

DID YOU KNOW?

Beginning in the last centuries before Christ, some Jews literally enacted the instruction given in Deuteronomy 6:6-8. They wrote portions of the Law of Moses on tiny pieces of parchment and put them in little boxes that they tied to their foreheads and their wrists with leather thongs. These are called *phylacteries*. Although Jesus never condemns this practice, Matthew 23:5 reports how Jesus remarked that some religious leaders liked to make their phylacteries bigger so people would notice them and consider them especially holy.

Pharisees and Sadducees: Keepers of the Law of Moses

The New Testament describes two groups of Jews who had great influence on the life of the community during the time of Jesus and the early church. Each one emphasized different parts of the Law of Moses and taught students according to their emphasis on the law. They were the Pharisees and the Sadducees. The Gospels report that Jesus had several run-ins with both groups (Matthew 23).

The word *Pharisee* means "the separated ones" in Hebrew. These were a group of pious teachers who had studied the Law of Moses and the oral tradition of the law. They had devised and compiled many exacting requirements of how the law was to be fulfilled. They were very serious and passionate in their beliefs.

The Sadducees, on the other hand, recognized the written Law of Moses and its commandments as being more important than oral tradition.

ANCIENT CURRICULUM

It's hard to say exactly when people first began to record thoughts in writing, but sometime before 3000 B.C., a pictorial method of recording language was used in Mesopotamia. The Phoenicians, a people who lived on the eastern coast of the Mediterranean Sea, are credited with having invented the alphabet around 1800 B.C. The Greeks and the Hebrews quickly adopted this style of writing.

In ancient times, people wrote with a stylus on wet clay, on wooden boards covered in wax and inscribed with a stylus (a pointed pen-shaped instrument as shown above), on papyrus rolled in long scrolls and inscribed in ink, or on leather scrolls made from sheep, goat, or calfskins that had been scraped to remove the hair, stretched, and dried on a frame.

WHAT KIDS IN ANCIENT ISRAEL MIGHT HAVE LEARNED

DID YOU KNOW?

In the 1983 movie *Yentl,* Barbara Streisand plays the part of a modern-day young woman who disguises herself as a man in order to study the Torah like the men.

The *Talmud* (sometimes called by the Aramaic name, *Gemara*) is a long commentary on the *Mishnah* (see next page). It exists in two major forms and its ancient teachings were put together over centuries.

- **Reading and writing** (if you were a boy)

- **Arithmetic**

- **The Ten Commandments** (Exodus 20:1-17), the ten important commandments given by God to Moses on Mount Sinai

- **Sections of the Torah** (the first five books of the Bible)

- **Oral law** (later known as the Talmud, an explanation of how the commandments and the Torah are to be carried out in everyday life)

- **The trade of your father** if you were a boy

- **Household duties** if you were a girl

THE ORAL LAW: Lessons Learned from Memory

Because the Law of Moses contained much more than the Ten Commandments, there was also the need for specific teachings about how to carry out these laws. Take, for example, the commandment not to work on the Sabbath (Exodus 20:8-11). What does *work* mean? Teachers of the law helped people understand how to carry out the Law of Moses. But so many rules and so many interpretations of rules were difficult to remember over the centuries. That's why, between A.D. 120 and 200, what the rabbis taught about the oral tradition of the law and how they interpreted the law were finally gathered together and recorded in a piece of literature called the *Mishnah*.

The Mishnah is divided into six parts (called *Shahs*):

- *Zera'im* (Seeds)—eleven sections of laws mostly dealing with agriculture
- *Mo'ed* (Festivals)—twelve sections of laws dealing with the Sabbath and festivals
- *Nash'im* (Women)—seven sections of laws dealing with marriage, divorce, and other contracts
- *Nezikin* (Injuries)—ten sections of laws dealing with civil and criminal law
- *Kodashim* (Holy Things)—eleven sections of laws dealing with the priesthood, sacrifices, and the temple
- *Tohorot* (Purifications)—twelve sections of laws dealing with purification rituals

THE SYNAGOGUE

The Pharisees and Sadducees taught in the Jerusalem temple and in local synagogues. A synagogue was a community gathering place of worship and prayer where the Torah, the Prophets, or the Talmud were read and studied. Synagogues may have begun during the time of exile (after 586 B.C.) when the people of Israel were scattered. At the time of Jesus, most synagogues were gatherings in people's homes. Later, especially after the temple in Jerusalem was destroyed in A.D. 70, Jews began to construct buildings especially for these gatherings. Like the word *church*, which also meant "gathering," the word *synagogue* in modern times has come to mean the building itself, rather than the gathering of people.

As faithful Jews, Jesus and the apostle Paul often taught in the synagogues (Luke 4:16; Acts 18:5-17). The leaders of synagogues had the authority to arrest people (Acts 9:2), or to keep someone from attending the synagogue. For example, a man who was born blind was eventually thrown out of the synagogue when he insisted that Jesus had cured his blindness (John 9:1-34).

Guimard synagogue, Paris, France

FOOD
What's for Dinner?

Food was not just a matter of survival in Bible times. It was how people showed hospitality to their guests, and it was the custom for the host to serve the best food he had—in generous portions.

So what might you find on the table?

Bread

This was one of the all-important foods of the ancient Near East. Bread was so basic a food that it meant the same as food. "Breaking bread" meant the same as "having a meal."

DID YOU KNOW?

» Manna was called the "bread of heaven." (See "Strange But True Food Stories.") Jesus referred to himself as "the bread that gives life" (John 6:35, 48).

» Bread was often used to scoop up soup, stew, or whatever main dish was served.

» The best breads were made from wheat flour. Barley, a hardier grain that could grow on poorer soil, was used to feed animals. Poor people often used this cheaper grain to make their bread. Jesus used barley bread to serve the five thousand people (John 6:9). (See "Strange But True Food Stories.")

» Bread was always pulled apart with the hands and not cut with a knife. That's where the phrase "to break bread" comes from.

Fruits

Another important food in Bible times, fruits were refreshing and healthy as seasonal additions to the menu. What couldn't be eaten was usually dried and saved for the winter months. Typical fruits included grapes and raisins; fresh and dried figs; pomegranates; citrus fruits such as limes, lemons and oranges; olives; and dates.

DID YOU KNOW?

» Dried figs were sometimes used for medicinal purposes (2 Kings 20:7; Isaiah 38:21).

» Olives were the most important crop in ancient Israel—not only for food but also the wood of the tree was used in construction, for ornaments, and for household utensils. Olive oil was used for medicinal purposes (Luke 10:34) and had a sacred use in the anointing of Israel's kings (1 Samuel 10:1; 16:12-13). It was also burned in lamps.

» Men called Nazirites had taken a lifelong vow to never drink or eat anything produced from a grape vine—that included grapes, grape juice, wine, and raisins (Numbers 6:3-4).

Photos.com

Meat

Most ancient people ate meat very sparingly. When company came, or there was something really special to celebrate, it was time to kill the fatted (or best) calf! Meats included mutton, kid (young goat), fatted calf, fish, and poultry.

DID YOU KNOW?

» Archaeologists have discovered images of chickens in Israelite art dating from before 700 B.C.
» Lamb was part of the Passover meal and would have been included in Jesus' last supper with his disciples. (See "Special Meals.")

Dairy

While meat was served sparingly and other foods were seasonal, there was always milk and cheese on the table. However, this milk and cheese came from goats. Goats were raised primarily for their milk.

DID YOU KNOW?

» Job stated that God had created his body "as cheese is made from milk" (Job 10:10).
» Right before driving a stake through Sisera's head, Jael gave him a bowl of camel's milk to drink, which put him right to sleep (Judges 4:19-21).

Desserts

You wouldn't find candy back in ancient Israel, but you would find your fill of fruits, nuts, and honey to make up some sweet treats to eat! In fact, the land God promised to Abraham and his descendants was sometimes called a land "rich with milk and honey" (Exodus 3:8).

DID YOU KNOW?

» Pistachios grew wild in the hills of ancient Israel. In Bible times, they were chopped and added to puddings, stuffings, and fruit dishes.

Veggies

If you're a kid who doesn't like the green stuff, you might have gone hungry. Often, vegetables were the only food available! Popular vegetables included peas, legumes (lentils, fava, lima, and garbanzo beans), cucumbers, garlic, onions, and salad greens

DID YOU KNOW?

» The typical breakfast in Egypt, where the Israelites lived for more than four hundred years, consisted of mashed fava beans with garlic, hard-boiled eggs, and a side of pickles and onions. These were some of the foods the Israelites missed most as they wandered in the desert (Numbers 11:5).

iStock.com

81

FORBIDDEN FOODS

When the people were wandering in the desert after leaving Egypt, God gave them a long list of do's and don'ts, including what foods to avoid eating—or even touching. Why did God forbid these foods? Partly to set the Israelites apart from other nations, but also to ensure the health of the people.

Below is a list of animals the people were told not to eat (Leviticus 11:1-47):

Not Kosher

Bats
Buzzards
Camels
Crows
Eagles
Falcons
Flying insects (but grasshoppers, crickets, and locusts are OK)
Geckos
Hawks
Lizards
Ostriches
Owls
Pelicans
Pigs
Rabbits
Rats
Ravens
Rock badgers
Seagulls
Shellfish of any kind
Snakes
Storks
Vultures
Weasels

PASSOVER AND THE SEDER

The Seder is a special meal held at the beginning of Passover—the celebration marking the exodus (or leaving) of the Israelites from slavery in Egypt. It is traditionally held in the Jewish family home and consists of six traditional foods:

- **MAROR AND CHAZERET**—Bitter herbs, to symbolize the bitterness and harshness of the slavery which the Jewish people endured in Egypt.
- **CHAROSET**—A sweet, brown, pebbly mixture, representing the mortar used by the Jewish slaves to build the storehouses of Egypt.
- **KARPAS**—A vegetable, such as parsley, celery, or boiled potato, which is dipped into salt water to represent the tears and pain felt by the Jewish salves in Egypt.
- **Z'ROA**—A roasted lamb shankbone, chicken wing or neck, to represent the *korban*, the lamb that was offered as a sacrifice in the temple in Jerusalem and eaten as part of the Seder.
- **BEITZAH**—A roasted egg, symbolizing the festival sacrifice offered in the temple and eaten as part of the Seder. The egg is a symbol of mourning since it is the first food served to mourners after a funeral.
- **MATZOT**—A stack of three matzohs are placed in the center of the table to represent the unleavened bread that the people took with them in their haste to leave Egypt.

Peter's Food Dream

Hundreds of years later, Peter, one of Jesus' disciples and a leader of the early church, had a very strange dream. Sitting on his rooftop before lunch, Peter saw a vision of the sky opening and a huge sheet being lowered from heaven. On the sheet, he saw every type of animal, including reptiles and birds. He then heard a voice instruct him, "Peter, get up! Kill these and eat them." Raised in a Jewish home, Peter was horrified. He replied, "Lord, I can't do that! I've never eaten anything that is unclean and not fit to eat." To which the voice replied, "When God says that something can be used for food, don't say it isn't fit to eat." (See Acts 10:9-43.)

So what did the dream mean? It really wasn't about the food so much as it was God's way of letting Peter know that no one was outside of God's love and care. All are welcome in God's family.

Strange, but true, food stories

But it's good protein!

(Mark 1:4–8)

John the Baptist made a name for himself not only for his strong preaching skills but also for his rather unusual lifestyle. He lived in the wilderness and wore clothes made from camel's hair. His food of choice? A steady diet of locusts and wild honey.

Dinner for five thousand?

(John 6:1–15)

Jesus once fed a crowd of five thousand people, who had gathered to hear him speak, with only five loaves of bread and two fish! After everyone ate, the disciples picked up twelve baskets full of leftovers.

A Heavenly Meal

(Exodus 16:1-36)

When the Israelites were wandering in the wilderness after leaving Egypt, they had nothing to eat. God provided them with a bread that seemed to appear from heaven, called manna. Every morning the people would gather the white flakes that covered the ground—and there always was enough for everyone.

The land God promised to Moses and his people lay between the coast of the Mediterranean Sea and the Jordan Valley. Sometimes this land is called "the Holy Land" or "the promised land." But the whole region is usually called "Palestine" because it was once the land of the Philistines (see Exodus 13:17; Joshua 13:2-3), who had settled along the southern coast and built cities there in the twelfth century B.C. When the Romans conquered the area in the first century B.C., they used the name "Palestine" to refer to the whole southern portion of Syria, stretching from the Lebanon Mountains to the Southern Desert, and from the Mediterranean Sea to the Arabian Desert.

Mountains

The following are the mountains mentioned in the Bible. Which is the tallest? Which do you think is the most interesting? Why?

Mountain	Location	Height	What Happened There?	Reference
Mount Nebo	Jordan	2,625 feet (800 m)	God showed Moses the promised land	Deuteronomy 34:1-4
Mount Carmel	Israel	1,792 feet (546 m)	Elijah challenged 850 prophets of Baal and Asherah	1 Kings 18:19-40
Mount Tabor	Israel	1,929 feet (588 m)	God helped Barak defeat Sisera	Judges 4:12-15
Mount of Olives	Israel	3-mile ridge (height varies)	Where Jesus prayed prior to his arrest, and where he later ascended into heaven	Luke 22:39; Acts 1:9-13
Mount Ararat	Modern-day Turkey	16,945 feet (5,165 m)	Believed to be where Noah's ark came to rest	Genesis 8:4
Mount Sinai	Egypt	7,500 feet (2,290 m)	Where God gave Moses the Ten Commandments	Exodus 19:16-20; 20:1-17

Fast Facts

▲ Mount Ararat, the highest mountain in Turkey, was once an active volcano.

▲ Mount Carmel has what is called a promontory— a shelf that juts out over the Mediterranean Sea.

▲ If you visit Egypt, you can follow the Path of Moses up Mount Sinai. It will take about three hours and around four thousand steps.

▲ The Garden of Gethsemane, the place where Jesus prayed the night before his death, is believed to have been located at the base of the Mount of Olives (Matthew 26:36-46; Mark 14:32-42; Luke 22:39-46).

▲ Moses saw the burning bush on Mount Sinai (Exodus 3:1-12).

Images by Photos.com

Valleys

Elah Valley

This valley, located about fifteen miles west of Bethlehem, is where David fought and defeated Goliath using a sling, a stone, and the power of God (1 Samuel 17:1-3; 41-54). Visitors to the area today still stop at the stream to choose their own stones as souvenirs.

Valley of Jezreel

This triangular area surrounded by Mount Carmel, Mount Tabor, and Mount Gilboa is the largest valley in Israel. Filled with lots of natural springs, the valley is a fertile farmland for wheat, corn, and other crops.

Mountains and valleys usually run from north to south in Palestine, but the Jezreel Valley runs east to west. As a result, it was vital to east-west travel and communication across Palestine. Control of the Jezreel Valley was important for invaders and defenders of Palestine, and the Bible mentions many battles in this area (Judges 4–5; 1 Samuel 28:4). Especially important was the area of Megiddo, which controls a major entrance to the Jezreel Valley. The valley was also one of the settings for the ministry of Jesus. In the village of Nain in the Jezreel Valley, Jesus raised a boy from the dead (Luke 7:11-17).

DID YOU KNOW?

While no one knows where Noah's ark may have come to rest on Mount Ararat, plenty of people have looked for it. Satellite pictures taken of an unusual looking area about 15,300 feet (4663 m) up toward the northwest corner of Mount Ararat have caused a big stir. This area looks about the same size as the ark. **Could it be the actual ark?** Or is it simply a ridge of ice, rock, or snow? At this point, no one knows for sure.

Great Rift Valley

This valley is approximately 3,000 feet long (4,830 km) and runs from northern Syria to Africa along a fault line. The river flowing from the new Jerusalem temple to the Dead Sea in Ezekiel's vision was probably located within the Great Rift Valley (Ezekiel 47:8-11).

The Eden Mystery

Adam and Eve leaving the garden, artist unknown

Where is the Garden of Eden? Experts have a few theories—it might be under water! They believe floods filled the area creating the Persian Gulf with Eden resting underneath. Others believe the garden is somewhere near Mount Ararat, where Noah's ark landed. Still others think the Garden of Eden may be located in present-day Tabriz, an industrial city in Iran. Its location, however, is still a mystery.

Rivers

River Name	Location	Length	Importance	Learn More
Euphrates	Southwest Asia	1,700 miles (2,740 km)	A border of the land God gave the Israelites	Exodus 23:31-33
Jordan	Northern Israel	200 miles (320 km)	Where the Israelites crossed to enter the promised land; where John baptized Jesus	Joshua 3–4; Mark 1:9-11
Nile	Egypt	4,160 miles (6,695 km)	Where Moses used the power of God to turn the Nile to blood	Exodus 7:14-21
Tigris	Southwest Asia	1,150 miles (1,850 km)	Where Daniel saw an angel in a vision	Daniel 10:1–11:1

Seas

Dead Sea

Is this sea between Israel and Jordan really dead? Well, the reason it's called the "Dead" Sea is because the water in the sea is so salty, nothing can live in it! In fact, the Dead Sea is one of the saltiest bodies of water in the world. In Bible times, the Dead Sea often served as a natural border for Israel (Numbers 34:12; Deuteronomy 3:12-17; Joshua 15:5). Check out Ezekiel 47:6-11 to read about Ezekiel's vision of the Dead Sea.

Red Sea

Is the Red Sea really red? The Red Sea, which lies between Africa and Arabia, is sometimes red due to the red algae present in it. But many people believe the Red Sea in the Bible is different from the Red Sea we know today. But whichever sea is which, God parted it for Moses and the Israelites (Exodus 14:21-31; Psalm 106:9-12).

Mediterranean Sea

This sea separates Africa and Europe. The apostle Paul traveled to areas all around the Mediterranean as a missionary. More than once, Paul faced major storms at sea. Read about one in Acts 27:13-44.

Largest, Longest, Lowest

At 1,144,800 square miles (2,966,000 sq km), the Mediterranean is the largest sea in the world.

The longest river in the world is the Nile. At 4,180 miles (6,650 km), it could stretch all the way across the United States from one coast to the other and part way back again. Wow!

How low can you go? The lowest spot on earth is the Dead Sea. Its water surface sits 1,349 feet (411 m) below sea level.

DID YOU KNOW?

The Jordan River once flowed backward! And something else unbelievable happened, too. You can read Psalm 114 to discover what the mountains were doing while the Jordan flowed upstream. The Jordan River also feeds into Lake Galilee, a freshwater lake with an abundant supply of fish (Luke 5:4). In the time of Jesus, the area around Lake Galilee was densely populated. Tradition identifies the northeast side of Lake Galilee as the place where Jesus performed the miracle of feeding the five thousand (John 6:1-14).

Deserts

Moses and the Israelites spent forty years wandering in deserts (Exodus 15:22—17:1; Deuteronomy 8:1-9). These are some of the deserts in the area.

Shur Desert

The Shur Desert, in the northwestern part of the Sinai Peninsula, was where the Israelites complained about being thirsty (Exodus 15:22-25). Here God told Moses to throw a piece of wood into the water to purify it.

Paran Desert

The Paran Desert was probably located in the northern or central part of the Sinai Peninsula. Moses and the Israelites traveled here after leaving the Sinai Desert (Numbers 10:11-13).

Zin Desert

This desert was located between Arabah and the Dead Sea. A natural boundary, the Zin Desert bordered Judah and Edom. Kadesh-Barnea, an oasis, was located in this desert. Here, an angry Moses struck the rock from which water flowed and was told that he would not enter the promised land (Numbers 20:1-11).

DiD YOU KNOW?

Camels are called "ships of the desert." Do you know why? If you need help figuring it out, check out Transportation, p. 222.

DiD YOU KNOW?

Wadis are small streambeds located mostly in western Palestine. Many streams in this area only flowed with water during the rainy seasons. The rest of the year, the streambeds contained stagnant pools or were completely dry. During dry periods, the wadis were like ravines or narrow gorges. Wadis were undependable as a source of water for people or for growing crops (Jeremiah 15:18), but when they were dry, wadis were useful routes for travelers. Some scholars believe that Abram entered the land of Canaan through the Wadi Farah in order to reach Shechem (Genesis 12:4-6).

Oases

So just what is an oasis anyway? It's an area of land in the desert that has a regular supply of water from underground springs. In an oasis, the ground has enough water so that plants can grow.

En-Gedi

This lush oasis—about twenty-five miles southeast of Jerusalem on the banks of the Dead Sea—made a perfect hideout for David. King Saul, who was jealous of David and wanted him killed, chased David there with three thousand of Israel's best soldiers. Read 1 Samuel 24:1-22 to find out how David escaped.

Kadesh, the largest oasis in northern Sinai, has a spring that puts out 250,000 gallons of water a day. Whoa! From Kadesh, Moses sent twelve men to check out the land of Canaan (Numbers 13:25-33).

GOD

In the Bible, you won't find the question "Does God exist?" Instead, the Bible assumes a God who not only exists but who also interacts with the people and the planet he made. The Bible teaches that there is only one true, all-powerful, and all-knowing God.

WHAT'S IN A NAME?

You probably have three names: your first, middle, and last name. Your name identifies you and your family. But in the Bible, the names for God describe his character.

NAMES OF GOD

NAME	EXPLANATION	OTHER FACTS
Yahweh	This is God's personal name. In Hebrew, it is written as four letters (YHWH), pronounced YAH-way, and is thought to mean "I Am" or "I am the one who is" or "I am the one who brings into being." God called himself this name when he spoke to Moses (Exodus 3:14-15). Because God's name is holy, Jewish people do not pronounce it and substitute the word *Adonai*, which means "my lord." Translators of the Bible show the Hebrew word "YHWH" as "LORD" in small capital letters.	Often *Yahweh* is combined with other words to show God's character. *Yahweh Sabaoth*—"The LORD All-Powerful" or "The LORD of hosts" (1 Samuel 1:3; 17:45) *Yahweh Ro'i*— "You, LORD, are my shepherd" (Psalm 23:1)

NAME	EXPLANATION	OTHER FACTS
EL	*El* is an ancient word for "God."	*El Shaddai*—"God All-Powerful" or "God, the One of the Mountains" (Genesis 43:14) *El Elyon*— "God Most High" (Daniel 7:18) *Immanuel*—"God is with us" (Isaiah 7:14)

NAME	EXPLANATION	OTHER FACTS
ELOHIM	This plural form of *El* means "strength" or "power." It tells of God's supreme rule, creative work, and the mighty things he did for Israel.	In Genesis 2:4—3:24, God is called *Yahweh Elohim* or "LORD God."

NAME	EXPLANATION	OTHER FACTS
Jehovah	Hundreds of years after the Scriptures were first written down, the vowels for *Adonai* were inserted under the consonants for *Yahweh*, creating a pronunciation that sounded like "Yehovah" or "Jehovah," but this is not a natural Hebrew pronunciation.	*Jehovah-nissi*— "The LORD is your banner" or "The LORD Gives Me Victory" (Exodus 17:15) *Jehovah-jireh*— "The LORD will provide" (Genesis 22:14) *Jehovah-shalom*— "The LORD is peace" or "The LORD Calms Our Fears" (Judges 6:24)

DID YOU KNOW?

After Bible times, Jews stopped saying Yahweh out loud, except at certain special occasions, because they considered the name too holy for everyday speech. They were afraid of breaking the commandment about misusing God's name (Exodus 20:7).

NAME

Adonai

EXPLANATION

Out of respect for God's holy name, when the Scriptures were read aloud, Yahweh was not pronounced and was replaced with the word *Adonai*.

OTHER FACTS

A Hebrew word meaning "my lord."

NAME

Father

EXPLANATION

When Jesus taught his disciples to pray, he taught them to call upon God as Father. Christians consider themselves to be children of God (John 1:12).

OTHER FACTS

Heavenly Father (Matthew 6:9,14)

Holy Father (John 17:11)

NAME

ABBA

EXPLANATION

An Aramaic word meaning "Father"

OTHER FACTS

A term Jesus used to call upon God when praying in the Garden of Gethsemane (Mark 14:36).

NAME

ALPHA AND OMEGA

EXPLANATION

These words are the first and last letters in the Greek alphabet and were used to mean "first" and "last" in any list of things. These names indicate the completeness of God, who is "the beginning and the end" (Revelation 21:6).

OTHER FACTS

The apostle John recorded that Jesus called himself by this title (Revelation 1:8, 17), and the prophet Isaiah also described God in this way (Isaiah 44:6; 48:12).

iStock.com

OTHER NAMES FOR GOD

Wonderful Advisor *(Isaiah 9:6)*

Mighty God *(Isaiah 9:6)*

Eternal Father *(Isaiah 9:6)*

Prince of Peace *(Isaiah 9:6)*

God of Israel *(Genesis 33:20)*

GOD'S CHARACTERISTICS

Getting to know people involves getting to know their characteristics. How do they behave in different situations? How do they treat others? Studying God's character traits allows you to understand him and see how he influences the world.

GOD'S CHARACTER

CHARACTERISTIC	WHEN IT WAS SHOWN	BIBLE REFERENCE
All-Powerful (omnipotent)	God described himself as "God All-Powerful" to Abraham.	Genesis 17:1; Malachi 3:6
Angry/ Wrathful	The rebellion of the people made God angry. God described his anger to the prophet Isaiah.	Isaiah 13:13
Faithful	Many psalm writers, including David, described God's faithfulness in their lives and in the lives of their people.	Psalm 40:11; Psalm 100:5
Forgiving	God promised King Solomon that he would forgive his people when they turned to him in prayer and agreed to stop sinning.	2 Chronicles 7:14
Generous	Jesus described God's generosity in the parable of the workers in the vineyard. The apostle Paul wrote that God is generous to everyone who asks for his help.	Matthew 20:1-16; Romans 10:12-13
Good	During the dedication of the temple commissioned by Solomon, the people declared that God was good. Goodness also is one of the fruit or characteristics of God's Holy Spirit.	2 Chronicles 7:3; Galatians 5:22
Just/Fair	God told Job that he was always fair.	Job 37:23
Loving	God showed his love by allowing his Son, Jesus, to die for the wrongs of all people. God is the source of love.	John 3:16; 1 John 4:8
Majestic and holy; fearsome and glorious; miracle worker	Moses and the Israelites sang a song about God's holiness.	Exodus 15:11
Merciful	The people of Israel experienced God's mercy many times while they wandered in the wilderness.	Exodus 34:6; Deuteronomy 4:31
Source of Wisdom	Solomon asked God for wisdom, knowing that wisdom came from God. James also encouraged people to ask God for wisdom.	1 Kings 3:9; James 1:5
Truthful	When Jesus prayed, he explained that God's word is the truth.	John 17:17
Unchanging	As the prophet Malachi explained, God never changes, but remains faithful to the descendants of Jacob.	Malachi 3:6

Photos.com

"God whispers to us in our pleasures, speaks in our conscience, but shouts in our pains: it is His megaphone to rouse a deaf world."

—C. S. Lewis
(C. S. Lewis lived from 1898–1963. He was a British scholar and writer whose *Chronicles of Narnia* have become Christian classics. The quote above is from his book, *The Problem of Pain*.)

"Never shall God be hidden, never shall God be wanting. Always shall He be understood, always be heard, nay even seen, in whatsoever way He shall wish."

—Tertullian
(Tertullian lived from about A.D. 160–225, and was an important early Christian writer and a leader of the Christian church in Africa.)

"A mighty fortress is our God, a bulwark never failing; a helper he amid the flood of mortal ills prevailing."

—Martin Luther
(Martin Luther was a German monk who lived from 1483–1546. He played a major role in the formation of Protestant churches. The quote above is from his hymn, *A Mighty Fortress Is Our God*. It is based on Psalm 46.)

91

GOD'S SPECIAL AGREEMENTS

Military or government leaders make pacts or agreements with each other (such as calling a truce, or allowing trade between countries). Throughout the Bible, we read that God makes agreements with his people, too. These are known as covenants. This chart tells you with whom the agreement was made and why.

GOD'S SPECIAL AGREEMENTS (COVENANTS)

AGREEMENT MADE WITH WHOM?	WHY?	BIBLE REFERENCE
Noah	God promised never again to destroy every living thing by a flood. As a sign of this agreement, he gave the rainbow.	Genesis 9:8-17
Abraham	God promised land to Abram (later renamed Abraham by God) and his descendants. He also promised that Abraham would be the father of many nations.	Genesis 15:7-21; 17:4-7
Moses and the people of Israel	God named Israel as his chosen people and promised to bless them as long as they obeyed him.	Deuteronomy 7:6-8
Phinehas	Phinehas, the grandson of Aaron, and his descendants would be God's priests.	Numbers 18:1-17; 25:10-13
David	God promised that a descendant of King David would always rule Israel.	2 Samuel 7:1-17; Psalm 108:1-36
Rebellious Israel	God promised to forgive them and write his law "on their hearts and minds." Christians understand Jesus to be the fulfillment of God's new agreement.	Jeremiah 31:31-34; Hebrews 8:7-12; 10:11-18

DiD YOU KNOW?

Some ways that agreements were sealed in biblical times included giving gifts (1 Samuel 18:3-4), setting up a stone or a pile of rocks (Genesis 31:43-55), offering one's sandal to another (Ruth 4:7-8), or by a simple handshake (2 Kings 10:15).

Photos.com

GOD SIGHTINGS

Jesus described God as "Spirit" (John 4:24). This means that God does not have a physical body, but exists in spirit form. Yet from time to time God was seen and heard in various ways by the people in the Bible.

GOD'S APPEARANCES

iStock.com

APPEARANCE	TO WHOM?	WHY?	BIBLE REFERENCE
A smoking pot and a flaming torch	Abraham	As a sign of God's agreement with Abraham	Genesis 15:17-18
A burning bush (the angel of the LORD)	Moses	To get Moses' attention. The ground around the bush became holy ground.	Exodus 3:1—4:17
A thick cloud (by day) and flaming fire (at night)	Moses and the people of Israel	To guide the people as they left Egypt and to give them light at night. The cloud was described as "the glory of the LORD" (Exodus 40:34).	Exodus 13:21-22; 40:34-38
A gentle breeze and a soft whisper	Elijah	To get the attention of his discouraged prophet, Elijah	1 Kings 19:9-13
A voice	Jesus, John the Baptist, and others present at Jesus' baptism	As a sign of God's recognition and approval of his son, Jesus	Matthew 3:17
A cloud and a voice	Peter, James, and John	At Jesus' Transfiguration, God again showed his approval of Jesus.	Matthew 17:5

FATHER, SON, AND HOLY SPIRIT

After his resurrection, Jesus told his followers to baptize people "in the name of the Father, the Son, and the Holy Spirit" (Matthew 28:19). Christians believe in one God (Ephesians 4:6), and many confess their faith in the words of the Apostles' Creed, which falls into three main sections dealing with God, Jesus Christ, and the Holy Spirit. Many Christians refer to these three aspects of the one God as the *Trinity*, a term that was introduced in the late second or early third century A.D. by the theologian Tertullian.

The apostle Paul, a first-century follower of Jesus, often referred to God the Father, Son, and Holy Spirit in his letters. His second letter to the Corinthians closes with this threefold blessing: "I pray that the Lord Jesus Christ will bless you and be kind to you! May God bless you with his love, and may the Holy Spirit join all your hearts together" (2 Corinthians 13:13). Check out Ephesians 1:3-14. How does Paul describe the Father? Jesus? The Holy Spirit? (For more about the Holy Spirit, see Holy Spirit, p. 124.)

GOVERNMENT

A STORY OF CHANGE

God helped Moses lead the Hebrew people out of Egypt. Yet the people were not yet a nation. They didn't really know the God who had chosen Abraham and who had called Moses to help free his people. Only after they received God's law and agreed to obey God did they become known as the people of God (Exodus 23:20–24:4).

THE LAW OF MOSES

The Law of Moses was a set of regulations given to the nation of Israel as it spent forty years in the desert after leaving slavery in Egypt. The most famous part of the law is the Ten Commandments, which Moses received from God on Mount Sinai (Exodus 20:1–17; Deuteronomy 5:1–21).

God established a covenant (agreement) with the people of Israel. The history of Israel was closely connected with this agreement—if the people obeyed, they would receive blessings; if they disobeyed, they would be punished (Deuteronomy 4:1–2, 39–40; 7:12–15; 8:19–20).

PURPOSE OF THE LAW OF MOSES

The Law of Moses was given to the people to guide them in their relationship with God. The people of Israel were already followers of God. The law would help them:

1. understand what God expected of them. He had made a covenant with them, a pledge to protect them and to make them a great nation. The Law of Moses helped them understand their part in that arrangement.
2. live together as a community.
3. have a foundation for a healthy, well-organized nation.

theocracy

In giving the Israelites this extensive law code, God also established their nation. He set up their government. God would rule the nation, and he would speak to a prophet or priest who would relay his message to the people.

Aspects of the Law

The Law of Moses addressed three aspects of their national life:

RELIGIOUS CODE
The religious laws dealt with how to worship God. In the Old Testament, sacrifices were required as payment for the penalty of the sins of the people. The Law of Moses explained how these rituals were to be performed.

MORAL CODE
The moral aspects of the law are perhaps the best known to us. The Ten Commandments were part of this, as were a number of regulations dealing with what was the right thing to do in a given situation (also known as ethics).

SOCIAL CODE
This section dealt with how the society was to function. Everything—from how legal disputes would be decided, to what to eat, to how to clean your house—was covered in these laws. As the life of God's people became more settled and less nomadic, rules for health and public safety were very important.

94

The Ten Commandments

God's commandments to the people of Israel were:

Do not worship any god except me.

Do not make idols that look like anything in the sky or on earth or in the ocean under the earth. Don't bow down and worship idols.

Do not misuse my name.

Remember that the Sabbath Day belongs to me.

Respect your father and your mother.

Do not murder.

Be faithful in marriage.

Do not steal.

Do not tell lies about others.

Do not desire to possess anything that belongs to another person.
(from Exodus 20:2-17)

THE PERIOD OF THE JUDGES

In Old Testament times, judges were special leaders called by God to help the people of ancient Israel. The judges sometimes settled legal cases (Judges 4:4-5), but most of them were known as military leaders chosen by God to lead the Israelites in battle against their enemies. The lives of these judges are described in Judges 3–16. The following chart lists the judges named in the book of Judges.

Judge	Length of Service	Chief Enemy	Accomplishments	Scriptures
Othniel	40 years	Northern Syria	Defeated Northern Syria and brought Israel forty years of peace	Judges 3:7-11
Ehud	80 years	Moabites and Amalekites	Killed King Eglon of Moab and defeated both the Moabites and Amalekites, who had joined forces against Israel	Judges 3:12-30
Shamgar	10 years	Philistines	Rescued Israel by killing six hundred Philistines	Judges 3:31
Deborah and Barak	40 years	Canaanites	Defeated the army of Canaanite King Jabin and his commander Sisera	Judges 4:1—5:31
Gideon	40 years	Midianites and Amalekites	Defeated the Midianites who joined forces with the Amalekites with only three hundred men	Judges 6:1—8:35
Tola	23 years	Not stated	Little information recorded other than he rescued Israel	Judges 10:1-2
Jair	22 years	Not stated	Little information recorded other than that he had thirty sons, each one in charge of a town in Gilead	Judges 10:3-5
Jephthah	6 years	Ammonites and Ephraimites	Defeated the Ammonites who had invaded Gilead; also battled the army of the Israelite tribe, Ephraim	Judges 11:1—12:7
Ibzan	7 years	Not stated	Little information recorded other than he had thirty daughters and thirty sons	Judges 12:8-10
Elon	10 years	Not stated	Little information recorded about this judge	Judges 12:11-12
Abdon	8 years	Not stated	Little information recorded other than that he had forty sons and thirty grandsons	Judges 12:13-15
Samson	20 years	Philistines	Took revenge on Philistine leaders and people who had burned his wife and family	Judges 13:1—16:31

Photos by iStock. Bacground photo by Getty Images

THE RISE OF THE MONARCHY: ISRAEL RULED BY KINGS

In 1 Samuel 8, the people of Israel asked for a king. Samuel, a wise priest and prophet who was sometimes called "Israel's last judge," was getting old, and Samuel's sons were viewed as unfit to take his place. Also, the people wanted to be more like the other nations of the region. Samuel did not like the idea. He believed that a king would not treat the people well (1 Samuel 8:9–18). He also thought that the people's request for a king showed a lack of trust in God as their leader (1 Samuel 10:17–19). But when Samuel prayed for guidance, God told him to give the people a king (1 Samuel 8:1–22). God told Samuel to anoint Saul as the first king of Israel in 1030 B.C. (1 Samuel 9–10).

DID YOU KNOW?

The Bible says that Solomon had one thousand wives, including an Egyptian princess. Unfortunately for Solomon, his many wives led him to worship other gods. Because of that disobedience, God told Solomon that he would take his kingdom away after he died. (1 Kings 11:1–13).

The early kings

Saul ruled well during the early years of his reign, but lost God's favor when he disobeyed God during a battle (1 Samuel 13–15). Saul became consumed with jealousy over David, a young shepherd who killed the Philistine giant Goliath (1 Samuel 17:1-54), and whom God had chosen to become the next king. David was placed on the throne of Israel instead of one of Saul's sons (2 Samuel 5:1-3). King David ruled the United Israelite Kingdom for many years. On his deathbed, David said that Solomon, one of his younger sons, would succeed him as king. Solomon became a great king who was known for his wisdom, his wealth, and for the magnificent temple that he built in Jerusalem.

King David playing the harp, 19th century chromolithograph

The Divided Kingdom

Solomon turned away from God at the end of his life. Upon his death, the northern tribes of Israel broke away from the kingdom. This kingdom was called Israel, while the southern tribes, who remained loyal to Solomon's son Rehoboam, were called Judah. Each had a king, and each went through a cycle of good and bad leaders. Both kingdoms met with tragic ends. The Assyrians defeated Israel in 722 B.C. Judah fell to the Babylonians in 587 B.C. Many of the people were taken captive and removed from their land. The next seventy years, when Israel was without a ruler of its own, is often called the exile (or the "Period of Captivity"). For a complete chart on the kings of both the northern and southern kingdoms, see Kings and Queens, p. 146.

Return from Period of Captivity

About a year after Cyrus of Persia conquered Babylon in 539 B.C., he gave the Jewish people permission to return to their homeland of Judea. The books of Ezra and Nehemiah in the Old Testament tell about the hundred-year period that followed the time of the exile. In the years following, Palestine (and Jerusalem) was governed by Alexander the Great of Macedonia (336–323 B.C.), who conquered much of the eastern Mediterranean world. Following his death, the lands were ruled for over a century by Alexander's generals or those who followed them. The most important of these rulers were the Seleucids, who controlled Syria, and the Ptolemies, who controlled Egypt. One of these two royal families ruled over Palestine, where the Jewish people lived and practiced their religion. However, in 168 B.C. the Seleucid king, Antiochus IV, tried to stop the Jewish people from practicing their faith. The people revolted against the king, and under the leadership of Judas Maccabeus, the small band of Jewish fighters defeated Antiochus's mighty army. (You can find out more about the Macabees in Calendar and Holidays, p. 32, and Jerusalem, p. 130.) The Maccabees then set up their own government, which lasted until the Roman general Pompey invaded Jerusalem and brought all the land under Roman control in 63 B.C.

PALESTINE AT THE TIME OF JESUS

By the time described in the New Testament, Israel had been under Greek and then Roman rule. Many of God's people were scattered throughout the world. However, even though their independence was gone, the people of Israel, under Roman rule, still held to the religious aspects of the law given to Moses.

RELIGIOUS LEADERS

The Great Sanhedrin (from a Greek word meaning "council") was composed of the top seventy-one religious leaders. Their job was to be sure the Law of Moses was carried out faithfully, and to supervise the smaller, local sanhedrins throughout the country. They were considered the highest members of society, and were the scholars and leaders in their communities.

After the exile (Period of Captivity), the religious leaders and scribes became responsible for interpreting the law. By the time of Jesus' ministry, hundreds of new rules and traditions had been added to God's law. Jesus himself changed certain rules of the law, not "to do away with them, but to give them their full meaning" (Matthew 5:17).

Photos by iStock.

97

Jesus and Government

Jesus was questioned about the role of the Roman government and the people of Israel's response to it. His followers were looking for him to overthrow the rule of Rome, which is something they thought the promised Messiah would do. Enemies of Jesus were seeking to trap him into saying something that they could use to have him prosecuted. He always answered carefully, however, instructing his followers to pay their taxes and to be good citizens. Read what Jesus had to say about this in Luke 20:20-26.

THE ROMAN EMPIRE

In 700 B.C., Rome was only a small city in Italy that controlled the area around it. By 508 B.C., it had developed the form of government known as a republic, in which the people chose the leaders they wanted to represent them. By the second century B.C., the Romans had conquered large parts of Greece and Asia Minor, as well as sections of North Africa, France, Spain, and many of the islands in the Mediterranean Sea. In 63 B.C., Roman troops, led by General Pompey, took over Palestine. After Julius Caesar, the first Roman emperor, died in 44 B.C., his successor, Augustus, extended the empire to include Egypt, most of Asia Minor, England, and parts of Germany.

Jesus was born in the town of Bethlehem in the province of Judea during the reign of Augustus Caesar, the first Roman ruler called "emperor."

Spread of the Message of Christ

The Tribute Money, James J. Tissot (19th century)

Photos.com

Because the Romans were well organized and had a strong army, their empire was actually very stable. Travel and trade between areas was easier than it had ever been. The international peace brought by Roman rule and the superior system of Roman roads helped the apostles to spread a new religion based on Jesus' teachings. Since Greek was spoken throughout the Roman Empire, there was no language barrier to overcome.

CAESARS

The Roman Empire was ruled by a series of leaders called "Caesars." This title started as a family name, as Julius Caesar attempted to become the emperor of Rome. At the time, Rome was a republic, and the political leaders, fearing a takeover by Caesar, assassinated him. Here are a few of the emperors who are mentioned in biblical accounts.

AUGUSTUS (OCTAVIAN)
The nephew of Julius Caesar, Augustus, became the first emperor of Rome in 27 B.C.– A.D. 14. He was emperor when Jesus was born. He is mentioned in Luke 2:1.

TIBERIUS
The adopted son of Augustus took power in A.D. 14 and reigned during the ministry and crucifixion of Christ. (See Luke 3:1)

GAIUS (CALIGULA)—A.D. 37–41
The young Caligula started his rule well, but is believed to have become insane. He was eventually murdered by the officers of his own guard.

CLAUDIUS—A.D. 41–54
(See Acts 11:28; 18:2) He was considered an unlikely candidate to become emperor because he reportedly had disabilities. However, he proved to be an able public administrator and builder of public works.

NERO
Took power in A.D. 54 after his mother allegedly killed his father, Claudius. He is known for two things: (1) the Roman public believed that he had set fire to Rome in A.D. 64; and (2) Nero tried to blame the fire on the followers of Christ, which eventually began the Roman policy of persecuting Christians. He is referred to but not explicitly named in Acts 25:10-12; 27:24; and 2 Timothy 4:16-17.

Photos by iStock.

In Sickness and in Health

When you're sick, perhaps your parents take you to the doctor or a pharmacy or pull out the homemade remedies. Maybe they look online for medical advice. But for the people of ancient Israel, the source of healing was God—see Psalms 38, 39, 88, and 102—and the best source for medical advice was the Law of Moses.

Photos.com

It's the Law!

The Law of Moses helped keep the people of Israel healthy and helped prevent the spread of diseases. Many of these laws can be found in Leviticus 12–18 and in some chapters of Numbers. Some conditions or diseases caused a person to be "unclean." This meant that the person was unable to participate in any religious or community activities until the person was made "clean" again.

Some health laws:

✚ Houses with strange growths, spots, or mildew on the walls had to be disinfected, cleaned, and repaired. They were torn down if the mold kept coming back. Clothing or blankets with mold or mildew had to be sanitized. If you couldn't get the mold out, you had to cut it out. If the mold grew or came back, you had to burn the cloth or leather (Leviticus 13:47-59).

✚ People with skin infections had to be quarantined outside the camp until they were cured. A priest had to examine the person to make sure of the cure (Leviticus 13:46; 14:2-3).

✚ Anyone who touched a dead body was unclean for seven days (Numbers 19:11-13).

✚ Clothing of soldiers returning from battle had to be disinfected. Any equipment brought home had to put through fire and not used for seven days afterwards (Numbers 31:22-24).

Reasons for Sickness

In the Bible, sickness or a disability was sometimes described as

✚ Something God does for reasons that people can't yet understand. Some parts of the Bible question the belief that sickness is a punishment from God, and instead point out that people cannot always understand God's reasons for bringing illness (Job 2; Ecclesiastes 8:10-13; 9:2; John 9:1-7).

✚ A punishment or discipline from God. In Numbers 12, Miriam (Moses' sister) was struck with leprosy when she rebelled against Moses. In Deuteronomy 28:21-23, 27, God explained through Moses that those who disobeyed him would suffer diseases.

✚ Something God can use to demonstrate his power. The disciples of Jesus asked him about a man who was born blind. Had the man or his parents sinned to cause his blindness? But Jesus replied, "Because of his blindness, you will see God work a miracle for him" (John 9:3).

iStock.com

Diseases in the Bible

Here are just a few illnesses mentioned in the Bible and some of the people who suffered because of them.

Disease or Condition	People Who Had It	Law or Advice Concerning the Disease	The Treatment
Dropsy (also known as *edema*—a disease where the body swells with fluid)	While at the home of one of the Pharisees, one of the guests had this condition (Luke 14:2).	This disease is mentioned only in the New Testament.	Although the Pharisees complained, Jesus healed the man on the Sabbath.
Fever	Peter's mother-in-law had a fever (Mark 1:30-31).	In the Old Testament, some fevers were considered punishment for disobedience (Leviticus 26:16).	Jesus healed Peter's mother-in-law (Mark 1:30-31).
Internal or regular monthly bleeding	Unnamed woman who touched the hem of Jesus' robe bled for 12 years (Mark 5:29).	The person was considered unclean for seven days or as long as the bleeding continued (Leviticus 15:25).	Two turtledoves or two pigeons had to be offered (Leviticus 15:28-30).
Leprosy (skin diseases, including Hansen's disease)	While traveling, Jesus met ten lepers (Luke 17:11-13).	The person had to tear his or her clothes and cry out "Unclean!" (Leviticus 13:45-46).	Jesus healed the ten lepers and told them to show themselves to the priest (Luke 17:14-17).
Sores or boils	Job suffered from painful sores (Job 2:7).	Leviticus 13:1-39	The priest has to examine the area. The person could be quarantined for seven days (Leviticus 13:2-21).
"Incurable" or "horrible" disease (This could be tuberculosis—"consumption" in the *King James Version*—or some other disease lacking a cure.)	The people of Israel who grumbled against Moses and Aaron (Numbers 16; Psalm 106:15)	This type of disease was considered a punishment for disobedience (Leviticus 26:16).	Obedience to God is the only way to prevent this (Leviticus 26:14-15).
Withered limbs	At the synagogue, Jesus saw a man with a withered hand (Matthew 12:9-10).	Because God promised to allow diseases as a result of disobedience, such a health issue might have been considered a curse (Deuteronomy 28:20-23).	Jesus healed the man to show his compassion.

The Priests: Your Clean Bill of Health

Photos.com

For the people of Israel in the ancient world, it was largely up to the priests to examine a person complaining about a rash or some other skin disease. They could then decide whether a person was clean (able to participate in religious or community life) or unclean. Check out Leviticus 13 for an example of how a priest determined whether a skin disease was infectious or not. Perhaps his notes looked like this:

For a Rash (Leviticus 13:1-8)

Day	Condition of Skin	Verdict: Clean or Unclean
Day 1	*White discoloration; only skin deep*	**Unclean** *(quarantine for 7 days)*
Day 7 *(second exam by the priest)*	*Rash unchanged (has not spread to the rest of the body)*	**Unclean** *(quarantine for another week)*
Day 14	*Rash faded*	**Clean** *(go on with normal life)*

For a Boil (Leviticus 13:18-23)

Day	Condition of Skin	Verdict: Clean or Unclean
Day 1	*White spot in center of boil, but not very deep*	**Unclean** *(quarantine for 7 days)*
Day 7 *(second exam by the priest)*	*Boil has faded.*	**Clean**

Midwives: Delivering Help

iStock.com

Perhaps you've heard of someone who used a midwife to help deliver a baby. Midwives have helped mothers deliver their babies for thousands of years. A midwife helped Rachel, the wife of Jacob, bring her son Benjamin into the world (Genesis 35:17). In ancient Egypt, two midwives—Shiphrah and Puah—refused to kill the Hebrew baby boys when ordered by a pharaoh who hoped to decrease the Hebrew population (Exodus 1:15-21). The midwives even lied about their actions to save the babies' lives!

The Doctor Is In?

There are more than a few references to doctors in the Old Testament. Job called his friends "useless doctors" (Job 13:4) who annoyed him with useless advice. King Asa of Judah consulted doctors "and refused to ask the LORD for help" (2 Chronicles 16:12). And because of the reputation of the region of Gilead as a producer of a healing ointment, God commented to the prophet Jeremiah, "If medicine and doctors may be found in Gilead, why aren't my people healed?" (Jeremiah 8:22).

But the Bible also portrays doctors and medicine in a positive light. The practice of medicine can be seen in part of the biblical command to love your neighbor (Leviticus 19:18; Luke 10:25-37). In fact, Jesus instructed his followers to go heal the sick (Luke 10:9). The Bible also teaches the value and dignity of human life, explaining that people are created by God and in God's likeness (Genesis 1:26-27). This belief has probably influenced the practice and ethics of modern medicine as well. In the New Testament, doctors are mentioned more frequently.

For example:

➕ Jesus, quoting a famous proverb, stated, "Doctor, first make yourself well" (Luke 4:23).

➕ When questioned about his habit of eating with "sinners and tax collectors," Jesus said, "Healthy people don't need a doctor, but sick people do. I didn't come to invite good people to be my followers. I came to invite sinners" (Mark 2:17; see also Matthew 9:12 and Luke 5:31).

➕ According to tradition, Luke, the writer of the Gospel of Luke and the book of Acts, was a doctor (Colossians 4:14).

➕ A woman who bled internally spent all of her money on doctors before being healed by Jesus (Mark 5:26-29).

It's a Miracle!

iStock.com

Sometimes God acted through people in an amazing way to make sick people well. He also caused dead people to live again! The Bible has many stories of people healed through the power of God. (For more miraculous healings, see the section on Jesus, page 136.)

➕ Miriam , Moses' sister, was healed of leprosy after Moses prayed for her (Numbers 12).

➕ The prophet Elijah brought the dead son of the widow of Zarephath back to life (1 Kings 17:17-24).

➕ The prophet Elisha told Naaman, the commander of the army of Aram, to wash in the Jordan River. Naaman was healed of leprosy (2 Kings 5).

➕ King Hezekiah of Judah prayed for healing and God told Isaiah to put figs on his boil. The king was healed (2 Kings 20:1-11).

➕ The apostles Peter and John used the power of God to heal a lame man at the temple gate in Jerusalem (Acts 3:1-10).

➕ Because apostles like Peter could perform miracles, many sick people believed they could be healed if Peter's shadow fell on them (Acts 5:15).

➕ In the city of Joppa, Peter brought Dorcas, a woman who performed kind acts for widows and the poor, back to life (Acts 9:36-42).

➕ The apostle Paul raised a young man named Eutychus from the dead after Eutychus fell out of a window (Acts 20:7-12).

Heaven

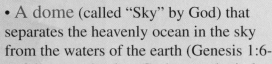

The word heaven has several meanings. The Bible refers to heaven as

What Is Heaven ?

• **A dome** (called "Sky" by God) that separates the heavenly ocean in the sky from the waters of the earth (Genesis 1:6-8). Rain was said to fall on earth when God opened windows in the heavenly ceiling (Genesis 7:11-12; Isaiah 24:18; Malachi 3:10).

• **Everything above the earth.** This includes not only weather, winds, sky, and stars (Genesis 1:1; Psalm 8:3; Psalm 19:1), but also signs from God, such as the rainbow (Genesis 9:12-17), and blessings from God, such as the bread God sent to feed the Israelites in the desert (Exodus 16:4).

• **The place where God rules** (1 Kings 8:30; Isaiah 66:1; Matthew 5:34) and where God's court meets (Genesis 1:26; 3:22; Job 1:6; 2:1; 15:7-8).

WHAT THE BIBLE SAYS ABOUT HEAVEN

The Bible actually says very little about what it looks like. The ancient Hebrews did not think of heaven as a place they would ever go after they died. To them it was simply the home of God. When Jesus taught about the kingdom of heaven, he was usually talking about God's purposes rather than a place (Matthew 5:3; 13:31-33). Jesus did, however, promise to prepare a place for the believers in his Father's house (John 14:1-3).

Many of the ideas we have about what heaven looks like come from the vision of a new heaven and a new earth described by John who was exiled on Patmos (Revelation 21:1—22:5).

DiD YOU KNOW?

An ABC News poll found that nine out of ten people in the United States say they believe in heaven.

Visions of Heaven from the Bible

In both the Old and New Testaments prophets and apostles had visions of heaven.

• The prophet Micaiah saw God sitting on his throne in heaven with all the members of heaven standing around him (1 Kings 22:19).

• The prophet Elijah was taken to heaven by a chariot and horses of fire while Elisha watched (2 Kings 2:11-12).

• The prophet Isaiah tells of seeing God seated on a high throne and wearing a robe that filled the temple (Isaiah 6).

• The prophet Ezekiel saw cherubim and a throne of sapphire (Ezekiel 1:1-25). Seated on the throne was "a figure in the shape of a human" (Ezekiel 1:26).

• The apostle Paul describes his vision of being taken up to "the third heaven" where he heard and saw things too wonderful to describe (2 Corinthians 12:1-4).

What John Saw

While exiled on the island of Patmos, the apostle John had a vision of the heavenly city of New Jerusalem while praying. In Revelation 21—22, the city

- Is like a bride (21:2).
- Is made bright by the glory of God with no need for the sun or moon (21:11).
- Has twelve gates with the name of one of the twelve tribes of Israel written over each one. Each gate is made of solid pearl and guarded by an angel (21:12).
- Is "shaped like a cube" about 1,500 miles high and 1,500 miles wide (21:16).
- Has walls 216 feet high made of jasper (21:17-18).
- Has twelve foundations made of precious stones with a name of one of the twelve apostles written on each (21:14;19-20).
- Has streets made of pure gold (21:21).
- Lacks a temple because God and the Lamb are its temple (21:22).
- Has a river of life flowing from the throne where God and the Lamb are seated (22:1).
- Has trees on each side of the river bearing a different life-giving fruit each month (22:2).

> The most ordinary moment in Heaven will be much better than the most special moment here! And we'll never worry that things are about to take a turn for the worse. Because they never will!
>
> —**Randy Alcorn**
> in *Heaven for Kids*

Thoughts about Heaven

Heaven vs. Hell

In ancient times, many believed the dead went to a place called *Sheol* (Hebrew) or *Hades* (Greek). This was considered a dark, silent place where no one knew or felt anything. Although not considered a place of punishment, it was thought to be the place where the dead waited for judgment (Ezekiel 31:16-18). About a century before Jesus was born, Jewish teachers began to speak of the fires of hell or a place of punishment for the wicked (see Matthew 5:22).

The New Testament describes a place of punishment and fiery torture called *Gehenna*, the Greek word for "hell" (Matthew 13:42, 50; 25:41). Jesus warned that this is where God would send evildoers (Luke 16:23-24). But for those who have faith in Jesus, he promises eternal life (John 3:16; 6:40). In describing life after death, the apostle Paul teaches that those who are raised to life will live forever and will have spiritual bodies that are beautiful and strong (1 Corinthians 15:42-44).

A Modern Vision of Heaven

Don Piper, author of the bestselling book *90 Minutes in Heaven*, was pronounced dead at the scene of a car accident near Houston, Texas. His body was left in his car on the side of the road for ninety minutes.

As Don describes it, he was taken to heaven where he was welcomed by a large crowd of people who had died during his lifetime. They welcomed him with open arms.

As he approached the gate of heaven, the sounds of a heavenly music filled the air. For Don, the music was the most inspiring and memorable part of his time there.

For ninety minutes Don experienced the sights and sounds of heaven. As he explained, "I get frustrated describing what heaven was like, because I can't begin to put into words what it looked like, sounded like, and felt like. It was perfect, and I knew I had no needs and never would again."

The Heroes Hall of Fame

When you think of heroes, who do you think of? Comic book heroes like Spiderman, Superman, Wonder Woman, or the Incredible Hulk? They can spin gigantic webs, leap tall buildings, and crush vehicles in the palms of their hands. But a hero isn't always a person who can do something amazing. A hero can be someone you see every day who overcomes great odds.

The people in the Bible weren't perfect. You might not even consider them heroic, because many made huge mistakes. But they had qualities like encouragement, honesty, faithfulness, and loyalty. Read on and decide who is *your* favorite hero.

Abraham

Ancestor of Israel; faithful and obedient; Genesis 12:1—25:10

When Abraham (still called Abram) was seventy-five years old, God told him to leave his country and his family and move to the land of Canaan. God further told Abraham to count the stars in the sky; that would be the number of Abraham's many descendants. Abraham believed him and God was pleased. God fulfilled that promise to Abraham when Sarah was well past her child-bearing years. Abraham was one hundred years old when his son Isaac was born (Genesis 21:5)!

God later tested Abraham by asking him to sacrifice his only son, Isaac, on an altar of fire. Because Abraham was so obedient and willing to offer his only son, God blessed him and through Abraham's descendants, the nation of Israel was born (Genesis 22:1-18).

Barnabas

Obedient encourager; Acts 4:36-37; 9:26-31; 11:22—15:41; 1 Corinthians 9:1-7

There were many leaders in the early church, but Barnabas (whose name means "one who encourages others") stood out because he always looked for the good in people. Because Barnabas was drawn to crowds that he could encourage, many people became believers of God. But Barnabas often put himself in danger. As he visited cities to spread the gospel, he was threatened and physically attacked. Even though he was uncomfortable at times, Barnabas was obedient to God and quietly and humbly served him by encouraging others.

Illustrations by Ron Wheeler

Daniel

Wise and faithful; Daniel 1–12

In his youth, Daniel, from the tribe of Judah, was taken captive by Nebuchadnezzar, king of Babylon. Daniel, renamed *Belteshazzar* (meaning "may Bel [god] protect his life"), was trained for court service. He quickly established a reputation for intelligence and absolute devotion to his God. After three years of training, Daniel began a career in the king's court that lasted seventy years and through three kings. During his service, Daniel proved his faithfulness to God by refusing to eat the rich food from the king's table, instead eating vegetables and water, and in the process, proving himself to be healthier and superior to the other young men. Later he interpreted the king's dream when the king's other wise men and magicians failed. Under the reign of Darius the Mede, Daniel was thrown into a pit of lions for praying to his God instead of Darius. Again, God protected him and Daniel was rescued.

Deborah

Wise and brave leader; Judges 4–5

God chose special leaders known as judges. Their job was to lead the people of Israel into battle, decide legal cases, and often perform religious duties. Deborah was the only woman chosen as a judge. After twenty years of oppression under the Canaanite King Jabin of Hazor, God told Deborah to lead the people into battle. She appointed Barak to lead an army of ten thousand men against the Canaanites. But he was afraid to go without Deborah. She agreed to go, but not before telling Barak that he would receive no honor in battle and that God would allow a woman to defeat Sisera, the Canaanite general. (Read about how this happened in Judges 4:11-21.) The people of Israel defeated the Canaanites in a rout, and together Deborah and Barak sang a victory song to God. (See Judges 5.)

Esther

Courageous and clever queen; Esther 1–10

When the queen of Persia, Vashti, disobeyed her husband, King Xerxes, he ordered that she never see him again. Then he selected officers in every province to bring beautiful women to the capital city of Susa in Persia, where he kept his wives. The woman who pleased him the most would become his queen. He fell in love with Esther and made her his queen. Even as queen, Esther had to obey the law that said anyone who visited the king without getting his invitation first would be put to death. Esther's uncle, Mordecai, one of the Jewish leaders in the land, would not bow down to Haman, the king's palace official. Infuriated, Haman suggested to the king that the Jewish people in Persia be killed and their property taken. Mordecai asked Esther to protect her people. She risked death by appearing before the king without invitation and asked him to reconsider (Esther 5:1-3). (See the bio on Mordecai for the rest of the story, p. 111.)

Gideon

Skeptical, but obedient servant; Judges 6:1–8:35

Gideon was secretly threshing wheat at night for fear of the Midianites stealing his food when God's angel appeared to him. The angel told Gideon to rescue the people of Israel from the Midianites, desert nomads who frequently attacked the country's land and livestock. Gideon was hesitant at first, but then he started to follow God's instructions. Even so, Gideon always asked God to prove himself. To show Gideon and the people that the victory belonged to him, God had Gideon reduce his army from thirty-two thousand men to three hundred. Following God's instructions carefully, Gideon and his small band of men were able to defeat the mighty Midianites by first confusing them with trumpets and torch lights! (Read about this amazing battle in Judges 7:1-25.)

Isaac

Second ancestor of Israel; faithful and obedient; Genesis 24; 25:19–26:35; 27:1–28:5; 35:27-29

Isaac was the promised son from God to his parents, Abraham and Sarah. Later in life, Isaac married Rebekah; they had two twin sons, Esau and Jacob. God blessed Isaac. He was successful and became very rich. King Abimelech told Isaac to leave their country because he was too powerful. Isaac left and settled in Gerar Valley. When Isaac went on to Beersheba, God appeared to him and told him not to be afraid and that he would bless him with many descendants. Isaac believed God, so he built an altar to worship God. At age one hundred and eighty, Isaac died at Hebron, also called Mamre. His sons buried him there in the land where their grandfather, Abraham, lived as a foreigner.

Jacob

Third ancestor of Israel; scheming, but faithful; Genesis 25:19-34; 27:1–35:29; 37; 42:1–50:14

Jacob was the father of twelve sons who later became the twelve tribes of Israel. God later changed Jacob's name to *Israel,* so he was considered the founding father of the ancient people of Israel. His older twin brother, Esau, was supposed to receive his father's blessing, but Jacob tricked his father into giving it to him instead. In Genesis 28:3-4, Isaac prayed that God would bless Jacob with many descendants and let him become a great nation. He also asked that Jacob would be blessed with the land once given to Abraham. God appeared to Jacob one night. Jacob promised God he would follow him as long as God never left his side.

Illustrations by Ron Wheeler

Jonathan

Loyal and brave friend
1 Samuel 13:16—14:46; 18:1-5; 19:1-8; 20:1-42; 23:14-18; 31:1-13.

Jonathan was the son of Saul, king of Israel. He also was a soldier in his father's army. Having faith that God would help him win a battle, he snuck out of camp with another soldier to attack the Philistines. Jonathan's plan to sneak up on the Philistine army from behind worked. The Philistines panicked and became confused. They even killed each other in the confusion. Later, when King Saul invited David to live in his home and work for him, David and Jonathan became best friends. Even when his father plotted to kill David because Saul was jealous of his battlefield successes, Jonathan remained loyal to his friend. Even though Jonathan was rightly next in line to be king, he knew that God had anointed David as the next king and pledged his loyalty to David. (See 1 Samuel 23:14-18.)

DID YOU KNOW?

Jonathan and his brothers were killed in a battle against the Philistines at Mount Gilboa (1 Samuel 31:1-2). Saul, however, took his own life. In 2 Samuel 1:17-27, David sings a song in memory of both Saul and Jonathan, paying tribute to his loyal friend.

Joseph

Man of honor, interpreter of dreams
Genesis 37:1-36; 39:1—50:26

Joseph was the eleventh son of Jacob and the firstborn of Jacob's beloved wife, Rachel. He was Jacob's favorite of all his children since Joseph was the son of his old age. But that made his brothers extremely jealous of him. Joseph only made matters worse for himself when he told his brothers that one day they would bow and worship him. They plotted to kill him, but decided instead to sell him as a slave to a caravan of traders. Joseph's journey into Egypt is a remarkable account of God's care and protection.

God gave Joseph an amazing ability to interpret dreams. Through a series of circumstances, this ability was brought to the attention of the Egyptian king, who had a puzzling dream about cows and grain. Joseph told the king the dream meant there would be seven years of plenty and seven years of starvation. He also told the king a plan that would save his people. The Pharaoh, liking his plan and thinking highly of him, made Joseph a governor of Egypt. Joseph was eventually reunited with his brothers and father when they traveled to Egypt, seeking food. As Joseph had predicted years before, his brothers did, in fact, bow to him when they first approached him, not knowing it was Joseph. At first, his brothers were afraid when they realized who he was. But Joseph reassured them. Read what he said in Genesis 50:20-21.

Joseph, Husband of Mary
Man of integrity
Matthew 1:16–2:23; Luke 1:26–2:52

While Joseph was engaged to Mary, an angel appeared to Mary and told her that she was going to have a baby, who would be God's Son (Luke 1:26-38). Mary was to name this child Jesus. Joseph knew the child could not be his. But he was a good man and decided to quietly break off the engagement (Matthew 1:18-19). An angel appeared to him in a dream and told him that Mary's baby was from the Holy Spirit and that Joseph should marry her. Trusting God, he did. Joseph took Mary to Bethlehem and was with her when she gave birth to Jesus. Through another dream, Joseph was told to leave Bethlehem and escape to Egypt because King Herod wanted to kill his son. Joseph led his family to safety until the death of King Herod.

Joshua and Caleb
A truthful and courageous duo
Numbers 13–14

When the Hebrew people left Egypt under Moses' leadership, God had assured them that he would lead them into Canaan, the land he promised to Abraham. Before they entered Moses chose twelve men—each one a leader of a tribe of Israel—to explore the land and report back on what they discovered. When the men returned, all spoke highly of the land, "a land rich with milk and honey"; but ten also reported that the land was strongly defended and filled with people so big "we felt as small as grasshoppers" (Numbers 13:31-33).

Only Joshua and Caleb urged the people to go forward and enter the land, saying "The Lord is on our side, and they won't stand a chance against us." But the people refused to listen, and because of their disobedience, God sent them back into the wilderness to wander for forty years. Not one of those people—with the exception of Caleb and Joshua—ever stepped foot in Canaan. Eventually, Joshua was chosen to succeed Moses as leader of the Israelites and he led them into battle, defeating the Amalekites and claiming Canaan as their home.

DID YOU KNOW?

Joshua was Moses' assistant. Moses invited Joshua to accompany him up to Mount Sinai where he received the law from God (Exodus 24:12-18). Joshua later was chosen to replace Moses as leader (Deuteronomy 31).

Illustrations by Ron Wheeler

Mordecai

Faithful servant and positive influence
Esther 1–10

Mordecai was an acknowledged leader during the captivity of the Jewish people in Persia. His cousin, Esther, whom he adopted after her parents died, had become queen to the Persian King Xerxes following a nationwide search and beauty contest. When Mordecai overheard two palace guards plotting to kill the king, he immediately alerted Esther and the king was saved. Later, when the king's prime minister, Haman, plotted to destroy the Jewish people because Mordecai had not bowed to him, Mordecai persuaded Esther to intervene for her people. Just as Mordecai was to be hanged for his disobedience, the king remembered how this man had saved his life and vowed to honor him. Esther exposed Haman's evil plot, revealing her own Jewish identify, and the king ordered Haman to be hanged instead and honored Mordecai by naming him one of highest officials in the land.

Moses

Deliverer and law-giver
Exodus, Leviticus, Numbers, and Deuteronomy

The man whose name in Hebrew means "He Who Draws Out" was drawn out of a people enslaved by the king of Egypt. The Egyptian king tried to decrease the Hebrew population by ordering the deaths of all Hebrew boys (Exodus 1:15-22). But Moses' mother, Jochebed (Exodus 6:20), hid and later set Moses afloat on the Nile River under the watchful eye of his sister, Miriam (Exodus 2:1-4). He was found and adopted by the daughter of Pharaoh, who also named him.

Moses' life can be divided into three periods of forty years:

First forty years: Prince of Egypt, learning military and civil law. But after murdering an Egyptian in a misguided attempt to help the Hebrews (Exodus 2:11-14), Moses fled to Midian to escape punishment.

Second forty years: Shepherd and husband of Zipporah, the daughter of the priest Reuel (also known as Jethro) (Exodus 2:16-25).

Last forty years: Shepherd of a new flock, the people of Israel—a task assigned by the God who called himself Yahweh (Exodus 3:14). After a long confrontation with the new king (or pharaoh), Moses drew the people out of slavery. But their disbelief in God's ability to grant them the promised land earned them a forty-year trip through the wilderness (Numbers 13–14). Because of his own disobedience, Moses was not allowed to enter the promised land. (Check out Numbers 20:1-13 for that story.) Still, Moses is considered one of Israel's greatest leaders.

Ruth

Woman of devotion
Ruth 1–4

Ruth was a woman from the land of Moab who married a man from Israel, one of the sons of Naomi. When Naomi's husband, Elimelech, died, and later both her sons (Mahlon and Chilion), Ruth made the courageous decision to leave her homeland and return with Naomi to Bethlehem. In an incredible statement of loyalty, Ruth declared, "Please don't tell me to leave you and return home! I will go where you go, I will live where you live; your people will be my people; your God will be my God" (Ruth 1:16). God rewarded Ruth's devotion and kindness to Naomi by providing her with a husband, Boaz. Their son Obed was the grandfather to David, Israel's greatest king.

DID YOU KNOW?

Ruth was from Moab, and the Moabites were long-time enemies of Israel. Ruth's name appears as part of Jesus' family lineage in Matthew 1:1-5.

Samson

Legendary warrior
Judges 13–16

You've heard of Hercules, right? Meet the original strongest man on earth—Samson. Before he was born, Samson's parents learned that he would live the life of a Nazirite. A Nazirite was set apart from others by their vow to God to abstain from strong drink, shaving or cutting their hair, and having contact with a dead body.

The Philistines were the enemies of Israel. God chose Samson to fight against these enemies. His strength enabled him to kill one thousand men with only a donkey's jawbone. But Samson was tricked by a woman named Delilah into revealing the secret of his strength: his hair. (Read about it in Judges 16:17.) Delilah immediately ran to the Philistines, and as she was cutting his hair while he napped, the Philistines captured and blinded Samson. But Samson asked for God's help once more and knocked down a Philistine temple by pushing his body against the structure's strong pillars, killing more Philistines in his death than he ever had during his life.

Silas

Faithful missionary
Acts 15:22–17:33

Silas was a leader in the Jerusalem church who traveled with Peter and Paul on separate missionary journeys. Once when he accompanied Paul on a trip to Philippi, they met a slave girl, who was possessed by a spirit that gave her the power to tell the future. When Paul and Silas cast the spirit out of her body, the owner complained that he had lost his source of income. So Paul and Silas were thrown into jail. While in jail, the two prayed and sang praises to God. Suddenly a strong earthquake shook the jail and the doors opened and the prisoners' chains fell off. The jailer thought all the prisoners had escaped and was about to kill himself, when Paul stopped him and told him that all the prisoners were still there. Immediately, the jailer fell down in front of Paul and Silas and asked, "What must I do to be saved?" The next day Silas and Paul were released from jail. (Check out Acts 16 for the whole story.)

Stephen

First Christian martyr and dynamic speaker
Acts 6–7

Stephen was highly respected by the apostles because he had great faith in God, so they chose him as a leader of the church. God gave Stephen the ability to perform great miracles among the people. Some men lied about Stephen, spreading rumors that he was telling terrible stories against Moses and God. Then they arrested him and presented him before the council. When the high priest asked if the rumors were true, Stephen gave an impressive speech (the longest in the book of Acts) that not only defended his ancestors (Abraham, Joseph, and Moses), but also helped to spread the gospel of Jesus. The council members became angry, so they stoned him to death. Saul, who would later be known as the apostle Paul, was present when Stephen was killed.

Timothy

Respected missionary
Acts 16:1-5; Philippians 2:19-30; 1 and 2 Timothy

Timothy, a native of Lystra, learned about the Scriptures from his mother, Eunice, and grandmother, Lois (2 Timothy 1:5). His father was Greek. When Paul made his second trip to Lystra, Timothy was already a well-respected disciple. Paul asked Timothy to join him on his journey. Often, Paul would send Timothy to represent him in places like Corinth and Philippi. Paul also gave Timothy some good advice: "Don't let anyone make fun of you, just because you are young. Set an example for other followers by what you say and do, as well as by your love, faith, and purity" (1 Timothy 4:12).

HISTORY

BACK IN THE DAY

The events of the Bible took place over thousands of years and in a very different world from ours today. Some events in the Bible took place long before calendars were invented, and many others were never recorded as "history" anywhere but in the Bible itself! Since the ways in which dates were recorded have changed over the centuries, we can guess when many of these events took place, and we only know approximately when others occurred. For other events, we can use clues found in the texts of the Bible to help us make more "educated guesses" about when they occurred. Here is a list of the events described in the Bible with dates that reflect the most accurate time periods we are able to determine. (For more information about calendars, check out Calendar and Holidays, starting on p. 32.)

Timeline: From Creation to Return from Exile

Time Period	Event	Book(s) of the Bible
The Beginnings		
Prehistory	Creation	Genesis
	Adam and Eve in the Garden of Eden	Genesis
	Noah and the Flood	Genesis
	The Tower of Babel	Genesis
The Ancestors of the Israelites		
1900 to 1700 B.C.	Abraham leaves his home (Haran) and journeys to Canaan.	Genesis
	Ishmael, ancestor of the Arab peoples, is born to Abraham and Hagar. Isaac, ancestor of the Israelite nation, is born to Abraham and Sarah.	Genesis
	Jacob and Esau are born to Isaac and Rebekah.	Genesis
	Twelve sons (ancestors to the twelve tribes of Israel) and one daughter are born to Jacob (Israel) and wives, Rachel and Leah.	Genesis
	Joseph, son of Jacob, is sold into slavery in Egypt; later becomes chief advisor to the king; the rest of brothers later move to Egypt.	Genesis
The Israelites in Egypt and the Wilderness		
1700 to 1290 B.C.	Israelites are made slaves in Egypt.	Exodus
1290 B.C.	Moses leads the Israelites out of Egypt.	Exodus
1290 to 1250 B.C.	The people of Israel wander in the wilderness. Moses receives the Ten Commandments and other laws at Mount Sinai.	Exodus, Leviticus, Deuteronomy

The Conquest and Settlement of Canaan

1250 B.C.	Joshua leads first stage of invasion of Canaan.	Exodus, Numbers, Joshua
1250 to 1030 B.C.	Israel conquers the rest of Canaan (Palestine) and is ruled by a series of judges.	Numbers, Joshua, Judges, 1 Samuel

The United Israelite Kingdom

1030 to 1010 B.C.	Saul becomes the first king of Israel.	1 Samuel
1010 to 970 B.C.	David becomes king of Israel.	1 & 2 Samuel, 1 Chronicles
970 to 931 B.C.	Solomon becomes king of Israel.	1 Kings, 2 Chronicles

The Two Israelite Kingdoms Before the Exile

931 to 687 B.C.	Israel divides into two kingdoms, Judah (southern) and Israel (northern). The prophet Elijah challenges and defeats the prophets of Baal. Israel (the northern kingdom) is conquered by the Assyrians in 722 B.C.	2 Kings, 2 Chronicles
687 to 586 B.C.	The last years of the kingdom of Judah: southern kingdom loses power and land until finally Jerusalem falls to Babylonia.	2 Kings, 2 Chronicles

The Exile

586 B.C.	Judeans are exiled in Babylonia.	2 Chronicles
539 B.C.	Persian rule begins.	2 Chronicles, Daniel

The People Return and Rebuild

538 B.C.	The edict of Cyrus allows Jews to return.	Ezra, Nehemiah
520 B.C.	Foundations of new temple in Jerusalem are laid.	Ezra, Nehemiah
445 to 443 B.C.	Walls of Jerusalem are rebuilt.	Nehemiah

DID YOU KNOW?

History can turn on the actions of just one person. What might have happened if Ruth—who became King David's great-grandmother—had decided not to follow her mother-in-law back to Bethlehem? To read about her simple, but history-changing life, check out the book of Ruth.

The **Second Temple** Period

Have you ever wondered what happened in Israel between the time the returning Jews began rebuilding Jerusalem and restoring worship in the Jerusalem temple and the time John the Baptist started announcing that a change would be coming? These events are described in books like 1 & 2 Maccabees, which aren't in every edition of the Bible. But these books, written in Greek, were part of the Old Testament used by most Christians in the early church. And they tell us a lot about what happened between the Old Testament period and the one described in the New Testament.

Timeline: From the Greek Conquest of Palestine to Paul's Imprisonment

Time Period	Event	Book(s) of the Bible
The Centuries Before the Birth of Christ		
333 B.C.	Alexander the Great establishes Greek rule throughout the known world, including Palestine.	
323 to 198 B.C.	Ptolemies, the descendants of one of Alexander the Great's generals, rule over Egypt, and now rule Palestine.	
198 to 166 B.C.	Seleucids, the descendants of another one of Alexander the Great's generals, rule over Syria, and now rule Palestine.	
166 to 63 B.C.	Jewish revolt under Judas Maccabeus reestablishes their independence and rule over Palestine.	
63 B.C.	Roman general Pompey conquers Jerusalem.	
37 to 4 B.C.	The Romans appoint kings—including Herod the Great—to rule over Palestine.	
New Testament Times		
6 B.C.	Jesus is born in Bethlehem.	Matthew, Luke
	John the Baptist makes quite a splash; Jesus is baptized and begins teaching, healing, and changing lives.	Matthew, Mark, Luke John
around A.D. 32	Jesus is killed on a cross, but he is resurrected to life again three days later.	Matthew, Mark, Luke, John
around A.D. 32	Filled with the Holy Spirit, the disciples minister in Jesus' name; the church starts to grow from Jerusalem outward.	Acts
A.D. 37	Saul of Tarsus meets the risen Christ on the road to Damascus and becomes Paul . . . and a Christian!	Acts
A.D. 41 to 65	Paul spreads the good news about Jesus.	Acts
A.D. 65	Paul is put in prison in Rome.	Acts
A.D. 70	The Romans suppress a Jewish revolt in Jerusalem and destroy the Second Temple.	

"Go to the people of all nations and make them my disciples."

That's what Jesus told his disciples (Matthew 28:19). The church that started with twelve disciples, plus a few more, has grown and expanded to cover the whole world! These two thousand years have brought amazing changes. Christianity has helped shape the growth of Western civilization. From about 1300 to 1750, Christian missionaries spread the good news about Jesus to North and South America, Asia, Australia, and southern Africa. By the beginning of the twenty-first century, Christianity had become the most widely publicized faith on the planet!

KEY EVENTS of the Early Christian Church

Time Period (all dates A.D.)	Year(s)	Event
The Early Church: 64 to 367	64 to 68	Nero blames the Great Fire of Rome on Christians; terrible persecution follows.
	70	The rebuilt temple at Jerusalem is destroyed by Roman emperor Titus to punish rebellious Jews.
	about 100	The Council of Jamnia decides on the official Hebrew Scriptures (Christian Old Testament).
		Reports of first Christians in Monaco, Algeria, Sri Lanka
	280 to 337	Constantine the Great is the first Roman emperor to convert to Christianity.
	325	First Council of Nicaea sorts out doctrines and produces the Nicene Creed (still used in some churches today).
	330	Constantine declares Byzantium (Constantinople) to be the capital of the Roman Empire.
	350	The faith of two Christians taken as slaves to Ethiopia leads to birth of Coptic Church.
	367	Athanasius's list of books of New Testament is accepted by church leaders.

DID YOU KNOW? What do you think is the most important invention of the past two thousand years? The electric light? The automobile? Rocketships that can travel outside our solar system? Some have said it's the invention of the moveable-type printing press by Johannes Gutenberg. It brought about a revolution in the way people gathered and shared knowledge. And do you know what the first book was that Gutenberg printed? That's right—a Bible! That was back in 1455. And the world has never been the same!

Where in the World?

The phrase "Holy Land" has been used by Christians since the sixth century. Back then, many Christians lived in and around Jerusalem and encouraged other Christians from around the world (mostly from Europe) to visit the places associated with the life and ministry of Jesus. Ever since, Christians have continued to make pilgrimages (religious journeys) to the Holy Land, just to "walk where Jesus walked." Even earlier, this part of the world was special for the history of the Jewish people—ever since their ancestor Abraham migrated to Canaan in obedience to God's call. Because Abraham is also an ancestor of the Arab peoples who follow Islam today, the Holy Land has special significance to three of the world's major religions: Judaism, Christianity, and Islam.

Church of the Holy Sepulcher, Jerusalem

Modern-Day Israel

In the Old Testament, Zion often stands for the city of Jerusalem (Isaiah 51:3; 64:10,11; Jeremiah 3:14-17; Zephaniah 3:14,15). Zion is also a poetic term for the land which God had promised to the descendants of Abraham. As a religious movement, "Zionism" represented the desire of God's people to return to the land promised in their covenant (agreement) with God.

As a political movement, "Zionism" sought to create a nation for the Jewish people in Palestine. In 1897, Theodor Herzl, an Austrian journalist and lawyer, convened the first Zionist Congress at Basel, Switzerland. In 1948—about 1,878 years after the Romans destroyed Jerusalem—the modern state of Israel became an independent nation. In that year statehood was proclaimed and recognized by twenty countries including the United States. In 1949, many more followed and Israel was admitted to the United Nations.

Important Cities in the Bible

Nineveh

This was the city Jonah tried to avoid. (Jonah 1:1-3). Nineveh was located along the east side of the Tigris River and was once the largest city in the world. It was one of the most important cities of the Assyrians. It was destroyed in 612 B.C.

Babylon

God allowed the people of Israel to be taken from their homeland to Babylon—the capital city of the Babylonian Empire under King Nebuchadnezzar (2 Kings 24:1-16). Located on the Euphrates River in Mesopotamia (now Iraq), Babylon was the site of the spectacular roof gardens known as the Hanging Gardens—one of the Seven Wonders of the ancient world. (See Buildings and Landmarks, p. 26.) In the seventh century B.C., the prophet Jeremiah declared that God would one day destroy this powerful city. By 141 B.C., there was not much left of Babylon.

Jerusalem

This city, sometimes called the City of David or City of Zion (after the hill on which it was built), is perhaps the most important and sacred place this side of heaven mentioned in the Bible. It is here where Jesus challenged the religious authorities of his day and where he was put to death on a cross. (To read more about this fascinating place, see Jerusalem, p. 130.)

Jericho

Jericho was the first city conquered by Joshua and the Israelites as they moved into Canaan. Not only is it the lowest city in the world (1,000 feet below sea level), it is also the oldest continually inhabited city. It was in existence thousands of years before Abraham came to Canaan and can be found north of the Dead Sea on the west side of the Jordan River.

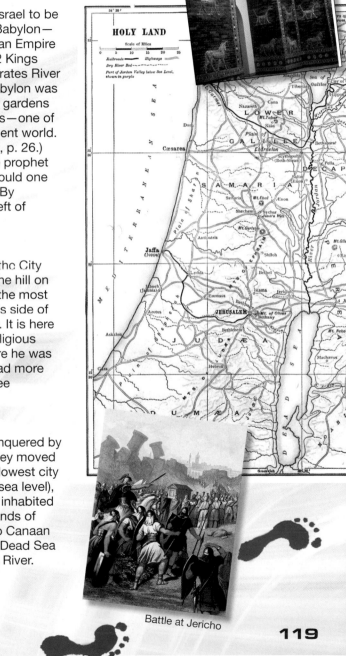

Ishtar Gate, Babylon B.C.

Photos by Photos.com

Battle at Jericho

The Holy Land in the Old Testament

Actually, the phrase *Holy Land* became popular centuries after Bible times. Starting in the sixth century, people talked about the Holy Land and meant Palestine, also known as Canaan, which God had promised to the descendants of Abraham.

Countryside scene in Israel

Canaan, the Promised Land

Can you imagine having a whole country named after you? Well, that's what happened to a man named Israel. Jacob, the grandson of Abraham and the son of Isaac and Rebekah, was also known as Israel. The twelve tribes that made up the nation of Israel were named after his sons (Genesis 48–49).

Over the centuries the tribes grew and a famine forced them to move south to Egypt, where their descendants became slaves. Years later Moses led the people out of slavery. For forty years they wandered in the wilderness of Sinai before crossing the Jordan River to enter the land God promised to their ancestor Abraham.

Joshua, their new leader, assigned land to each tribe.

The LORD gave the Israelites the land he had promised their ancestors, and they captured it and settled in it. There still were enemies around Israel, but the LORD kept his promise to let his people live in peace (Joshua 21:43-44).

Photos by Photos.com

Hebrew University in Jerusalem

DID YOU KNOW?

God provided *Safe Towns*, where a person who accidentally killed someone else could go to be protected from the angry family members of his unfortunate victim. All Israelites agreed that anyone seeking safety in one of these *cities of refuge* would remain untouched until he had received a fair trial. These Safe Towns were spread throughout Canaan (no fleeing Israelite would have to ride for more than a day or two to reach one) and were entrusted to the care of the priestly tribe, the Levites. They were Kedesh, Shechem, Hebron, Golan, Ramoth, and Bezer (Numbers 35:6-15; Deuteronomy 4:41-43; 19:1-13).

Son of Israel/ Tribe	Borders and Other Facts	Key City or Town	Key Bible References
Reuben	Middle of the Arnon River Valley, east of the Dead Sea; as far north as Medeba; bordered by the Jordan River at the west	Beth-Peor	Joshua 13:15-23
Simeon	Tribal land was inside Judah's borders	Beersheba	Joshua 19:1-9
Levi	Priests of Israel did not own land. Instead they were given control of forty-eight towns located throughout the entire country.	The six Safe Towns, most notably Hebron	Numbers 35:1-8; Joshua 13:14; 14:6-15; 21:1-42
Judah	One of the most powerful tribes; borders were the Mediterranean and the Dead Sea	Jerusalem, Gaza, Gath (taken from Philistines), Bethlehem	Joshua 15:1-12
Dan	Between Ephraim and Judah, with Joppa at the northwest; lost land to Philistines, then moved north	Laish (Dan)	Joshua 19:40-48
Naphtali	North and west of Lake Galilee; includes the Huleh Valley. Jesus spent much of his public life here.	Hazor; later, Capernaum	Joshua 19:32-39; Matthew 4:12-16
Gad	At the western border of the Jordan River (between Manasseh's and Reuben's allotments)	Jabesh, Rabbah	Joshua 13:24-28
Asher	Along the Mediterranean coast; Mount Carmel at the south	Tyre, Sidon	Joshua 19:24-31
Issachar	Land-locked with Mt. Tabor in north and the Jordan River at the east	Jezreel	Joshua 19:17-23
Zebulun	West of Lake Galilee; included the Valley of Jezreel in Lower Galilee	Jokneam; later, Gath-Hepher, Nazareth	Joshua 19:10-16
Joseph (tribal land split between sons— Ephraim and Manasseh)	Ephraim—from Bethel to Shechem (at the north); from the Jericho River west	Bethel, Shiloh	Joshua 16–17; 1 Samuel 7:15-16; Jeremiah 7:12-14
	Manasseh—divided into west and east (of Jordan River)	Megiddo, Ashtaroth	Joshua 13:29-31; 17:1-13
Benjamin	Allotted land between Judah and Ephraim that included essential cities	Jericho, Ai, Gibeah	Joshua 18:11-28

Palestine in Jesus' Time

The region that many today call the Holy Land changed hands many times in the twelve centuries from the Israelites' entry into Canaan to the birth of Jesus. The Roman Empire marched on and finally ruled all of the region they called Palestine.

Jesus' life on earth began and ended in the Roman province of Judea. The northern province of Galilee, however, was where he did most of his teaching and healing.

CAPERNAUM

The town of Capernaum, located at the north of Lake Galilee, was Jesus' home away from home (Matthew 4:13; 9:1). Some of Jesus' disciples—Peter, James, John, and Matthew—were born here. Because of the unbelief of the people living there, Jesus predicted that this town would be destroyed. It was.

Synagogue at Capernaum

NAZARETH

This town in the province of Galilee was Jesus' home for about thirty years, until the people there rejected him (Luke 4:16-30). Nazareth was near several trade routes, bringing the local population into contact with the outside world. Because of Nazareth's association with outside influences, some religious Jews distrusted anyone from this town. When one such Jew (who would later become a follower of Jesus) first met Jesus, he asked, "Can anything good come from Nazareth?" (John 1:46).

SAMARIA

The name "Samaria" was more than just a geographical label for the province between Galilee and Judea. Samaria had been the capital city of the northern kingdom of Israel. The Samaritans of Jesus' day were descended from the intermarriage of the northern Israelites and the foreigners that the Assyrian empire had placed there after the defeat of the northern kingdom. Because of this history, in Jesus' time, the Jewish people and the Samaritans did not get along. That's why Jesus' conversation with a Samaritan woman at the well (John 4:3-42) surprised his Jewish disciples. And when Jesus chose a Samaritan to be the hero of one of his most famous parables (Luke 10:25-37), his listeners likewise would have been puzzled and shocked.

Mary's Well, Nazareth

JERICHO

The city of Jericho in New Testament times was a short distance south of its Old Testament location, and the road that connected it to Jerusalem was steep and treacherous. Jesus healed the blind in this ancient city, including a man named Bartimaeus (Mark 10:46-52). The mugging described in the parable of the Good Samaritan happened on the dangerous road outside Jericho (Luke 10:30-37).

View of Jericho

Photos by Photos.com

BETHANY

This village just east of the Mount of Olives was along the road to Jericho. Jesus' friends Mary, Martha, and Lazarus lived there. It was here that Jesus raised Lazarus from the dead (John 11:17-44). At the home of Simon in Bethany, Jesus was anointed by a grateful woman (Mark 14:3-9).

BETHLEHEM

Bethlehem was the hometown of David, Israel's greatest king. And it was from this humble town that the prophet Micah said Israel's Messiah would one day come (Micah 5:2). Centuries later Jesus' birth fulfilled this prophecy (Matthew 2:5-6). Although Joseph and his pregnant wife Mary lived in Nazareth, Joseph was required to go to Bethlehem to be recorded in a census, because he was a descendant of David. This is how it happened that Jesus was born in Bethlehem rather than at home in Nazareth (Luke 2:1-7).

Church of St. Lazarus, Bethany

View of modern-day Bethlehem

HOLY SPIRIT

WHO IS THE HOLY SPIRIT?

God was always active in the world, giving life to plants, animals, and humans (Psalm 104:27-30). The LORD's Spirit gave power to Israelite leaders in ancient times (Numbers 11:24-25).

Names for the Holy Spirit

▶ **The Spirit** (John 14:17)

▶ **Advocate/Helper/Comforter** (John 14:16)

▶ **Holy Ghost** (a name found in Bible passages like Hebrews 2:4 in the *King James Version* of the Bible)

The Holy Spirit is God's presence at work in the world. Before his death, Jesus told his followers that he would send the Holy Spirit to help and teach them (John 14:16). After his resurrection, Jesus told his followers that the Holy Spirit would give them power to tell others about him (Acts 1:8).

DID YOU KNOW?

The word for "a mighty wind" (or "Spirit of God") that moved over the water when God created the world is from the Hebrew word *ruach*, which means "breath" or "wind" or "spirit."

What the Holy Spirit Does

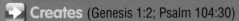

➡ **Creates** (Genesis 1:2; Psalm 104:30)

➡ **Guides** (John 16:13)

➡ **Teaches** (John 14:26)

➡ **Inspired the writing of the Scriptures** (2 Timothy 3:16)

➡ **Gave power to anointed kings and prophets** (1 Samuel 16:13; Isaiah 61:1; Micah 3:8)

➡ **Produces fruit** (Galatians 5:22-23; see "Fruit of the Spirit")

During Jesus' life, the Holy Spirit
» descended upon him in the form of a dove at his baptism (Matthew 3:16).
» led him into the desert where he was tested by the devil (Matthew 4:1).
» gave him the power to drive out demons (Matthew 12:28).

The Church Is Born

When Jesus was raised from death, he appeared to his disciples, breathed on them, and said, "Receive the Holy Spirit" (John 20:22). And fifty days later, on the day of Pentecost, God sent the Holy Spirit, just as Jesus had promised (Acts 2:1-13). Arrival of the Holy Spirit was signaled by
» a mighty wind (Acts 2:2).
» tongues of fire over each person (Acts 2:3).
» people speaking other languages (Acts 2:4).
Now all God's people would be empowered with the Spirit, not just leaders or kings (Acts 2:38-39).

FRUIT OF THE SPIRIT

PLANTS AND TREES SHOW THEIR HEALTH BY BEARING FRUIT. THE HOLY SPIRIT PRODUCES FRUIT IN THE LIVES OF GOD'S PEOPLE. THIS ISN'T THE KIND OF FRUIT YOU EAT. THE FRUIT OF THE SPIRIT IS:

LOVE · PATIENCE · GOODNESS · GENTLENESS · JOY · PEACE · KINDNESS · FAITHFULNESS · SELF-CONTROL

THESE ARE THE CHARACTERISTICS DESCRIBED IN GALATIANS 5:22–23.

GIFTS OF THE SPIRIT

Who does not want a gift? The gifts of the Spirit are not like the newest video game system or the greatest action figure, but are ways that the Holy Spirit acts through God's people. With these gifts, God's people help one another. Here are some of the gifts of the Spirit mentioned in the Bible:

- Service (Romans 12:7; Ephesians 4:12)
- Teaching (Romans 12:7)
- Encouragement (Romans 12:8)
- Giving (Romans 12:8)
- Leadership (Romans 12:8)
- Compassion (Romans 12:8)
- Wisdom (1 Corinthians 12:8)
- Knowledge (1 Corinthians 12:8)
- Faith (1 Corinthians 12:9)
- Healing the sick (1 Corinthians 12:9)
- Working miracles (1 Corinthians 12:10)
- Prophecy (1 Corinthians 12:10; Romans 12:6)
- Discernment (1 Corinthians 12:10)
- Speaking in an unknown language (1 Corinthians 12:10)

The Holy Spirit decides which gifts to give each of us (1 Corinthians 12:11). According to these gifts, people are chosen by the Spirit to be

- Apostles
- Prophets
- Missionaries
- Pastors
- Teachers

They are ways that the Holy Spirit graciously acts through the members of the church. We call these "spiritual gifts." Through these abilities, the members of Christ's body help one another.

DID YOU KNOW?

God's gathered people are known as the Church or as "the body of Christ." Read more about what it means to be a member of the body of Christ in 1 Corinthians 12:12-31.

PRAYING IN THE SPIRIT

In certain ways we are weak, but the Spirit is here to help us. For example, when we don't know what to pray for, the Spirit prays for us in ways that cannot be put into words (Romans 8:26).

This verse comes from the apostle Paul's letter to the church in Rome. It explains the Spirit's role in prayer. Praying in the Spirit means that God's Spirit will guide you as you pray.

125

Idols and Foreign Gods

Who's on First?

In Old Testament times, the people of the ancient Near East worshiped many different gods and goddesses. These gods were believed to serve different purposes and to oversee different aspects of life—like the weather, warfare, agriculture, and the movement of the sun and moon. These divine beings were often represented by statues called idols, and some cultures believed the god actually inhabited the idol. The worship of these idols was closely tied to the kings that ruled the land. In fact, kings and queens were sometimes seen as the "go-betweens" for the gods. In some cases, this identification was so strong that the people actually considered their earthly rulers to be gods themselves.

The Law of Moses commanded God's people to remain loyal to the one true God, who had led them out of slavery in Egypt and into the promised land of Canaan (Exodus 20:1-5). Once they settled there, they were often tempted to follow the other gods, and often did.

Main Gods and Goddesses of the Ancient Near East

BAAL

The term *Baal* is a title from the ancient Near East that means "lord." It was used by many different cultures of the region when addressing their gods. In Canaan, Baal was the name of the storm god who was believed to provide rain for the crops. Because of this important role, the Canaanites thought of him as the king of all the gods. King Ahab of Israel and his queen, Jezebel, encouraged the people to worship Baal. (See 1 Kings 16:29-33.) A very dramatic encounter between the God of Israel, Yahweh, and two foreign gods can be found in 1 Kings 18, where the prophet Elijah challenges 450 prophets of Baal and 400 prophets of Asherah (see next section).

Baal, bronze figurine (14th-12th centuries B.C.)

ASHERAH

The Canaanites believed Asherah to be the mother of the earth. She was their highest-ranking female deity and was often honored with an Asherah pole—a large pole decorated with carvings and set into the ground. These poles were often placed next to altars of Baal. When Gideon was chosen to be a leader (judge) in Israel, God told him to cut down the Asherah pole and burn the wood when making an offering to God (Judges 6:25-32).

Asherah (c. 1300 B.C.)

The Prophets of Baal are Slaughtered, Gustave Doré (c. 1865)

DAGON

The Philistines who lived along the shore of the Mediterranean Sea worshiped Dagon, a god who was depicted as half man, half fish. Like Baal, Dagon was the god of rain and fertility and considered to be the top god. In 1 Samuel 5:2-5, strange things happened to a statue of Dagon. When the Philistines captured the Israelites' sacred chest (the ark of the covenant), they placed it in a temple of Dagon (1 Samuel 4–5). In the morning, the statue had fallen over in front of the sacred chest. When the statue was set upright, it was found the next morning in the same place with its head and hands broken off.

A modern interpretation of Dagon

MOLECH

Molech was the main god of the Phoenicians. In statues, he was shown as a man with the head of a bull. The followers of Molech practiced human sacrifice and were known to sometimes offer their first-born children to be burned on an altar. Israel was warned not to give any of their children to Molech or they themselves would be killed (Leviticus 20:2-5). In spite of this warning, however, King Solomon created an altar to Molech on the Mount of Olives (1 Kings 11:7). Sixteen generations later, King Josiah finally destroyed the altar (2 Kings 23:13).

Molech worshipers, 19th century engraving

Solomon worshiping idols, 19th century engraving

DID YOU KNOW?

In the ancient Near East, when one country conquered another, the conquering nation often took the defeated countries' most important idol back to their capital, and held it captive in their own capital. If the two countries made peace at a later time, the idol was returned, but usually with the name of the victorious king inscribed on it. In the same way, the sacred chest was taken by the Philistines during battle and placed in Dagon's temple (1 Samuel 4).

High Places

Historically, altars to gods were built on mountains or other high areas. This was to give the gods a position of elevated status.

In the Law of Moses, God did not permit the Israelites to build altars on high places. In fact, the Israelites were instructed to tear down all the altars that other nations had built on high places (Deuteronomy 12:1-4). God said that he would provide a special place for them to go to make sacrifices to the Lord, so that their worship would be distinct from that of other religions. "Don't worship the LORD your God in the way those nations worship their gods" (Deuteronomy 12:4).

The History of Costume,
Braun & Schneider

The Ephod

After Gideon's small army defeated the Midianites (Judges 7), the people of Israel called for him to become their king. He refused, but requested the gold that had been taken from the Midianites in battle. With part of this gold, he created a statue in the shape of an ephod—a garment worn by the high priest of Israel. After he placed this statue in his hometown of Ophrah, the Israelites began to worship it as a god. In Judges 8:27, we find that "even Gideon and his family were trapped into worshiping the statue."

Gideon leading his army of 300 against the Midianites

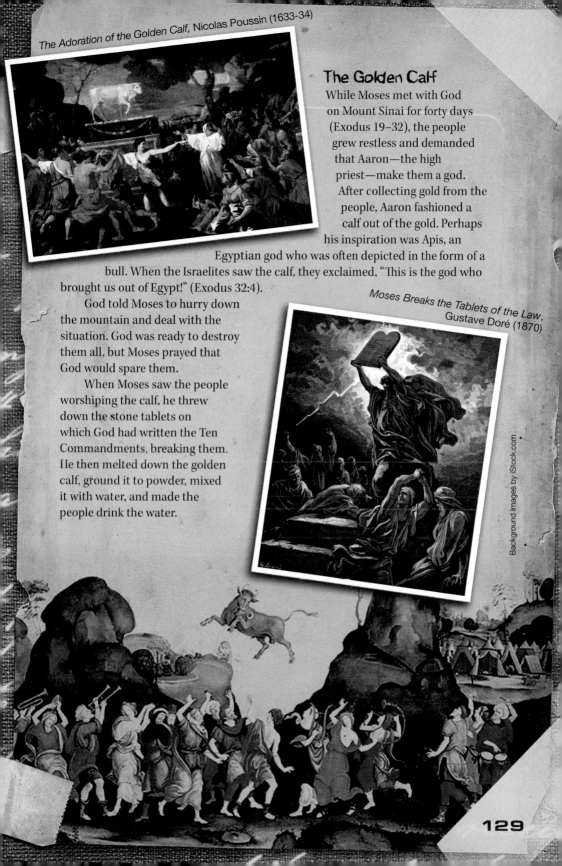

The Adoration of the Golden Calf, Nicolas Poussin (1633-34)

The Golden Calf

While Moses met with God on Mount Sinai for forty days (Exodus 19–32), the people grew restless and demanded that Aaron—the high priest—make them a god. After collecting gold from the people, Aaron fashioned a calf out of the gold. Perhaps his inspiration was Apis, an Egyptian god who was often depicted in the form of a bull. When the Israelites saw the calf, they exclaimed, "This is the god who brought us out of Egypt!" (Exodus 32:4).

God told Moses to hurry down the mountain and deal with the situation. God was ready to destroy them all, but Moses prayed that God would spare them.

When Moses saw the people worshiping the calf, he threw down the stone tablets on which God had written the Ten Commandments, breaking them. He then melted down the golden calf, ground it to powder, mixed it with water, and made the people drink the water.

Moses Breaks the Tablets of the Law, Gustave Doré (1870)

Background images by iStock.com

JERUSALEM

O JERUSALEM, JERUSALEM!

When you turn on your television to watch the world news, it will often include a story about the city of Jerusalem or its surrounding area. Sometimes you will see people who are angry, people who are crying, and even people who have been hurt or killed. Maybe you ask yourself, *Why is everybody so upset over who owns this city?* To answer this question you must start at the beginning, over 5,500 years ago, around 3500 B.C.

The Dome of the Rock, on the Temple Mount in Jerusalem

Hilltop view of Jerusalem

A long time ago in a desert far, far away . . .

Archeological evidence suggests that the site of what would later become Jerusalem was settled by a Stone Age people around the year 5000 B.C. They stayed there for about 1,500 years before being driven off by a people known as the Canaanites, who established a settlement there around the year 3500 B.C. This makes Jerusalem one of the oldest cities in the world. It was situated on a small hill below what would come to be known as the Temple Mount, and was protected by steep slopes on three sides: the Kidron Brook on the east, the Hinnom Valley on the south, and the Tyropoeon valley on the west. Gihon Spring, one of the few available fresh water springs in the area, provided water for the settlements' inhabitants. Two and a half millennia later, that same spring would play a vital role during the time of King David.

Ancient tomb in Jerusalem

Pharaoh, the Habiru Are Coming, the Habiru Are Coming!

The first mention of Jerusalem in writing takes place in three different texts. One is found in Genesis 14:18-20 where Abraham (called Abram then), who lived between 2000 B.C. and 1500 B.C., meets Melchizedek, the mysterious king from Salem (a named derived from Jerusalem). An Egyptian text from around 1900 B.C. also speaks of Jerusalem.

The Amarna Letters, written on clay tablets, were sent back and forth from King Amenhotep III of Egypt and the Canaanite king of Jerusalem, Abdi-Heba, around 1400 B.C. Found in an archeological dig in 1887 in the ruined city of Tell El-Amarna, the letters reveal that King Abdi-Heba was being attacked by a mysterious group of people called the Habiru. He needed Egypt's military help. Nobody knows for certain whether the Habiru really refers to the Hebrews or not.

DID YOU KNOW?

The *Amarna Letters* consist of over 406 clay tablets—at least, that's how many have been found so far. Many appear to have been diplomatic letters written to other kings in the region. That's a lot of text messaging!

THE BIG APPLE OF DAVID'S EYE

By the year 1200 B.C., Jerusalem was under the control of a group of people called the Jebusites. When Joshua led the people of Israel into the promised land (Canaan), they settled in the areas surrounding Jerusalem. But they never managed to drive the Jebusites out of the city because it was so well fortified.

Enter King David! Around 1000 B.C., David was looking for a way to unite and rule not only his tribe (Judah) but also all the tribes of Israel (2 Samuel 2). Jerusalem's location along the border would allow him to establish a political, spiritual, and economic capital that would unite the Israelites. The only problem was how would he get inside the city to remove the Jebusites?

The Jebusites bragged that Jerusalem, sitting atop three steep slopes, could never be conquered. (See 2 Samuel 5:6-12) But David had thoroughly scouted out the city and its surroundings. Seeing that the Jebusites did not have to go outside the city walls to fetch water, David realized that Gihon Spring must run underneath the city to a well. Taking a group of brave men, David's general, Joab, went to the spring and began digging a tunnel big enough for his men to fit through. Upon finding the entrance to the well, they climbed its walls and were able to take the city without having to knock down its gates!

DIFFERENT NAMES OF JERUSALEM:

- Jebus— "Of the Jebusites"
- Kiryat Hannah David— "City Where David Camped"
- Ariel— "Lion of God"
- Ir Ha'Elohim— "City of God"
- Neveh Zedek— "Righteous Dwelling"

The Queen of Sheba visits King Solomon, Julius Schnorr von Carolsfeld (19th century)

FROM RICHES TO RAGS

Under David's son, Solomon, Jerusalem reached its most glorious height. The city's most important building, the temple, was completed around 959 B.C. Only thirty-five years after the completion of the temple, Jerusalem was under siege by King Shishak of Egypt, who plundered everything from the temple treasuries (2 Chronicles 12:1-9).

Two hundred years later, the Assyrian King Sennacherib laid siege to Jerusalem when Hezekiah was king of Israel. However, the Bible records in 2 Kings 19:20-34 how God came to the rescue of the people of Jerusalem.

Finally, nearly one hundred years later in 586 B.C., Jerusalem was utterly destroyed by the Babylonian king, Nebuchadnezzar. The last king of Judah, Zedekiah, was placed in chains, as were many of his subjects, and taken to Babylon (2 Kings 25:1-21).

iStock.com

Background image by iStock.com

HOMECOMING

For seventy years, the Babylonians held the Israelites captive, while Jerusalem lay in ruins. By the time King Cyrus of Persia allowed the people of Israel to return home (Ezra 1), most of the original captives who had lived in Jerusalem had died. So the majority of people returning to Jerusalem had never seen it! They returned over a period of fifty years to the ruins of Jerusalem. Ezra, a scribe, was one of the people who returned. That wasn't until the year 445 B.C., when Nehemiah and a group of armed men approached the outskirts of Jerusalem to survey the damage.

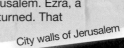
City walls of Jerusalem

DID YOU KNOW?

It took Nehemiah, the governor of Judah, and others fifty-two days to complete the rebuilding of the walls (Nehemiah 2:11-20; 6:15). Men from every clan helped. And when the builders were threatened by their hostile neighbors, each builder worked with only one hand so that his other hand would be free to grab a weapon should their enemies attack (Nehemiah 4:16-18).

DROPPING THE HAMMER

During the four hundred years between the rebuilding of the walls of Jerusalem and the time Herod the Great came to power, the nation of Israel was governed by Syrians. In 167 B.C., a brave Jewish family called the Maccabees (a name meaning "hammer") led a revolt agains the Syrians. Waging a guerrilla military campaign, Judas Maccabeus and his followers eventually defeated the Syrians in 164 B.C., regained control of Jerusalem, and rededicated the temple, which the Syrians had defiled through the worship of false gods. The Maccabees ruled for one hundred years until the Romans invaded in 63 B.C., when a series of emperors in Rome appointed a series of governors and provincial leaders to rule over the city and region.

HEROD THE BUILDER

Enter Herod the Great, who was appointed king by the Romans in 37 B.C. Though he was a Jew, Herod was very cruel to his own people, favoring his own selfish ambitions over the care of the people. Though he did expand Jerusalem greatly through impressive building projects, the majority of the projects were done to protect him from invading forces, or so that his own magnificence as a ruler would be remembered. These projects included:

Bust of Herod the Great

- Remodeling the fortress north of the Temple Mount and naming it the Antonia Fortress, in honor of Mark Anthony.

- Building a second fortress along the western side of Jerusalem.

- Building an upper and lower palace for himself within the city.

DID YOU KNOW?

Herod was not always selfish. In Jerusalem, he also constructed baths, a theater, and a stadium known as a Hippodrome, where he promoted both Roman and Greek games.

OUT WITH THE OLD...

By the time Jesus began his ministry around A.D. 28, Jerusalem had been the center of Jewish faith and worship for over one thousand years. Before that, it was a hot, dusty little city on a hill with a well. It wasn't until King David brought the sacred chest (ark of the covenant) into the city and his son Solomon built the temple there that the city really began to be seen as the spiritual center of the Israelite community. In their mind, the people saw God transporting the covenant he established at Mount Sinai to the Temple Mount in Jerusalem. Therefore, the City of David soon became the city of the LORD, and the temple became the place where God could reside among his people.

...IN WITH THE NEW

When Jesus decided to travel to Jerusalem (Luke 9:51), he knew that he would not be going there to receive popular praise as Messiah, but to be rejected by its rulers, and ultimately to die there (Mark 8:31). It is for this reason that he wept over the city and predicted that it would be surrounded by Roman armies and destroyed—even its temple. Why? "Because you did not see that God had come to save you" (Luke 19:44). The city prepared by God to welcome his presence had, in fact, rejected him. They no longer recognized him.

Sermon on the Mount,
Carl Heinrich Bloch
(19th century)

IMPERIAL DOMINATION

By the time the temple was destroyed in A.D. 70 during a war called the Great Jewish Revolt, the Romans had turned Jerusalem into an insignificant outpost in the growing Roman Empire. The Emperor Hadrian renamed the city Aelia Capitolina, after himself and the Roman god Jupiter. Any Jews who had not already been forced to move across the Mediterranean after the revolt were allowed in the city only one day a year, when they could mourn the destruction of the temple by going to the only wall it had left standing: the Western Wall, or "Wailing Wall," as it is sometimes called.

Constantine the Great, mosaic in Hagia Sophia (c. 1000)

A ROMAN EMPEROR REBUILDS JERUSALEM

For one hundred and fifty years, Jerusalem remained an unimportant town until the first Christian emperor, Constantine, rebuilt it as a Christian center of worship, building the famous Church of the Holy Sepulcher in A.D. 335. Jews, however, were still banned from the city until a brief period in A.D. 614-629, when Jerusalem fell under the rule of Persia.

DID YOU KNOW?

The Old City of Jerusalem is just thirty-five square miles and has been divided up into four distinct quarters.

The Storm from the Desert

Jerusalem fell to the first Muslim conquest in A.D. 638. Why? Islam's key prophet and founder, Muhammad, claimed he had received a vision from God in A.D. 621. In his vision, the archangel Gabriel appeared to him and took him up into heaven and then to Jerusalem, where he told him to lead other prophets in prayer there. When Muhammad died in A.D. 632, his followers continued to grow in strength and numbers until they were able to assemble armies that marched all across the Middle East, North Africa, Eastern Europe, and even to Spain. One of the first cities they conquered was Jerusalem. Sixty years later the Dome of the Rock was completed, a shrine located on the Temple Mount that houses a rock that is said to have been the place where Muhammad ascended into heaven with Gabriel. This is one of the reasons why the Muslims consider Jerusalem one of their religion's sacred cities.

Muhammad's Call to Prophecy and the First Revelation; Compendium of Histories, (ca. 1425)

ToDay's JeRusaLEM

Today, Jerusalem is a culturally vibrant city with over 740,000 people living within its boundaries, and is the capital of Israel. When Israel became a state in 1948, Jews who had been scattered across the world for nearly two thousand years were once again able to return to their ancestral home.

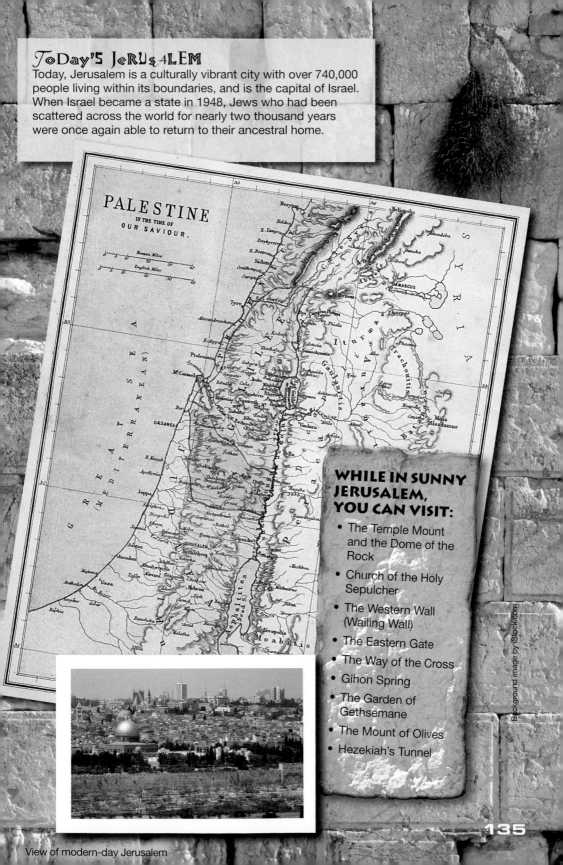

WHILE IN SUNNY JERUSALEM, YOU CAN VISIT:

- The Temple Mount and the Dome of the Rock
- Church of the Holy Sepulcher
- The Western Wall (Wailing Wall)
- The Eastern Gate
- The Way of the Cross
- Gihon Spring
- The Garden of Gethsemane
- The Mount of Olives
- Hezekiah's Tunnel

Background image by iStock.com

View of modern-day Jerusalem

JESUS

Photos.com

Who Is Jesus?

Many people throughout the centuries have asked themselves this question. You probably hear about Jesus most especially during the Christmas and Easter seasons. There are movies and books about him. The system of dating historical events was changed because of his birth. So, who is Jesus? What influence has he had throughout history, and how does he influence life today?

Happy Birthday, Jesus!

When was Jesus born? No one really knows for sure. If you read the section on Christmas (p. 38), you know that Jesus was not born on December 25. That date was established in the fourth century when Christianity became the official religion of the Roman Empire. The date was probably chosen as a way to oppose the festival surrounding the winter solstice and the pagan feast celebrating the birth of the sun god (*Sol Invictus*). Clement of Alexandria, a church leader in the second century, thought Jesus was born on May 20, while Hippolytus of Rome, a church leader during the second and third centuries, believed that Jesus was born on January 2.

Photos.com

WHAT'S IN A NAME

In the New Testament, various names and titles are used for Jesus. Some are in the list below. These names tell you what many believe about him.

Photos.com

ALPHA AND OMEGA
(Greek terms for "first and last," used in Revelation 1:8; 22:13)

THE BREAD THAT GIVES LIFE
(John 6:35; 48)

THE BRIDEGROOM *(Matthew 9:15)*

THE CHRIST, THE SON OF GOD
(John 11:27)

THE GATE FOR THE SHEEP *(John 10:7-9)*

THE GOOD SHEPHERD *(John 10:11-18)*

THE GREAT HIGH PRIEST
(Hebrews 4:14)

I AM In John's Gospel, Jesus uses the term "I am" to show that he has been in God's plan from the beginning when he said, "even before Abraham was, I was, and I am" *(John 8:58)*. When God commanded Moses to lead the Israelites out of slavery in Egypt, Gold told Moses that his name is "I Am" *(Exodus 3:14)*.

iStock.com

IMMANUEL
("God is with us"—Matthew 1:23)

KING OF KINGS AND LORD OF LORDS
(Revelation 19:16)

LAMB OF GOD *(John 1:29)*

LIGHT OF THE WORLD *(John 8:12)*

LION FROM THE TRIBE OF JUDAH
(Revelation 5:5)

LORD *(Acts 2:36; Romans 10:9; Philippians 2:11)*

MESSIAH *(Matthew 16:16)*

THE MOST IMPORTANT STONE
(Ephesians 2:20)

THE ONE WHO RAISES THE DEAD TO LIFE *(John 11:25)*

SAVIOR *(Luke 2:11)*

SON OF DAVID *(Luke 18:38)*

SON OF GOD
(John 1:49; Hebrews 4:14)

SON OF MAN
(Matthew 8:20; 20:18; 24:30)

THE TRUE VINE *(John 15:1)*

THE WAY, THE TRUTH, AND THE LIFE *(John 14:6)*

THE WORD *(John 1:1)*

THE WORD OF GOD *(Revelation 19:13)*

Photos.com

PROPHECIES OF THE MESSIAH

There were many prophecies in the Old Testament about the coming Messiah (the Savior) that Christians point to being fulfilled in Jesus' life, death, and resurrection.

PROPHECY	FULFILLED BY JESUS
A virgin would give birth to a son named Immanuel (Isaiah 7:14).	Mary, a virgin, gave birth to Jesus (Luke 2:1-7). He was called Immanuel (Matthew 1:23).
A ruler would be born in Bethlehem even though it is the smallest of towns (Micah 5:2).	Jesus was born in Bethlehem (Luke 2:1-20).
A prophet would come out of the desert and prepare the way for the LORD (Isaiah 40:3-5; Malachi 3:1).	John the Baptist started preaching in the desert and telling people to turn back to God (Matthew 3:1-3; Mark 1:1-4; Luke 3:3-6).
The prophets Isaiah and Jeremiah spoke out against corruption in the temple (Isaiah 56:7; Jeremiah 7:11).	Jesus entered the temple and drove out all who were buying and selling there (Matthew 21:12-13; John 2:13-22).
The king would enter Jerusalem on a donkey (Zechariah 9:9).	Jesus rode into Jerusalem on a donkey (Matthew 21:1-11; Mark 11:1-11; Luke 19:28-40; John 12:12-16).
David lamented over the betrayal of a friend (Psalm 41:9).	Jesus, a descendant of David, quoted this verse when he predicted his betrayal (John 13:18). Judas was the betrayer (Matthew 26:20-25, 47-50; John 13:18-30; Acts 1:16-18).
The suffering servant (the Messiah) would be wounded for the sins of others (Isaiah 53:5).	Jesus, the suffering servant, was put to death for the sins of others (Matthew 27:32-66; Mark 15:21-41; Luke 23:26-56; John 19:17-37).
In this psalm of David, enemies provided vinegar to drink (Psalm 69:21).	While on the cross, Jesus was offered some wine mixed with vinegar to ease the pain (Matthew 27:34).
The servant would be buried in the tomb of a rich man (Isaiah 53:9).	Joseph of Arimathea, a rich man, buried Jesus in his own tomb (Matthew 27:57-61).
David spoke of living forever in God's presence (Psalm 16:8-11).	The apostle Peter quoted these verses when preaching about Jesus' resurrection from the dead (Acts 2:25-31).

iStock.com

137

Like stories? Jesus often used stories about common, everyday things to communicate important truths about God and his kingdom. Here are some of the stories Jesus told.

PARABLES OF JESUS

STORY	MATTHEW	MARK	LUKE	JOHN
Friend at midnight			11:5-13	
Good Samaritan			10:25-37	
Good Shepherd				10:1-18
Lost coin			15:8-10	
Lost sheep	18:12-14		15:4-7	
Mustard seed	13:31-32	4:30-32	13:18-19	
Pearl of great price	13:45-46			
Pharisee and tax collector			18:9-14	
Prodigal son			15:11-32	
Renters of a vineyard	21:33-46	12:1-12	20:9-19	
Rich fool			12:16-21	
Rich man and Lazarus			16:19-31	
Sheep and goats	25:31-46			
Ten bridesmaids	25:1-13			
Ten talents	25:14-30		19:11-27	
The sower	13:3-9, 18-23	4:3-9, 13-20	8:4-8, 11-15	
Two builders	7:24-27		6:47-49	
Two debtors			7:41-43	
Unmerciful servant	18:21-35			
Unprepared builder			14:28-30	
Vine and branches				15:1-17
Weeds in field	13:24-30, 36-43			
Widow and judge			18:1-8	
Workers in the vineyard	20:1-16			

The Sermon on the Mount

Jesus was considered a great teacher. Many of his most well-known teachings are included in the Sermon on the Mount (Matthew 5–7). Here you'll find the **BEATITUDES** (5:1-12), the Lord's Prayer (6:9-13), and other important teachings. Here are a few quotes from this sermon that you may recognize:

♦ "When someone slaps your right cheek, turn and let that person slap your other cheek" (5:39).

♦ "Don't condemn others, and God won't condemn you" (7:1).

♦ "You can see the speck in your friend's eye, but you don't notice the log in your own eye" (7:3).

♦ "Treat others as you want them to treat you. This is what the Law and the Prophets are all about" (7:12).

MIRACLES OF JESUS

Jesus could do amazing things! He did the following feats and many others to show that he was the promised Savior and the Son of God.

iStock.com

WHAT JESUS DID	WHERE YOU CAN FIND IT
Cured a woman who bled for twelve years	Matthew 9:20-22
Fed over 5,000 people	Matthew 14:13-21; John 6:1-14
Walked on water	Matthew 14:22-33
Healed a crippled man	Mark 2:1-12
Calmed a storm	Mark 4:35-41
Cured a man of evil spirits	Mark 5:1-20
Raised a dead girl to life	Mark 5:21-24, 35-43
Healed a deaf and mute man	Mark 7:31-37
Raised a widow's dead son to life	Luke 7:11-17
Healed ten lepers	Luke 17:11-19
Turned water into wine	John 2:1-11
Healed a man born blind	John 9:1-41
Brought Lazarus back to life	John 11:17-44

Key Events in Jesus' Life

Jesus was born in the town of Bethlehem during the reign of Augustus Caesar, the Roman emperor, and when Herod the Great was king of all Palestine. This places the date of Jesus' birth at or around 6 B.C. At age twelve, Jesus attended the Passover in Jerusalem with his parents, and he began his public ministry when he was around thirty years old. His earthly ministry is estimated to be anywhere from one to three or more years. This would place the date of his crucifixion and resurrection around A.D. 30.

When Jesus Was a Kid

BETHLEHEM: Jesus is born and the shepherds witness it. Later, wise men from the east visit him *(Matthew 1:18-25; 2:1-12; Luke 2:1-20).*

JERUSALEM: Mary and Joseph bring Jesus to the temple *(Luke 2:21-40).*

GALILEE/EGYPT: Mary and Joseph take Jesus to Egypt to escape Herod the Great; they return when it is safe *(Matthew 2:13-23).*

JERUSALEM: Jesus visits the temple as a boy *(Luke 2:41-52).*

Jesus' Public Ministry

JORDAN RIVER: Jesus is baptized by John the Baptist *(Matthew 3:13-17; Mark 1:9-11; Luke 3:21-22; John 1:29-34).*

DESERT: Jesus is tempted by Satan *(Matthew 4:1-11; Mark 1:12-13; Luke 4:1-13).*

CANA: For his first miracle, Jesus changes water into wine at a wedding *(John 2:1-11).*

LAKE GALILEE: Jesus calls his first disciples *(Matthew 4:18-22; Mark 1:16-20; Luke 5:1-11).*

CAPERNAUM: Jesus chooses his twelve disciples (Matthew 10:1-4; Mark 3:13-19; Luke 6:12-16).

NEAR THE LAKE GALILEE: Jesus gives the Sermon on the Mount *(Matthew 5:1–7:29).*

LAKE GALILEE: Jesus calms a storm *(Matthew 8:23-27; Mark 4:35-41; Luke 8:22-25).*

NEAR BETHSAIDA: Jesus walks on water *(Matthew 14:22-33; Mark 6:45-52; John 6:16-21).*

CAESAREA PHILIPPI: Jesus predicts his death *(Matthew 16:21-26).*

Three of the disciples see Jesus' glory *(Matthew 17:1-13; Mark 9:2-13; Luke 9:28-36).*

BETHANY: Jesus raises Lazarus from the dead *(John 11:1-44).*

JERICHO: Jesus heals blind Bartimaeus *(Matthew 20:29-34; Mark 10:46-52; Luke 18:35-43).*

Jesus' Final Week
See also Easter, p. xxx.)

JERUSALEM: Jesus enters Jerusalem on a donkey *(Matthew 21:1-11).*

Jesus chases the moneychangers out of the temple *(Matthew 21:12-17).*

BETHANY: Jesus is anointed at Bethany *(Matthew 26:6-13).*

JERUSALEM: Jesus eats the Passover meal, the last supper *(Matthew 26:17-30; Mark 14:12-26; Luke 22:7-23).*

JERUSALEM: Jesus washes his disciples' feet *(John 13:1-20).*

Jesus prays in Gethsemane *(Matthew 26:36-46; Mark 14:32-52; Luke 22:39-46).*

Jesus prays for his followers *(John 17:1-26).*

Jesus is arrested *(Matthew 26:47-56; Mark 14:43-52; Luke 22:47-53; John 18:3-14).*

JERUSALEM: Jesus is tried and sentenced to death *(Matthew 26:57—27:30; Mark 14:53—15:21; Luke 22:66—23:25; John 18:19—19:16).*

GOLGOTHA *(near Jerusalem)***:** Jesus is crucified *(Matthew 27:31-56; Mark 15:22-41; Luke 23:26-49; John 19:17-37).*

NEAR JERUSALEM: Jesus is buried *(Matthew 27:57-66; Mark 15:42-47; Luke 23:50-56; John 19:38-42).*

Jesus is raised to life *(Matthew 28:1-10; Mark 16:1-8; Luke 24:1-12; John 20:1-18).*

Jesus' Final Forty Days on Earth

NEAR JERUSALEM: Jesus appears to his followers *(Luke 24:13-49; John 20:19—21:25; Acts 1:3-5).*

A MOUNTAIN IN GALILEE: Jesus gives his disciples final instructions *(the Great Commission—Matthew 28:16-20).*

BETHANY: Jesus returns to heaven *(Luke 24:50-53; Acts 1:6-11).*

Quotes about Jesus
"Who Do People Say That I Am?"

Jesus asked his disciples this question. (See Matthew 16:13-20; Mark 8:27-30; Luke 9:18-21.) Here are some of the ways people have described him.

MAHATMA GANDHI, early twentieth-century leader in India:

"[Jesus]—a man who was completely innocent, offered himself as a sacrifice for the good of others, including his enemies, and became the ransom of the world. It was a perfect act."

Gandhi on Non-violence, by Mahatma Gandhi, edited by Thomas Merton.

H. G. WELLS, late nineteenth to twentieth century author, writer of *The Time Machine*:

"I am an historian, I am not a believer, but I must confess as a historian that this penniless preacher from Nazareth is irrevocably the very center of history. Jesus Christ is easily the most dominant figure in all history."

Quoted in *Vintage Jesus: Timeless Answers to Timely Questions*, by Mark Driscoll and Gerry Breshears.

BLAISE PASCAL, seventeenth-century physicist and mathematician:

"Jesus is the God whom we can approach without pride and before whom we can humble ourselves without despair."

Pensées, by Blaise Pascal, translated by A.J. Krailshaimer.

C. S. LEWIS, twentieth-century author and scholar:

"You must make your choice. Either this man was, and is, the Son of God: or else a madman or something worse."

Mere Christianity by C. S. Lewis.

Will Jesus Return?

Jesus returned to heaven before his disciples' startled eyes. But two angels at the site explained that Jesus would return to earth someday (Acts 1:9-11).

Before his betrayal, Jesus told his followers that he was going to prepare a place for the disciples and then come back for them (John 14:1-3). He said there would be a time of suffering and distress before he comes back and that no one knows the time or place of his return (Matthew 24:36-44; Mark 13:32-37). Jesus' return is often connected with a time of judgment, when those who have done wrong will be punished and those who have done right will be rewarded (Matthew 13:41-43; 16:27-28; 25:31-46). The apostle Paul describes Christ's return as a time when the faithful will be raised to life (1 Corinthians 15:23; 1 Thessalonians 4:14-18). Christians continue to expect and wait for Jesus to return.

KIDS IN THE BIBLE

If you could hop into a time-travel machine and transport yourself back to ancient times, how different do you think a kid's life would be? You probably wouldn't recognize many things that were commonplace thousands of years ago. Here are some brief recaps of well-known children from Bible times.

CAIN AND ABEL

The births of Cain and Abel, sons of Adam and Eve, doubled the population of the world—from two people to four. Not much is known about the childhoods of Cain and Abel. Abel became a shepherd and Cain was a farmer. But when Cain offered part of his harvest to God and Abel offered a first-born lamb, God was more pleased with Abel's offering. Out of anger, Cain killed his brother. That act made Cain and Abel "first" again—the first murderer and the first person to die (Genesis 4:1-16).

Death of Abel, Gustave Doré (1880)

ISHMAEL

Ishmael was the son of Abraham and Hagar, an Egyptian maid of Abraham's wife, Sarah (Genesis 16:1-4). Years after Ishmael's birth, Sarah and Abraham had their own son, Isaac (Genesis 21:1-4). But Sarah did not want Ishmael to inherit Abraham's property. So Ishmael and his mother were sent into the desert with just a little water and food. When the water ran out, Hagar feared that Ishmael would die. However, the angel of God promised that Ishmael would grow up to be the father of a great nation (Genesis 21:9-21).

Hagar and Ishmael in the Wilderness, Karel Dujardin (c.1662)

DID YOU KNOW?

Ishmael's descendants became nomads in northern Arabia (now Yemen, Oman, Saudi Arabia, and Jordan). The traders to whom Joseph was sold were descendants of Ishmael (Genesis 37:25). Muslims trace their lineage to Abraham through Ishmael.

ISAAC

Imagine being born to parents old enough to be your great-grandparents. Before Isaac was born, God told Abraham that his wife, Sarah, would have a son (Genesis 18:10). This was the son God promised, and Sarah laughed when she heard the news. After all, Abraham was ninety-nine years old and Sarah was eighty-nine at the time! But when the baby was born, Sarah named him Isaac, which means "he laughs" (Genesis 21:1-7).

Abraham and Isaac Before the Sacrifice, Jan Victors (1642)

DID YOU KNOW?

Abraham and Sarah used to be called Abram and Sarai. After Ishmael was born, their names were changed by God (Genesis 17:4-15-16) as a sign of their status as the father and mother of nations. *Abraham* is a Hebrew word meaning "father of many nations." *Sarah* means "princess."

142

JACOB AND ESAU

Jacob and Esau were twin sons born to Isaac and his wife Rebekah. Their personalities could not have been more different. Esau, the hunter, was a favorite of Isaac, while the quieter Jacob was closer to Rebekah. Since Esau was born first, he would inherit a double portion of his father's property, according to the Law of Moses (Deuteronomy 21:17). But before Rebekah gave birth, the LORD told her that the older son would serve the younger (Genesis 25:23). This occurred when Esau sold his birthright to his brother for a bowl of stew (Genesis 25:27-34)! To strengthen his claim to the birthright, Jacob tricked Isaac into giving him the blessing of the first-born (Genesis 27).

JOSEPH AND HIS BROTHERS

Jacob, the son of Isaac, had twelve sons who did not always get along. His favorite son was Joseph, a child he had with his wife, Rachel (Genesis 30:22-24). Jacob gave Joseph a very fancy coat to show that Joseph was his favorite son (Genesis 37:3-4). His brothers, many of whom were born to Jacob's other wife, Leah, became jealous and plotted to get rid of Joseph. Instead of killing him, they sold him to Ishmaelites (descendants of Ishmael) on their way to Egypt. But God had big plans for Joseph, and many years later the brothers would meet again (read the story in Genesis 39–47).

MIRIAM

Hundreds of years after the time of Joseph, the king of Egypt (pharaoh) began to fear the growing population of Jacob's descendants. He gave orders to enslave the people in order to decrease the population. When that didn't work, he ordered all Hebrew baby boys to be killed. Girls like Miriam, however, could live (Exodus 1:1-16). Imagine how Miriam and her mother felt after the birth of Miriam's baby brother, Moses. (For more about Moses, see Heroes, p. 106.) To save his life, Miriam's mother put the baby in a watertight basket and set it afloat on the Nile River. Miriam watched over the basket, which was found by the daughter of Pharaoh (Exodus 2:1-10). When Miriam grew up, she became a prophet (Exodus 15:20).

Shemuel, questioning the prophet Eli, engraving, H. Robinson

SAMUEL

Samuel was the son born to Hannah (the wife of Elkanah of the tribe of Ephraim), after she begged God to give her a child (1 Samuel 1:1-20). When Samuel was still a young child, Hannah brought him to live in the temple, in fulfillment of her vow to give her son to God. Years later, when Samuel was probably a preteen, he heard the voice of God calling to him during the night (1 Samuel 3). When he became a man, Samuel had three jobs: prophet, priest, and Israel's last judge. When the people of Israel demanded a king, he anointed the first king of Israel—Saul (1 Samuel 10:1).

DAVID

Ever feel ignored in your family? David was sometimes overlooked in his family. He was the youngest of the eight sons of Jesse, the grandson of Ruth, the widow from Moab (Ruth 4:17, 22). Like his father, David was a shepherd who took good care of the flocks, using his sling to kill wild animals that tried to attack the sheep.

But while he was little more than a youth, two amazing events occurred in his life: (1) he was chosen to replace Saul, whom God rejected as the king of Israel (1 Samuel 16:1-13); (2) he became famous for killing a giant named Goliath (1 Samuel 17). David was skilled at playing the harp and often entertained King Saul when Saul was in a bad mood (1 Samuel 16:14-23). David's best friend was Jonathan, Saul's son (1 Samuel 19:1-8; 23:14-18).

A WISE SERVANT GIRL

Even enemies can sometimes become allies. The Arameans (Syrians), located northwest of Israel, frequently raided Israel and took captives. On one such raid a young Israelite girl was kidnapped and became a slave of the wife of Naaman, an army commander. But instead of being bitter, this girl was a huge help to Naaman. Knowing that Naaman had a disease called leprosy, the girl advised Naaman to seek help from Elisha, a prophet in Samaria. Following her advice led to a cure (2 Kings 5:1-19). (For more information on leprosy, see Health and Body, p. 100.)

Jeremiah, Michelangelo Buonarroti, (Sistine Chapel Fresco, c. 1508-1512)

JEREMIAH

Jeremiah came from a line of priests and could trace his roots through his father Hilkiah back to Abiathar, a priest who served during the time of King David (1 Samuel 23:6). During the time when Zedekiah was king of Judah, Jeremiah was chosen by God to be a prophet. Although Jeremiah thought he was too young to be a prophet and tried to talk his way out of the task, he obeyed God's call (Jeremiah 1:1-19). (For more about prophets, see Prophets and Prophecies, p. 212.)

Photos by iStock.com

DANIEL AND HIS FRIENDS

When the Babylonians conquered Judah in 586 B.C. (2 Kings 25:1-21), Daniel and his friends, Hananiah, Mishael, and Azariah (later renamed Shadrach, Meshach, and Abednego), were carried off to Babylon with many of their people. Although they were probably teens at the time, they were chosen by King Nebuchadnezzar to be trained as court officials. They had the best of everything, including the king's meat and wine. But since the food and wine had been offered to the gods the Babylonians believed in, Daniel and his friends wanted to honor God by eating only vegetables and drinking water (Daniel 1). After a ten-day trial, the four young men were found to be healthier and look better than their peers, so they were allowed to keep their diet.

When the three years of training was completed, King Nebuchadnezzar interviewed all the young men and discovered none were as outstanding as Daniel and his three friends. So they were given positions in the royal court.

JESUS

Although most of the stories of the Bible are about Jesus as an adult, a few show glimpses of his childhood: his birth in Bethlehem (Luke 2:1-20), the visit of the wise men (Matthew 2:1-12), and how the family fled to Egypt when Herod tried to find and kill him (Matthew 2:13-18). The only other story in the Bible about Jesus' childhood took place when he was twelve years old. During the yearly visit to Jerusalem for the Passover, Jesus became separated from Mary and Joseph. He was found in the temple, asking questions that amazed the temple leaders (Luke 2:41-50). (For more information on Jesus, see Jesus, p. 136.) When his frantic parents discovered him in the temple, Jesus calmly told them, "Why did you have to look for me? Didn't you know that I would be in my Father's house?" (Luke 2:49). He returned to Nazareth with Mary and Joseph, and he became wise and grew strong (Luke 2:51-52).

Jesus and the doctors of the Faith, entourage of Giuseppe Ribera (1783)

A BOY WITH A LUNCH

Ever wish you could do something amazing? A boy during the time of Jesus took part in one of the most amazing miracles described in the Bible—simply by offering his lunch. What was his name? How old was he? Where did he live? The Bible doesn't tell us any of those things. All we know is that Jesus used this boy's lunch (fives loaves of barley bread and two fish) to feed over five thousand people (John 6:1-15)!

Photos.com

DID YOU KNOW?

When the disciples tried to stop people from bringing their children to Jesus, he said, "Let the children come to me!" (Mark 10:13-14)

PAUL'S NEPHEW

How do you help the people in your family? The apostle Paul's nephew helped him by acting to save Paul's life. Because of Paul's boldness in preaching about Jesus, many people tried to harm Paul. When the Romans arrested Paul, a group of men in Jerusalem took a special vow to kill him! Paul's nephew heard about the plot and told his uncle and a Roman commander about it. The commander believed the boy, and with a large number of soldiers sneaked Paul out of Jerusalem in the middle of the night (Acts 23:12-35).

GAMES CHILDREN PLAYED

Very old people with walking sticks will once again sit around in Jerusalem, while boys and girls play in the streets (Zechariah 8:4-5).

Zechariah, the Old Testament prophet, spoke these words about a future time of peace where children would play once again. But maybe you're wondering what the boys and girls played in ancient times. Paintings in tombs from ancient Egypt show children playing leapfrog and tug-o-war—games you've probably played.

The Bible mentions very little about the games kids in Israel played. Most games were probably played outdoors, like running races or aiming stones into a pit. Singing songs was probably also a favorite pastime. Jesus compared the people of Israel to children who sang songs to one another (Matthew 11:16-17).

145

THE GOOD, THE BAD, AND THE SO-SO

Some kings and queens mentioned in the Bible tried to follow God's commands and rule with fairness and justice. They were the good rulers. But some were very bad, thinking only of themselves, and more importantly, were unfaithful to God. Others were so-so, and didn't accomplish much according to the biblical authors.

Look at the following cast of characters and see if you can sort out ☑ THE GOOD, ☑ THE BAD, AND ☑ THE SO-SO.

ONE KING TO RULE THEM ALL

Israel was a united nation governed by a single monarch for fairly a short period of time—only about a century. (For more information, see Government, p. 94.)

SAUL

God chose Saul to be Israel's first king after the Israelite leaders demanded a king like the other nations around them. So God sent the prophet Samuel to find and anoint one (1 Samuel 8:5-9). Although he was from the small tribe of Benjamin, Saul looked the part of a king: he was tall and handsome. Saul started out as a good ruler, but soon suffered a mental breakdown, resulting in his famous temper tantrums, extreme jealousy of David, and disobedience to God.

The beginning of the end for Saul occurred when he disobeyed God's direct order from the prophet Samuel during a battle against the Amalekites. (Check out 1 Samuel 15 to see how this played out.) So God rejected Saul as king and sent Samuel to find and anoint a more suitable candidate to be Saul's successor. That person turned out to be the young shepherd boy David. After more than a decade of trying to end his rival's life so David couldn't become king, Saul ended up killing himself after losing a battle to the Philistines. Read all about the decline and fall of Israel's first king in 1 Samuel 9:1—31:13.

DAVID: A KING AFTER GOD'S HEART

David was the most famous king of Israel. He became an instant hero after defeating the Philistine giant Goliath with a slingshot (1 Samuel 17), but he was also a musician, a poet, and a just ruler. Many of the psalms in the book of Psalms were written by David, most likely because he eagerly worshiped and obeyed God. Many of the psalms seem to express what David probably experienced as the leader of God's chosen people—his struggles and his gratitude toward God. His love of God was well known (2 Samuel 6).

THE LONG ROAD TO THE THRONE

Although David was anointed king as a young man (1 Samuel 16:1-13) and ruled his own tribe (Judah) for many years, David did not become king over all of Israel until he was thirty years old (2 Samuel 5:1-5; 1 Chronicles 11:1-3). He spent years on the run from the jealous Saul, but even though he knew he was to be king, David had far too much respect for "God's anointed one" to claim the throne while King Saul was still alive.

NOT PERFECT BUT FORGIVEN

As much as David loved God, he wasn't perfect. At one point, he had an affair with Bathsheba, the wife of one of his generals and even had a hand in causing the general's death so that he could marry Bathsheba (2 Samuel 11). Although God forgave David, there were consequences that lasted the rest of his life (2 Samuel 12). Another time, he ordered a census of the fighting men of Israel against God's wishes, which resulted in a plague that killed 70,000 people (2 Samuel 24:15-16). The never dull story of David can be found in 1 Samuel 16:1—1 Kings 2:12 and 1 Chronicles 11–29.

SOLOMON

Solomon, the second son of David and Bathsheba, was Israel's third king. After Solomon asked God for wisdom, God gave him both wisdom and great wealth (1 Kings 3:9). Although he had commanded cities and seaports to be built, Solomon was especially recognized for building the temple in Jerusalem (1 Kings 6). Solomon is believed to have written many of the proverbs in the book of Proverbs, and the book of Ecclesiastes was written in his honor. Although he had great wisdom, Solomon behaved foolishly by marrying women who turned him away from God (1 Kings 11).

Solomon dedicates the temple, Oleograph (1870)

Photos.com

DID YOU KNOW?

David's name appears over one thousand times in the Bible.

A Tale of Two Kingdoms

REHOBOAM

Solomon's son, Rehoboam, was supposed to be king over all twelve tribes of Israel. Because Solomon worshiped false gods and idols, the prophet Ahijah predicted that Jeroboam (one of Solomon's officials) would rebel and take the ten tribes away from Rehoboam (1 Kings 11:26-40). That's exactly what happened. Because Rehoboam listened to bad advice and kept trying to force the people to work very hard, the ten northern tribes revolted. From that time on Israel was divided into the northern kingdom called Israel and the southern kingdom of Judah. You can read Rehoboam's story in 1 Kings 12:1-24.

SOME NOTABLE (AND NOTORIOUS) KINGS AND QUEENS

☐ GOOD
☐ BAD
☐ SO-SO
(CHECK ONE)

AHAB AND JEZEBEL: THE DASTARDLY DUO

Ahab was the seventh king of Israel. Jezebel, a Baal-worshiping princess from nearby Phoenicia, was his wife. Ahab is mostly remembered for his arguments with the prophet Elijah (1 Kings 16:29—22:40). (For more about Elijah, check out Prophets and Prophecies, p. 212.) First Kings 21:28 gives a very clear picture of what kind of rulers this king and queen were: "No one was more determined than Ahab to disobey the Lord. And Jezebel encouraged him."

Idol of Baal (14th-12th century B.C.)

147

☐ GOOD
☐ BAD
☐ SO-SO
(CHECK ONE)

ATHALIAH:
THE WICKED QUEEN

When Athaliah's husband, King Jehoram of Judah died, her son became king, reigning about one year before he was killed. When Athaliah heard that this last surviving son was dead, she murdered all but one of her grandsons: Joash. She would have murdered Joash too, but his aunt rescued him before Athaliah could carry out the murder. Having no male heirs, Athaliah proclaimed herself the ruler of Judah. Her wicked, idol-worshiping reign lasted for six years before she met her doom (2 Chronicles 22:1-12; 23:12-14).

HEZEKIAH:
THE REFORMER

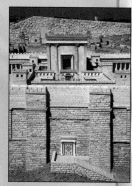

Model of Herod's Temple (the second temple), Israel Museum in Jerusalem

Hezekiah could be called the "reformer" king of Judah. He had to reform all the corruption and disobedience to God that Ahaz, his Baal-worshiping father, had allowed during his reign. Hezekiah had the temple in Jerusalem cleansed so that the Passover could once again be properly celebrated there (2 Chronicles 29–31). When the Assyrians threatened invasion and later when an illness nearly killed him, God rescued Hezekiah both times (2 Chronicles 32).

iStock.com

But Hezekiah's reign did not end well. Proud of his riches, he showed his treasury to visitors from Babylon (2 Chronicles 32:27-31). Big mistake! The prophet Isaiah predicted that one day everything would be taken to Babylon. You have only to read 2 Kings 25 to see that Isaiah was right. (You can also find Hezekiah's story in 2 Kings 18–20 and Isaiah 36–39.)

JOSIAH:
THE BOY KING

Josiah became the king of Judah when he was eight years old. During his reign, Josiah removed all the idols and sinful things from the southern kingdom. He tried to renew the kingdom by rededicating it to God, and ordered the temple in Jerusalem to be repaired. While the broken-down temple was being renovated, *The Book of God's Law* was found. Josiah called together the people and read to them from *The Book of God's Law*. After reading the laws to the people, Josiah asked them to obey God and follow his commands. For more about this "reformer" king, read 2 Kings 22:1–23:30 and 2 Chronicles 34.

Photos.com

ZEDEKIAH:
THE LAST KING

Zedekiah was the last king of Judah, serving as a local ruler under the control of King Nebuchadnezzar of Babylonia. In spite of the prophet Jeremiah's warnings, Zedekiah rebelled against Nebuchadnezzar. The Babylonian army destroyed Jerusalem. Zedekiah tried to escape, but was captured and blinded after witnessing the execution of his sons. He was then sent to Babylon in chains, where he remained a prisoner until he died (2 Kings 24:14–25:7).

Photos.com

THE KINGS OF JUDAH AND ISRAEL

Here is a chart of all the kings of both the northern (Israel) and southern (Judah) kingdoms and a map of both kingdoms.

THE KINGDOMS OF ISRAEL AND JUDAH

SCALE OF MILES
0 10 20 30

This map can be viewed at:
www.bible.ca
Steven Rudd (2007)

The Great Sea

Egypt

Egyptian protectorate until 106 AD

JUDAH (SOUTHERN KINGDOM)	ISRAEL (NORTHERN KINGDOM)
Rehoboam (931–913 B.C.)	Jeroboam (931–910 B.C.)
Abijah (913–911 B.C.)	Nadab (910–909 B.C.)
Asa (911–870 B.C.)	Baasha (909–886 B.C.)
Jehoshaphat (870–848 B.C.)	Elah (886–885 B.C.) Zimri (7 days in 885)
Jehoram (848–841 B.C.) Ahaziah of Judah, 841 B.C.	Omri (885–874 B.C.)
Queen Athaliah (841–835 B.C.)	Ahab (874–853 B.C.)
Joash (835–796 B.C.)	Ahaziah (853–852 B.C.)
Amaziah (796–781 B.C.)	Joram (852–841 B.C.)
Uzziah (781–740 B.C.)	Jehu (841–814 B.C.)
Jotham (740–736 B.C.)	Jehoahaz (814–798 B.C.)
Ahaz (736–716 B.C.)	Jehoash (798–783 B.C.)
Hezekiah (716–687 B.C.)	Jeroboam II (783–743 B.C.) Zechariah (6 mos. in 743) Shallum (1 mo. in 743)
Manasseh (687–642 B.C.)	Menahem (743–738 B.C.)
Amon (642–640 B.C.)	Pekah (737–732 B.C.)
Josiah (640–609 B.C.) Joahaz (3 mos. in 609)	Hoshea (732–723 B.C.)
Jehoiakim (609–598 B.C.) Jehoiachin (3 mos. in 598)	Assyrians defeat Israel and capture its capital, Samaria, 722 B.C. The kingdom of Israel ends.
Zedekiah (598–587 B.C.)	
Babylon defeats Judah and destroys Jerusalem, 587 or 586 B.C. The Period of Captivity in Babylon, 586–538 B.C.	

iStock.com

CYRUS THE GREAT

iStock.com

Cyrus the Great, also known as Cyrus II, ruled from 560–530 B.C. He was the greatest conqueror in the ancient Near East (until Alexander the Great, two centuries later). He created the Persian Empire and expanded its boundaries from the Aegean Sea (between Greece and Turkey) in the west, to the Egyptian border (in the south), and to the Indus River in the east. Cyrus II was known for his generous attitudes toward captive peoples and their customs. He is an important figure in the Bible, where he is remembered as the one said to be chosen by God to end the captivity of the Israelites and restore the temple in Jerusalem (Ezra 1:1-4; Isaiah 45:13).

■ **GOOD**
■ **BAD**
■ **SO-SO**
(CHECK ONE)

DID YOU KNOW?

Today we think of messiah as a title for Jesus, but the Hebrew word *messiah* means "anointed one," and is sometimes translated as "chosen one." (Anointing is the practice of pouring oil on the head of a person who is chosen to serve God and God's people.) The ancient Israelites saw Cyrus II as the liberator foreseen in their prophecies. He is the only non-Israelite in the Bible to be referred to as the "chosen one" or messiah (Isaiah 45:1).

ESTHER

Photos.com

King Xerxes wanted a new queen after Vashti embarrassed him. Even though Esther was a Jewish woman born in captivity, King Xerxes chose her to replace Vashti. Mordecai, a relative of Esther, advised her to avoid telling Xerxes that she was a Jew. But later Esther became famous for saving her people from extinction due to a plot by Haman, one of the king's high-ranking officials. After the Jews were saved, a new holiday—Purim—was developed to remember the brave queen who risked her life to save her people. Esther's story is told in the book of Esther.

Esther Confounding Haman, Gustave Doré (1865)

Photos.com

XERXES

Xerxes was the Persian name of Ahasuerus, the oldest son and successor of Darius I. Xerxes was king from 486–465 B.C. He is best known for his unsuccessful invasion of Greece, described in the book *Persian Wars*, by the Greek historian Herodotus. You can read about him in the book of Esther.

DARIUS

Darius I was also called Darius the Great. Many building projects were completed during his reign. Darius was the king during the time of two Israelite leaders, Ezra and Nehemiah. He allowed Ezra to lead a large group of Jews back to Israel to rebuild the temple. The prophets Haggai and Zechariah mentioned him in their books. He ruled from 521–486 B.C. (Haggai 1:1, 15; Zechariah 1:1).

Darius I, king of Persia from 521, with attendants (1881)

Photos.com

THE HERODS

The Herod family had strong connections to Rome and had become involved in the affairs of the Jewish state, Palestine. Members of this family ruled Palestine from about 55 B.C to the mid-first century A.D. Notable family members found in the Bible are listed below.

NAME	DATE	KNOWN FOR	REFERENCE
Herod the Great	40–4 B.C.	Rebuilding the temple in Jerusalem; ordering all baby boys in Bethlehem to be killed in hopes of preventing Jesus from becoming "king of the Jews"	Matthew 2:1-18
Herod Antipas	4 B.C. to A.D. 39	Beheading John the Baptist; taking part in Jesus' trial	Matthew 14:1-12; Luke 23:6-12
Herod Agrippa I	A.D. 41–44	Had the apostle James executed and put the apostle Peter in prison	Acts 12:1-5; 20-25
Herod Agrippa II	After A.D. 50	Presided over the apostle Paul's trial; asked him, "In such a short time do you think you can talk me into being a Christian?"	Acts 25:13—26:32

151

LANGUAGES

The Confusion of Tongues, engraving by Gustave Doré (1865)

Why So Many Languages?

Language is an essential part of being human. From the very beginning of human civilization, people used words to create and to communicate. At the time of creation, God's words caused events to happen. "God said, 'I command light to shine!' And light started shining" (Genesis 1:3). When he created people, God communicated with them in a language they could understand.

In many cities of the world today, you might hear several different languages spoken. But the Bible describes a time when all the people on Earth spoke the same language (Genesis 11:1). A group of people banded together to build a city "with a tower that reaches to the sky" (Genesis 11:3-4). They wanted to make a name for themselves and become famous, but God confused their language (Genesis 11:8-9). Unable to understand one another, and frightened by their sudden inability to communicate, the people scattered. The tower they built became known as the Tower of Babel. It was located between the Tigris and Euphrates Rivers.

DID YOU KNOW?

Babel sounds like the Hebrew word *balal*, which means "confused." Sounds a lot like the English word *babble*, doesn't it?

Speak the Language

This chart shows some words and phrases in the Bible and the languages used.

Word or Phrase	Language	English translation
Abba	Aramaic	Father (Mark 14:36)
"Eli, Eli, lema sabachthani?"	Aramaic	"My God, my God, why have you deserted me?" (Matthew 27:46; Mark 15:34)
Pistis, elpis, agape	GREEK	Faith, hope, and love (1 Corinthians 13:13)
Shalom	HEBREW	Peace (Judges 6:24)

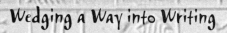

Wedging a Way into Writing

Compared to spoken language, written language is new. And it didn't start with letters, it started with wedge-shaped symbols!

Cuneiform writing was developed before 3000 B.C. It was associated with the Sumerians and was the first widely used system of writing in the ancient Near East. The modern word, *cuneiform*, comes from the Latin *cuneus*, which means "wedge." The individual characters of cuneiform—word pictures of animals or objects like spears or grain—were made by creating wedges in tablets of moist clay. When writing in cuneiform, a scribe would press a stylus with a triangular tip into the tablet. Many surviving cuneiform tablets appear to be inventory or shopping lists. The cuneiform system spread through the ancient Near East and changed to meet the needs of several ancient languages.

The language of the Phoenicians also gained popularity, thanks to Phoenician traders whose routes surrounded the Mediterranean Sea. By 1000 B.C., the Phoenician language was written in cuneiform by the populations along the coasts of Syria, Palestine, and other Phoenician colonies in the Mediterranean.

The people of Ugarit (in northern Syria) and the Persians also used wedges for their writings. The Ugarit cuneiform system has thirty signs or characters, which were used to record documents in languages similar to Phoenician and Hebrew.

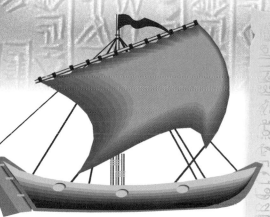

Alphabet Soup Invented!

The alphabet that we use today—where a set of written symbols (letters) stand for "phonemes" (sounds that are part of a syllable)—took shape in the ancient Near East, probably among the Phoenicians. Scholars call this first complete alphabet the "Semitic alphabet."

The ancient Greeks invented a basic alphabet—where a set of written symbols (letters) stand for the syllables in a spoken language. Scholars believe that the first basic alphabet was "Linear B," a Greek alphabet thought up around 1400 B.C. Now you really know your ABCs!

Write Like an Egyptian

Hieroglyphics is a way of writing in pictures that originated with the Egyptians. The lengthy history of the Egyptian language has been broken into five periods:

- Old Egyptian (before 3000 B.C. to about 2200 B.C.)
- Middle Egyptian (about 2200 B.C. to about 1600 B.C.)
- Late Egyptian (about 1550 B.C. to about 700 B.C.)
- Demotic (about 700 B.C. to about A.D. 400)
- Coptic (about A.D. 100 through at least 1600).

These periods describe only the five written languages of Egyptian. Within each period, the spoken dialects were often quite different from the written word!

153

LaNGuagEs oF thE Bible

There are several languages associated with the history of the Bible, but the earliest biblical manuscripts were written in Hebrew and Aramaic (for the Old Testament), or Greek (for the New Testament).

Engraving of a scroll of the Penteteuch, British Library.

HEBREW

The history of the Hebrew language can also be broken into distinct periods:

BIBLICAL OR CLASSICAL HEBREW. This was spoken from about 1200 B.C. through the third century B.C., and was the language in which most of the Old Testament was written.

MISHANIC OR RABBINIC HEBREW. This was never a spoken language, but was used only to write the Mishnah, a collection of Jewish traditions.

MEDIEVAL HEBREW. This was spoken between roughly the sixth and thirteenth centuries A.D., and includes many words borrowed from Greek, Spanish, and Arabic.

MODERN HEBREW. The language of Israel in modern times.

DiD YOU KNOW?

The oldest form of Hebrew is found in some Old Testament poems, like the Song of Deborah in Judges 5.

Text from Joshua 1:1 in the *Aleppo Codex*, a 10th century Hebrew Bible

Aramaic

Aramaic and Hebrew share a lot of the same vocabulary. In fact, by 500 B.C., Aramaic had replaced Hebrew as the language of the people of Israel. Aramaic was used by the common Jewish people, while Hebrew remained the language of religion, government, and the educated upper class.

Aramaic began in Syria and spread in part by Babylonian merchants who spoke the language during their travels. It eventually became the language of international communication.

DiD YOU KNOW?

Yiddish is a fairly modern language with strong connections to earlier forms of Hebrew. Yiddish is the language of the Ashkenazim—Jewish men and women who lived in the Rhineland valley (Germany) and France before migrating east after the Crusades. Yiddish has a rich literary tradition and along with Hebrew and Aramaic, is one of the three major languages in the history of the Jewish people.

"*Arabic*" in the Arabic Al-Bayan Script

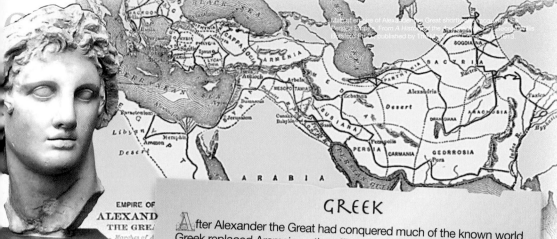

EMPIRE OF
ALEXAND
THE GRE

Alexander the Great

GREEK

After Alexander the Great had conquered much of the known world Greek replaced Aramaic as the official language throughout the former Persian Empire. The *koine* (common) dialect of Greek was spoken by the common person. The documents that eventually were gathered together in the New Testament were written in koine.

Adopting the Greek language and culture carried a number of benefits for conquered people. Jewish men and women in Egypt who spoke Greek could count on a much higher social standing. Acts 21:27-40 recounts a time when a commander of Jerusalem greatly changed his attitude toward the apostle Paul once he learned that Paul could speak Greek.

DID YOU KNOW?

Images of Christ's crucifixion often show the letters *INRI* written above his head on the cross. These letters stand for *Iesves Nazarenvs Rex Ivdaeorvn*, which is Latin for "Jesus of Nazareth, the King of the Jews." But John reports in his Gospel that these words were also written in Greek and Hebrew so that everyone present could read and understand them.

Latin

Just as Greek spread with Alexander's empire, Latin spread with the rise of the Roman Empire. It is the mother of the Romance Languages—a group of modern languages connected to Rome. These include French, Spanish, Italian, Portuguese, and Romanian.

And just as aspects of Roman culture continue to live on long after the Empire died (the calendar and system of government, for example), by the end of the twentieth century, more than 900 million people identified a Romance language as their native language, and over 300 million as their second language.

For centuries, Latin was the language most used in the West for scholarly purposes. Until the latter part of the twentieth century, the Roman Catholic Church required its use in liturgy (religious worship).

Calligraphy in a Latin Bible (A.D. 1407)

What's in a Word?

"In the beginning was the one who is called the Word. The Word was with God and was truly God" (John 1:1).

Greeks used the term *word* to mean the spoken and unspoken word, but also the "words" of the mind, or reason. To philosophers and thinking people of Jesus' day, this term meant "the rational principal that governs all things." Jewish people at that time used the term as a way of referring to God without actually saying God's name. The apostle John knew the power of words. In using *Word* to refer to Jesus, he was intentionally using a term that would be meaningful to both Jews and Gentiles.

One Good Book Inspires Another ... and Another

Throughout its history, the Bible has inspired countless people, from many cultures, to write other books. In fact, the Bible has inspired so many other books in so many languages that it's impossible to measure its effect on literature. Let's take a look at just a few of the famous ones and find out what made their books so special.

iStock.com

Augustine of Hippo? Yes...Hippo!

St. Augustine of Hippo, Lippo Memmi (c. 14th century)

Augustine was born in A.D. 354 in a little town on the North African coast. His father was a minor Roman official and his mother was a Christian. Augustine's parents made sure he got a top-notch education. He became a teacher in Carthage, Rome, and Milan. In Milan, he heard the sermons of Ambrose, a famous Christian speaker, whose sermons helped convert Augustine to Christianity.

When Augustine returned to Africa, he became a priest in a port city called Hippo, where he remained for the rest of his life. He wrote a famous autobiography called *Confessions* that tells how he became a Christian and made peace with God.

With this book and many others, Augustine is considered one of the most influential Bible scholars of all time!

Photos.com

Dante Alighieri: The Poet Who Went Everywhere

Dante Alighieri (1265–1321) was born in Florence, Italy. He grew up in a country torn by power-hungry individuals. By age thirty, Dante was exiled. During his exile from Florence, Dante wrote one of the greatest works in world literature—an epic poem, in three parts, called *The Divine Comedy*.

What's So Funny about an Inferno?

The Divine Comedy is a trip with three stops: Hell, Purgatory, and Heaven. In this case, the word *comedy* doesn't mean the poem is funny. It means the story has a happy ending. *The Divine Comedy* is an allegory where fictional characters or things represent ideas or values. This chart shows a few of the people who represent objects or ideas.

Statue of Dante, Uffizi Gallery in Florence, Italy

iStock.com

Person	What He or She Symbolizes
Dante	A soul struggling to know God
Virgil	The limited human mind
Beatrice	God's grace

John Bunyan: He Traveled While in Prison

John Bunyan (1628–1688) was the son of a metalworker and utensil repairman. His father didn't provide a good education for his son. But that didn't stop Bunyan from trying to study important and inspiring texts. By the time he was thirty, he had joined the Baptist church and was preaching in nearby villages. This was considered unlawful because Bunyan was not a member of the Church of England. He was caught and thrown into prison for three months. When he promised to continue preaching after he was released, Bunyan's sentence was extended to twelve years. In prison, John Bunyan began writing his greatest work, *The Pilgrim's Progress.*

The Angel Secret delivers a message to Christiana from *The Pilgrim's Progress,* colored lithograph (c. 1850)

Written in a simple style, *The Pilgrim's Progress* uses names like Christian, Evangelist, Worldly Wise-Man, and places like Hill Difficulty, the Delectable Mountains, and the Doubting Castle, all of which are named after the types of people and things they represent. The story follows a man named Christian as he flees from the City of Destruction (Earth) and finds his way to Celestial City (Heaven), all the while encountering places and characters that help or hinder his progress.

DID YOU KNOW?

Next to the Bible, *The Pilgrim's Progress* is the most widely published book, having never gone out of print. It has been translated into over two hundred languages. That's staying power!

John Milton: A Poet of Epic Proportions

John Milton (1608–1674) is considered one of the greatest English poets. Having a command of at least eight languages, he was appointed to a government position, where he wrote political pamphlets in support of the new Puritan government in England under Oliver Cromwell. However, when the monarchy took back control of England, Milton was out of a job and in despair about the failure of the revolution and the new government. From about 1658 to 1663, Milton wrote what many think is the greatest epic in any modern language, *Paradise Lost.*

What's So Epic about Eating Fruit?

For inspiration, Milton went to the book of Genesis in the Bible, making Adam and Eve his main heroes. The action spans Heaven, Earth, and Hell. *Paradise Lost* has an epic purpose: to show that when Adam and Eve ate that forbidden fruit, it set the conditions for Jesus, God's Son, to become human and to redeem (pay the price for) our sins. For Milton, the point was that God is always in control and can turn any of Satan's evil plans to a good outcome.

Another epic feature of *Paradise Lost* is Milton's portrait of Satan. Talk about a bad guy! At the beginning of the poem, Satan shows up as a super-smart super-villain. But the longer Satan stays away from the creative, intelligent presence of God, the duller and slower he seems.

Caedmon: "I Have No Songs"

Caedmon (pronounced Cad-men) lived at a monastery in Yorkshire, England from A.D. 657–680, where he worked as a simple herdsman. According to the famous historian Bede, the monks at the abbey were singing and playing a harp one night and asked Caedmon, who was illiterate, to sing. He replied that he didn't know any songs and left to go sleep among the flock he tended. While he slept, someone appeared to him in a dream and asked him to sing "the beginning of creation." (See Genesis 1.) He composed a short poem that praised God's creation. When he woke up, he remembered the poem and even added lines to it.

Caedmon was sent to the leaders of the abbey where they were told what happened. Wanting to make sure the gift was from God, they asked him to write a new poem about the history of Scripture. Next morning, Caedmon gave them a beautiful poem. The head of the monastery asked Caedmon to study as a monk. According to Bede, Caedmon wrote several works of poetry on Christian topics, but only a fragment of one of his poems, "Caedmon's Hymn," has been found.

Whitby Abbey, where Caedmon was believed to live and work.

Caedmon's Hymn

Now we must honor the guardian of heaven,

the might of the architect, and his purpose,

the work of the father of glory

—as he, the eternal lord, established the
    beginning of wonders.

He, the holy creator,

first created heaven as a roof for the children
    of men.

Then the guardian of mankind, the eternal lord,

the lord almighty, afterwards appointed the
    middle earth,

the lands, for men.

iStock.com

C. S. Lewis:
Not Just the Narnia Guy

Clive Staples Lewis (1898–1963) is considered by many to be one of the best defenders of Christianity in the twentieth century. Born to a Church of Ireland family in Northern Ireland, he fought in World War I before attending university at Oxford. He was a very good student, and later he became a teacher at Oxford.

When he was in his early thirties, having fallen away from his childhood faith, Lewis re-converted to Christianity. He wrote many nonfiction books, like *Miracles* and *Mere Christianity*, that explain his views of Christian life.

In his fiction, Lewis loved to write allegories like *The Screwtape Letters*. His best-known work of fiction is the *Chronicles of Narnia* series. The seven books in *The Chronicles of Narnia* series have sold over one hundred million copies in over forty languages. Following the lives of several different children and their adventures in the fantasy world of Narnia, these books are classics of children's literature. Many Narnia books have been adapted as movies, plays, radio broadcasts—and there are even Narnia video games!

iStock.com

Books in the Series

Like the *Star Wars* movies, the Narnia books were released out of sequence. If you want to read them in the order in which the events take place, use the following list. If you want to read them in the order in which Lewis wrote them, follow the publishing dates given.

The Magician's Nephew (1955)

The Lion, the Witch and the Wardrobe (1950)

The Horse and His Boy (1954)

Prince Caspian (1951)

The Voyage of the Dawn Treader (1952)

The Silver Chair (1953)

The Last Battle (1956)

DID YOU KNOW?

Lewis also wrote a series called The Space Trilogy. The books in that trilogy are *Out of the Silent Planet* (1938), *Perelandra* (1943), and *That Hideous Strength* (1945).

Magic AND FORTUNETELLING

What's Up with Fortunetellers?

In ancient kingdoms such as Babylonia and Egypt, people who claimed the power to foretell events were given tremendous privilege and honor. These magicians, enchanters, sorcerers, diviners (fortunetellers), and astrologers often were members of the king's royal court. They held positions as "advisors" to the king, and were required to know his deepest fears. Ancient magicians knew that if they couldn't provide information the king wanted, their own lives could vanish in a puff of smoke.

When the pharaoh of Egypt and King Nebuchadnezzar of Babylonia had troubling dreams, they demanded interpretations from their magicians. When royal advisors failed to produce results, the kings were forced to turn to other sources—to Israelite exiles who worshiped only the God of Israel. Who were those men? Joseph in the pharaoh's court and Daniel in Nebuchadnezzar's. Check out Genesis 41 and Daniel 2 and 4 for their full stories.

READ ALL ABOUT IT

Quick! Think of a book where spells are cast and magic powers are invoked. Perhaps you're thinking of one of the Harry Potter books. Believe it or not, the Bible has lots to say on the subject.

DID YOU KNOW?

The wise men (magi) who searched for Jesus were most likely astrologers. Having studied the stars, they identified the appearance of a new star. They understood it to be a sign that something amazing was about to take place—the birth of a great leader (Matthew 2:1-12).

iStock.com

iStock.com

What Does God Say About Magic or Fortunetelling?

Quite a bit, actually. Aside from the examples just discussed, the Scriptures usually identify magic and fortunetelling as bad behaviors—something to be discouraged among God's people. Some of the following Scripture verses are laws that were established to protect God's people.

• "Don't practice any kind of witchcraft" (Leviticus 19:26).

• "Don't try to use any kind of magic or witchcraft to tell fortunes or to cast spells or to talk with spirits of the dead" (Deuteronomy 18:10-11).

Misadventures in Magic

Many listened to God, but some did not. Check it out in the stories below.

You Had to Ask, Didn't You?

When the Philistine army threatened Israel, King Saul was desperate for advice. But God's prophet Samuel was dead. And after King Saul angered God by his disobedience (check out 1 Samuel 15:1-30), God stopped answering Saul's prayers. Even though he knew that fortunetelling was against God's law, Saul searched for a woman—a medium—who could speak to the dead. One was discovered about six miles away at a place called Endor. Although Saul went in disguise, the woman recognized him as the king when the spirit of Samuel appeared. Samuel reminded Saul that God would take away his kingdom. He also told Saul that he would die the next day—and he did! For the whole story, read 1 Samuel 28.

MAGICIANS MISMATCHED

Confrontations between God's people and court magicians or popular prophets often ended with the court magicians on the losing side. Wondering why? The power of God made all the difference.

Moses and Aaron vs. Pharaoh's Magicians: God sent Moses and his brother, Aaron, to Pharaoh, the king of Egypt, to tell him to free the people of Israel from slavery. God warned them that Pharaoh would challenge them to perform miracles. When Aaron's staff (also called a walking stick) turned into a snake, the magician's staffs turned into snakes. But Aaron's snake ate their snakes. Later, when God turned the water of the Nile River into blood, the magicians also were able to perform the same feat, as well as the next plague (frogs). But God's superiority to their magic was proved when they could not duplicate or stop any of the other plagues (Exodus 8:16-24; 9–11; 12:29-30).

Copy Cats Get Clobbered

Ephesus, a city in Asia Minor, was the home to many sorcerers. Sceva, a Jewish high priest, was one of them. When Paul visited Ephesus, many of the local people were fascinated by Paul's ability to drive out evil spirits using the name of Jesus. Some tried to copy him. When Sceva's sons tried to drive the evil spirit out of a man, the evil spirit told them, "I know Jesus! And I have heard about Paul. But who are you?" (Acts 19:15). The man leaped up and attacked Sceva's sons. After this episode, more people realized that Paul used the true power of God. Many who practiced witchcraft brought scrolls containing magic formulas to burn in a public bonfire (Acts 19:16-20).

Elijah vs. the Prophets of Baal: In a confrontation on Mount Carmel, the prophet Elijah represented the God of Israel. On the other side were the eight hundred fifty prophets of Baal and Asherah from the court of King Ahab and Queen Jezebel of Israel. (For more about Baal or Asherah, see Idols and Foreign Gods, p. 126.) Both sides prepared their altars and readied their sacrifices. The only thing missing from this barbeque was a little fire. Both sides knew that the deity who answered their prayers by sending fire was the real and supreme God. Guess who won? If you can't guess, read 1 Kings 18:1-40.

Peter vs. Simon Magus: Simon Magus couldn't get over himself. Throughout Samaria in the first century A.D., Simon used his sorcery to amaze everyone who watched him. But Simon's magic act came to a halt when many of Simon's followers became Christians. When Simon saw the miracles they could perform in God's name, he offered the apostles money if they would teach him how to perform them as well. But the Holy Spirit was not for sale! Peter saw through Simon and warned him about his greed (Acts 8:9-25).

161

Photos.com

MIRACLES

It's a Miracle!

A miracle is an astonishing or awesome event that shows the presence of God in the universe. Miracles can be small and local events, or gigantic upheavals in nature that change history. In the Bible, God's miracles are often contrasted with the situation of those who looked to other gods, relied on magic, or called on the spirits of the dead.

MIRACLES IN THE OLD TESTAMENT

In the Old Testament, God sometimes used times of great miracles to signal the beginning of a new era in history.

JOURNEY TO THE PROMISED LAND

God used many miracles in answering the prayers of his people who were held as slaves in Egypt. From the time the people of Israel left Egypt until they entered the land God promised to their ancestors, God performed many miracles on their behalf. Here are some of them:

God turned Moses' walking stick into a snake (Exodus 4:1-5; 7:8-13).

God caused ten plagues to come upon the Egyptians (Exodus 7:14—12:30; see Disasters and Catastrophes, p. 64, for a full list of these miracles).

Photos.com

God led the people of Israel through the desert, appearing as a pillar of cloud in the daytime and a pillar of fire at night (Exodus 13:21-22).

God parted the Red Sea and allowed the people of Israel to walk across on dry ground. God then stopped the Egyptians from following the Israelites by causing the walls of water to come tumbling down on the Egyptian army (Exodus 14:1-31).

God changed bitter water into fresh water for drinking (Exodus 15:22-25).

God fed the children of Israel for the entire forty years they were in the desert by providing manna (a sweet-tasting bread-like substance) for them each morning. He also provided fresh quail (a type of bird) when they grew tired of the manna (Exodus 16; Numbers 11:31-32).

God caused water to come out of a rock (Exodus 17:5-6; Numbers 20:1-13).

iStock.com

At Joshua's request, God caused the sun to stand still for nearly a day to give the Israelites enough time to defeat the Amorites. When the Amorites tried to run away, God sent a hailstorm that killed more enemy soldiers than the Israelites themselves had killed (Joshua 10:1-15).

God caused the walls of the city of Jericho to fall as the army of Israel marched around it (Joshua 6:1-25).

iStock.com

162

MIRACLE MEN—
ELIJAH AND ELISHA

In the Old Testament, God often used miracles to turn the hearts of the people of Israel back to him and to help them believe his promises. Through the prophet Elijah and his successor, Elisha, God performed many miracles to help his people.

Elijah

A LITTLE BIRD TOLD HIM

God sent Elijah to confront Ahab, king of Israel, about his evil ways. As a punishment for the people's wickedness and to demonstrate that God, not the god Baal, was in charge of the rains, Elijah announced there would be no rain or dew until he gave the word. Then God sent Elijah into the wilderness to hide from the angry king. There Elijah drank from a small stream and God sent ravens to feed him each day. (For more about this, read 1 Kings 17:1–7.)

THE FLOUR THAT DIDN'T RUN OUT

During the drought, God sent Elijah to a widow about to prepare her last meal for herself and her son. Elijah asked her to prepare some bread for him also. He assured her that "everything will be fine," and that God would not allow the flour and oil to run out until the rains returned. So the woman did exactly as Elijah told her, and for the next several years, she never ran out of flour or oil (1 Kings 17:8–16).

Photos.com

Elijah Taken Up to Heaven in a Chariot of Fire, woodcut by Gustave Doré

Elisha

SWING LOW FIERY CHARIOT

As the time came for Elijah to be taken to heaven, God chose Elisha as prophet to take Elijah's place. When the two of them were walking together, Elijah was taken up into heaven by a whirlwind. Elisha saw him leave in a chariot and horses made of fire. As Elijah disappeared from sight, Elisha found the cloak Elijah had left behind. Elisha took the cloak and struck the surface of the Jordan River. The waters parted to let him cross (1 Kings 19:19–21; 2 Kings 2:1–15).

Elisha and the widow, 19th century engraving

SHE STRUCK OIL!

A poor woman went to Elisha to beg for help. Her husband had died, she was in debt, and her sons were being forced into slavery to pay the debt. When Elisha learned she had a little oil in the house, he told her to borrow as many pots and jars as she could. Then she was to fill them all from her own jar of oil. The woman did as Elisha told her. She filled every pot and jar to the brim. The woman was able to sell the oil to pay her debt and had enough left to live on (2 Kings 4:1–7).

163

WATER FROM NOWHERE

The kings of Israel, Judah, and Edom were marching through the desert to attack Moab. Along the way they ran out of water. Elisha gave orders to dig ditches in the valley. Even though there would be no wind or rain, Elisha promised that God would provide. The next morning the ditches were full—there was more than enough water for the soldiers and their animals (2 Kings 3:4–20).

Elisha touches the water, 19th century engraving

HE TOOK THE PLUNGE

Naaman, a commander in the Syrian army, was a brave and highly decorated soldier. There was just one problem. He had leprosy. (See Health and Body, p. 100, for more on leprosy.) His servant girl, an Israelite who had been captured during a raid, told Naaman's wife that her husband could be cured

if he found Elisha. So Naaman went in search of Elisha. When Naaman arrived at Elisha's house, Elisha sent word for Naaman to wash seven times in the Jordan River. Insulted that Elisha wouldn't come out to talk with him in person and that Elisha suggested a river in Israel, Naaman left in a huff. But Naaman's servants begged him to give it a try. At their urging Naaman went down to the Jordan and plunged seven times into the water. When he surfaced for the seventh time, he had been completely healed (2 Kings 5:1–14).

Naaman in the Jordan River, 19th century engraving

A PROMISE KEPT

In his travels, Elisha often stopped to eat and rest with a rich woman and her husband in the town of Shunem. Because of his hostess's kindness, Elisha promised that God would give her what she did not have—a son. About a year later, the woman gave birth. But one day when the boy was still young, he was working with his father in the fields and complained of a headache. Within a few hours the boy was dead. Immediately, the woman went to find Elisha. Elisha returned with the woman and shut himself in the boy's room with the body. He prayed and then stretched himself over the boy's body two times. Then the boy opened his eyes. Elisha returned the boy, healthy and happy, to his mother (2 Kings 4:8–37).

Elisha stretches over the boy, 19th century engraving

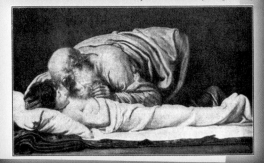

MIRACLES IN THE NEW TESTAMENT

The New Testament records many miracles of Jesus. Jesus used miracles show God's love for the people like 4.18-21) and to announce the presence of the kingdom of God. (See us, p. 136 for more on his miracles.) During his ministry on earth, us sent his disciples out to preach out the coming of God's kingdom, heal the sick, and to drive out emons ((Matthew 10:1; Mark 6:7-13; Luke 9:1-6). Part of the special mission he gave them as he left the earth to return to the Father in heaven was to continue this work (Mark 16:15-18).

A POWER-PACKED CHURCH

In the early church, public miracles helped people recognize that God was at work. The apostle Paul claimed that God helped him perform miracles to confirm the good news about Jesus (2 Corinthians 12:12). He also told people about Jesus' miracles to help them believe (Romans 15:15-19). Read below for more on specific miracles the apostles performed.

Peter and John walked into the temple and saw a crippled man begging. Peter had no money to give him. Instead, he told the man to get up and walk in the name of Jesus. The man picked up his bed and began walking and leaping and praising God as he went (Acts 3:1-10).

Because of the works done by the apostles, the people brought the sick into the streets and laid them on mats so that Peter's shadow would fall on them. The crowds brought their sick and those who were bothered by evil spirits, and all of them were healed (Acts 5:12-16).

The apostles were arrested and put in jail by some jealous religious leaders. During the night, an angel of the Lord came and led the apostles safely out (Acts 5:17-42).

In Joppa there lived a woman named Tabitha who was always helping the poor. When Tabitha became sick and died, her friends immediately called for Peter. When the apostle arrived, he got down on his knees and prayed. Facing her, he said, "Tabitha, get up!" Immediately Tabitha opened her eyes and got up (Acts 9:36-43).

Peter was visiting the believers in Lydda. There he found a man named Aeneas who was paralyzed. Aeneas had been sick in bed for eight years. Peter said to him, "Jesus Christ has healed you! Get up and make up your bed." Immediately, Aeneas picked up his bed and walked (Acts 9:32-35).

Late one night as Paul was speaking in an upstairs room, a young man named Eutychus was seated in the window and fell asleep. In his sleep he fell three floors to his death. Paul rushed down, threw his arms around Eutychus and said, "Don't worry! He's alive." All of Eutychus's friends were relieved to see him alive and well again (Acts 20:7-12).

Peter had been arrested by King Herod for preaching the good news of the kingdom of God. While he was in prison, the church prayed for him. The night before his trial, Peter was sleeping in his cell, guarded by no less than four soldiers. An angel appeared to him and led him out of the prison and down the street. When Peter went to the house where many were praying, they were shocked to see him and praised God for his safe return (Acts 12:1-17).

Traveling aboard a ship headed for Crete, Paul was visited by an angel. The angel warned Paul the ship would be wrecked but no one would die. Safely on the shore of Malta, a huge fire was built to warm those who had escaped the wreck. A poisonous snake came out of the fire and bit Paul on the hand. The islanders waited for Paul to die, but he didn't. Instead he was able to pray for them and heal many of their sick (Acts 28:1-10).

Paul on the island of Malta, 19th century copperplate

165

TYPES OF MIRACLES

God does not work miracles just to show off. Each miracle has a purpose—sometimes more than one.

Demonstration of Power and Authority

As the sacred chest (ark of the covenant) was being carried across the Jordan River into the promised land, the river stopped flowing to allow the people of Israel to walk across on dry ground (Joshua 3:14-17). When Jesus spoke sharply to the wind during a storm, the winds immediately died down (Luke 8:22-25).

Judgment for Evil

The people of the earth became so evil that God destroyed them all in a flood—all except righteous Noah and his family (Genesis 6–9). In the New Testament, two members of the Jerusalem church, Ananias and Sapphira, were struck dead for lying (Acts 5:1-11).

Help to Women Who Want Children

God gave Abraham's wife, Sarah, a son when she was in her nineties (Genesis 21:1-2). Hannah, the wife of Elkanah, prayed for a son so passionately that Eli the priest thought she was drunk. But God honored her prayer with a son she named Samuel (1 Samuel 1:12-20).

Help in Battle

God helped David kill Goliath with a single stone thrown from a sling (1 Samuel 17:41-54). Gideon and an army of three hundred Israelites defeated thousands of Midianites with only torches and trumpets (Judges 6:33—8:3).

Provision

God provided manna and quail for the children of Israel in the desert (Exodus 16). Jesus told Peter he would find the money for taxes in the mouth of a fish (Matthew 17:27). Jesus fed more than five thousand people with five loaves of bread and two small fish (John 6:1-15).

Background image by iStock.com

Safety and Deliverance

King Nebuchadnezzar tried to execute Shadrach, Meshach, and Abednego by tossing them into a fiery furnace. God protected them in the furnace and amazed Nebuchadnezzar (Daniel 3).

Visions

The prophet Isaiah had a vision of God seated on his throne, surrounded by angels who worshiped him (Isaiah 6:1-5). Paul had a vision of Jesus on the road to Damascus that changed his life (Acts 9).

Healing

When a widow's son died, she carried the dead boy to Elijah. Elijah put the boy on his bed, stretched himself out over him three times, and prayed. God heard Elijah's prayer and the boy came back to life. (For the full story, read 1 Kings 17:17-24.) Jesus gave sight to a man who was born blind (John 9:1-7) and restored a man's ability to hear and speak (Mark 7:31-37).

Raising the Dead

God used Elisha to raise the Shunammite woman's son from the dead (2 Kings 4:18-37). Jesus raised his friend Lazarus to life (John 11:17-44).

Special Gifts for Chosen People

God gave Joseph the ability to explain the meaning of dreams (Genesis 41:1-41). God called and prepared a boy named Samuel to one day assume a position of leadership in Israel (1Samuel 3). God gives spiritual gifts to all believers (1 Corinthians 12:1-11).

DID YOU KNOW?

Although Jesus performed many miracles during his time on earth, the Gospels only record about forty of them.

MOVIES

PASS THE POPCORN

Did you know that movies based on Bible stories are among the most popular movies of all time? Clearly, the lives of Jesus and his disciples, Moses, and other biblical characters are popular choices for movie-goers.

JESUS AT THE MOVIES

Some movies focus on Jesus' ministry, teaching, and the events leading up to his crucifixion and resurrection. Others focus on other characters from the Gospels. When you watch these movies, see if you can identify which parts of the stories come directly from the Bible and which ones are the creative inventions of the moviemakers.

The Robe

Director: Henry Koster, 1953

This film, based on a novel by Lloyd C. Douglas, stars Richard Burton as a Roman officer (Marcellus) in charge of crucifying Jesus. Marcellus wins Jesus' robe after gambling for it. But the robe causes nothing but problems for him. Later, Marcellus becomes a follower of Jesus. This dramatic story is based on just two verses of Scripture— John 19:23-24.

Ben Hur

Director: William Wyler, 1959

Based on a novel by Lew Wallace, this movie is a remake of a 1925 silent movie. It tells of a Jewish prince, Judah Ben-Hur (played by Charlton Heston), who is betrayed by his childhood friend Messala and sold to the Romans as a slave. Although the movie is about Judah's coming to faith in Jesus, it depicts some key events from the life of Jesus, such as his birth and his crucifixion.

King of Kings

Director: Nicholas Ray, 1961

This film focuses on the political background of the events described in the Gospels. It contrasts the life of Jesus with that of Barabbas, a Jewish rebel who fought to free his people from the Romans. It stars Jeffrey Hunter as Jesus and Henry Guardino as Barabbas. In Matthew 27:15-26, Barabbas is identified as the guilty prisoner the people asked Pontius Pilate to set free instead of Jesus.

OTHER MOVIES ABOUT JESUS

Godspell (1973)

The Messiah (1976)

Jesus of Nazareth (1977)

The Passion of the Christ (2004)

The Greatest Story Ever Told

Director: George Stevens, 1965

This movie tells a big story—the life of Jesus from the cradle to the cross. The all-star cast includes Max von Sydow as Jesus and Bible-flick superstar Charlton Heston as John the Baptist. This over-sized movie, however, was considered a box-office flop because it cost more than it made. Decades would pass before Hollywood dared make another big-budget Bible movie.

Jesus

Directors: Peter Sykes and John Krisch, 1979

This film about Jesus is unique in that it depicts events and uses dialogue found in only one of the four Gospels—Luke. Effective for reaching people who have never heard about Jesus Christ, this film has been dubbed into over one thousand different languages. Brian Deacon portrays Jesus. Since 1979, "the Jesus movie," as its fans like to call it, has been shown over six billion times.

The Nativity Story

Director: Catherine Hardwicke, 2006

This movie is a highly detailed account of Jesus' birth starting from when an angel tells Mary (played by Keisha Castle-Hughes) she would give birth to the Messiah. It recounts the many trials and tribulations she and her husband Joseph (played by Oscar Isaac) faced as first-century Jews living under Roman rule. The biblical record of these events is found in only two Gospels: Matthew 1–2 and Luke 1–2.

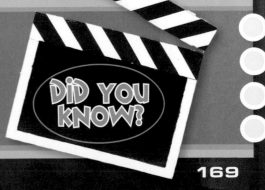

Director Cecil B. DeMille also made a movie called *The King of Kings* in 1927. But he's best known for the movie *The Ten Commandments* (See the section "Movies about Moses.")

DID YOU KNOW?

MOVIES ABOUT MOSES

The powerful Old Testament story of Moses leading the Hebrews out of slavery in Egypt toward a life of freedom in the land promised to their ancestors is another popular subject for Hollywood.

The Ten Commandments
Director: Cecil B. DeMille, 1956

This movie tells how Moses led the Hebrew people out of slavery in Egypt. It includes a very dramatic scene when Moses parts the Red Sea and shows how the people wandered through the wilderness and were given the Ten Commandments at Mount Sinai. The people's rebellion and desire to worship a golden calf is another famous scene. Although the movie recounts much of what is told in Exodus 2–32, a number of additional story lines have been included. Charlton Heston (yes, him again) stars as Moses. *The Ten Commandments* grossed more money in 1956 than any other movie.

The Prince of Egypt
Directors: Brenda Chapman, Steve Hickner and Simon Wells, 1998

The Prince of Egypt is an animated version of Moses' life and the exodus from Egypt. *The Prince of Egypt* follows Moses' life up to and including the parting of the Red Sea and the presentation of the Ten Commandments at Mount Sinai. (Moses was voiced by Val Kilmer.) As with the Cecil B. DeMille production, the movie features a friendship between Moses and Ramses, an Egyptian prince who would later become the pharaoh of Egypt. But you won't find that friendship in the Bible!

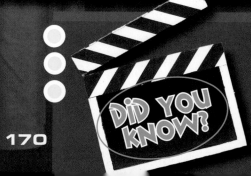

DID YOU KNOW?

While diving in the Gulf of Aqaba (or of the northern arms of the Red Sea), Peter Elmer, a mechanic from Keynsha England, found what he believes are chariot wheels from the Egyptians who pursued the Israelites (Exodus 14:5—15:10).

One Night with the King won a CAMIE award in 2007. CAMIE stands for Character and Morality in Entertainment.

DID YOU KNOW?

MOVIES ABOUT ESTHER

What about the women in the Bible? Besides Jesus' mother Mary, Esther, the beautiful wife and second queen to the powerful King Xerxes of Persia, has been a popular choice in Hollywood. Esther has a whole book of the Bible named after her. How's that for star treatment?

One Night with the King
Director: Michael O. Sajbel, 2006

One Night with the King is an adaptation of the story of Hadassah (Esther's Jewish name), the main character of the book of Esther. As in the Bible book, this beautiful young Jewish woman was recruited into the king's harem and later chosen to be his queen. Esther risks her life to appear before her husband, King Xerxes, in an attempt to save her people from a plot to destroy them devised by Haman, an evil and jealous court official.

OTHER MOVIES

Joseph and the Amazing Technicolor Dreamcoat
Director: David Mallet, 1999

This movie, with lyrics by Tim Rice and music by Andrew Lloyd Webber, is based on the Broadway musical of the same name. Both are loosely based on the story of Joseph found in Genesis 37–50. Joseph's brothers sell him into slavery because they are jealous of their father Jacob's love for Joseph. After all, Jacob had given Joseph a very special and colorful coat. Donny Osmond starred as Joseph in the movie and also played him on Broadway.

171

MUSIC

Music was important in biblical times in much the same way it is important today. With or without words, music enlivens the celebration of special events and offers comfort in hard times. Music plays a key role in the worship experience. Hymns and songs of praise provide ways of helping people hear God's Word in a new way.

MAKE SOME NOISY JOY!

Shout praises to the LORD, everyone on this earth. Be joyful and sing as you come in to worship the LORD!

(Psalm 100:1-2)

DID YOU KNOW?

The first musician named in the Bible was Jubal. He "was the first to play the harps and flutes" (Genesis 4:21).

Photos.com

DID YOU KNOW?

The "Hallelujah Chorus," often sung during the Christmas season, is really from the Easter portion of Handel's oratorio, *Messiah*. It is based on Revelation 19:6, 19.

Where's the Praise Band?

You won't find full orchestras and bands in the Bible. Still, many different instruments were around thousands of years ago and many were similar to instruments we play today.

Shofar (ram's horn, or sometimes referred to as a trumpet), made from a goat's horn, number-one instrument in the Bible; still used in synagogues today (Leviticus 23:24; Numbers 29:1; Joshua 6:4-20; Judges 3:27; 6:34).

Khatsotsrah (trumpet), made of bronze or silver, measuring one foot long; usually played by pairs of priests to celebrate religious festivals (Numbers 10:10), to signal the people to gather (Numbers 10:3-8), to give commands during battle (Numbers 10:9).

Kinnor (lyre), often called a harp, but much smaller with a few strings; David's instrument. Many kinds and sizes of lyres were played in the ancient Near East (Genesis 4:21; 1 Samuel 16:14-23; Psalm 137:2).

Nebel, another stringed instrument, either a harp with angles or a lyre with an unusual sound-box (Genesis 31:27; Psalm 150:3).

Khalil (flute or pipe), made of reed, metal, or ivory; two pipes together, each with a mouthpiece holding either a single (clarinet-type) reed or a double (oboe-type) reed (1 Kings 1:40; Jeremiah 48:36; Matthew 11:17).

Ugab (flute), looked much like flutes today (Genesis 4:21; Psalm 150:4).

Toph, also called tabor, timbrel, tabret (tambourine), but no jingles on it (Exodus 15:20; 2 Samuel 6:5).

Other percussion instruments: small bronze cymbals (1 Chronicles 16:5), castanets (2 Samuel 6:5), and jingling bells that were attached to a priest's robe (Exodus 28:33-35; 39:24-26).

Give a Shout-Out . . . Over the Centuries!

Time Period	Musical Style or Innovation	Some Key People
Until A.D. 500	Chanting, continuation of Jewish cantor traditions, singing psalms, using Greek music theory	
325 and later	During the reign of Constantine, Christianity becomes the official religion of Roman Empire; European music develops as Christianity spreads	
About 600 and later	Gregorian Chant established, made regular (also called plainsong, plainchant)	Notker Balbulus, Hildegard von Bingen
1100–1450	Polyphony ("many voices"), parts move at same intervals	Guillame de Machaut, John Dunstable, Guillame Dufay
1450–1600	Renaissance: chanson (French song), madrigal, Antiphony (two or more choirs)	Josquin Des Prez, Thomas Morley, Giovanni Pierluigi da Palestrina
1600–1700	Baroque period: strict musical forms, ornamental works, first operas, oratorios Anthems develop from antiphony; first "modern" hymns written	Claudio Monteverdi, Marc-Antoine Charpentier, Antonio Vivaldi
1700–1750	Late Baroque period: well-tempered tuning, modulation between keys, chromatic harmony; all the main styles, forms, and national traditions of preceding generations united	Johann Sebastian Bach, George Frideric Handel
1750–1820	Classical period: simpler, clearer formal style, the sonata form, symphonies, more elaborate operas	Wolfgang Amadeus Mozart, Franz Joseph Haydn, Ludwig van Beethoven, Franz Schubert
Late 1700s to late 1800s	Folk traditions, shape-note singing, spirituals, leading to gospel	

PITAGORAS   PYTACORA

PHYLOLAVS

DAVID AND THE BIBLE'S SONGBOOK

King David really loved God and really loved music! He soothed King Saul by playing his harp (1 Samuel 16:14-23). David appointed the Levites to serve as musicians whenever the people gathered for worship (1 Chronicles 6:31-47). In later times, the Levite musicians chose and sang psalms that were appropriate for particular occasions, sacrifices, or festivals. You'll find details about the Levites' responsibilities in 1 Chronicles 25:1-31.

The book of Psalms takes its name from the Greek word *psalmos*, which means "song," and is the Bible's songbook. The songs and prayers in the book were used by the Hebrew people to express and celebrate their relationship with God. Some psalms indicate that they were written by David, but others were written by poets over a period of centuries. Many psalms include musical directions such as "Use flutes" (Psalm 5) and "To the tune 'Lilies of the Agreement'" (Psalm 80).

I will sing and play music for you with all that I am.
I will start playing my harps before the sun rises.
I will praise you, LORD, for everyone to hear;
I will sing hymns to you in every nation (Psalm 108:1-3).

Give a Shout-Out . . . Over the Centuries!

Time Period	Musical Style or Innovation	Some Key People
1820–1910	Romantic period: more emotional, expressive works, program music, tone poems	Ludwig van Beethoven, Franz Schubert, Felix Mendelssohn, Gioacchino Rossini
	Growth of orchestras, concert halls, opera houses, century of classic hymns	Hector Berlioz, Johannes Brahms, Anton Bruckner, Giuseppe Verdi
	Exporting Western musical traditions in missions to Africa, Asia, South America	
	1877—Edison invents sound recording	
	1890s—Ragtime is born	Scott Joplin
1910–1950	Modern period: experimental forms, new harmonies, traditional pop	Arnold Schoenberg, Igor Stravinsky, George Gershwin
	Growth of gospel	Thomas Dorsey, Charles Tindley, Rosetta Tharpe
	Birth of jazz, country, rhythm and blues	Jelly Roll Morton, Louis Jordan, Jimmie Rodgers
	Encouraging other countries' own musical traditions in worship	
	Radio and recording technology advances	Hank Williams, Bing Crosby, Frank Sinatra
	1936—first electric guitars	Charlie Christian, Les Paul, Leo Fender
1951–today	Continuation of modern forms	Luciano Berio, Philip Glass, John Adams
	Growth of gospel	Mahalia Jackson, James Cleveland, Soul Stirrers
	Birth of rock	Elvis Presley, Aretha Franklin, The Beatles
1970s–1980s	Birth of contemporary Christian music	Malcolm & Alwyn, 2nd Chapter of Acts, Amy Grant

Johann Sebastian Bach, Elias Gottlob Haussmann (1746)

Photos.com

DiD YOU KNOW?

The words to "Joshua Fit de Battle of Jericho," a traditional spiritual, were changed to "Marching 'round Selma Like Jericho" during the 1965 civil rights marches in Alabama.

Soli Deo Gloria

Giving God the Glory

Here are some famous hymn writers and a few of the well-known hymns they wrote.

Fanny Crosby
(1820–1915)
American poet, blind since infancy
"Safe in the Arms of Jesus,"
"Blessed Assurance"

Thomas A. Dorsey
(1899–1993)
American songwriter, singer, pianist;
"father of gospel music," toured
with Mahalia Jackson
"Precious Lord, Take My Hand,"
"There'll Be Peace in the Valley"

Frances Ridley Havergal
(1836–1879)
English poet and writer
"Take My Life and Let It Be,"
"Like a River Glorious,"
"Thou Art Coming, O My Savior"

John Newton
(1725–1807)
English minister, antislavery activist;
conversion from life as captain of a
slave ship led to his writing "Amazing Grace"
"Glorious Things of Thee Are Spoken,"
"How Sweet the Name of Jesus Sounds!"
"Amazing Grace"

Isaac Watts
(1674–1748)
English minister, first great
English hymn writer
"O God, Our Help in Ages Past,"
"Joy to the World,"
"Jesus Shall Reign"

Charles Wesley
(1707–1788)
English minister, started
Methodist Church with
brother John *"Hark! the
Herald Angels Sing,"*
*"Christ the Lord Is Ris'n
Today"*

Charles Wesley, artist unknown

Top Twenty Praise and Worship Songs . . . So Far*

1. "How Great Is Our God," Chris Tomlin
2. "God of Wonders," Third Day/Caedmon's Call
3. "You Are My King (Amazing Love)," Newsboys
4. "He Reigns," Newsboys
5. "We Fall Down," Chris Tomlin
6. "Here I Am to Worship," Phillips, Craig & Dean
7. "Blessed Be Your Name," Tree63
8. "Breathe," Michael W. Smith
9. "Indescribable," Chris Tomlin
10. "You're Worthy of My Praise," Jeremy Camp
11. "Friend of God," Phillips, Craig & Dean
12. "Holy Is the Lord," Chris Tomlin
13. "How Can I Keep from Singing," Chris Tomlin
14. "Open the Eyes of My Heart," John Tesh
15. "Shout to the Lord," Darlene Zschech
16. "Forever," Chris Tomlin
17. "Lord, I Lift Your Name on High," Petra
18. "Come, Now Is the Time to Worship," Phillips, Craig & Dean
19. "The Heart of Worship," Matt Redman
20. "Made to Worship," Chris Tomlin

* Song title and writer; according to *20 The Countdown Magazine* (as compiled by Christian Radio Weekly)

The Power of Names

יהוה

"Yahweh"
Tetragrammaton

Do you know why your name was chosen for you? Many children are named after a relative, a close friend, or even someone their parents admire. Characters from books or movies are also a source for names. Some parents will name their children based on people mentioned in the Bible.

For the people of the ancient Near East, a person's name was more than just a label—it actually expressed who the person was on the inside. When you read your Bible, you will often find that a person's name shows his or her character or an event when he or she was born. For example, the name Moses means "drawn out of the water"—which is exactly how Pharaoh's daughter found Moses (Exodus 2:10)!

Biblical Names and Their Meanings

Here is a list of some key people in the Bible and what their names mean.

Name	Meaning	Read About It
Abraham	Father of many	Genesis 17:4
Adam	Humankind; man	Genesis 1:26-27; 3:20
Amos	Burden bearer; to carry	Amos 1:1
David	Favorite; beloved	1 Samuel 16:11-13
Elijah	Yahweh is my God	1 Kings 17:1
Eve	Life; life-giving	Genesis 3:20
Esther	Star; myrtle	Esther 2:1-18
Ezekiel	God will strengthen	Ezekiel 1:1; 2:1-10
Hezekiah	God gives strength	2 Kings 19–20
Hosea	Deliverance, salvation	Hosea 1:1
Isaac	Laughter	Genesis 21:6
Isaiah	Yahweh is salvation	Isaiah 1:1; 2:1-5
Jacob	He grasps the heel; the supplanter	Genesis 25:26
Job	Afflicted; persecuted	Job 1:1–2:10
Melchizedek	King of justice	Genesis 14:17-24
Micah	Who is like the LORD?	Micah 1:1; 7:18-20
Noah	Rest; comfort	Genesis 6–9
Peter	Rock; stone	Matthew 16:13-20
Ruth	Friend; companion	Ruth 1
Samson	Sun	Judges 13–16
Sarah	Princess	Genesis 17:15-16

DID YOU KNOW?

The name Jesus (in Hebrew, Yeshua or Joshua) means "the LORD Saves." The Bible says that God has "honored his name above all others" (Philippians 2:9).

Can You Spell that for Me Again, Please?

The prophet Isaiah bestowed upon his son the longest name in the Bible: Maher-Shalal-Hash-Baz (Isaiah 8:3). The name means "suddenly attacked, quickly taken."

Popular Names in the Bible

✦**Deborah.** Two people in the Bible are named Deborah. One was a devoted servant to Rebekah, the wife of Isaac (Genesis 35:8); another was an Israelite prophet and leader who joined Barak in battle and helped defeat one of Israel's enemies (Judges 4–5).

✦**John.** John the Baptist called people to turn to God and to prepare for the coming of Jesus. He baptized Jesus in the Jordan River (Matthew 3). One of the twelve apostles was also named John (Matthew 10:2).

✦**Joseph.** There are several Josephs mentioned in the Bible. The son of Jacob and Rachel, who later became governor of Egypt (Genesis 30:24; 41:37-57); an Israelite priest who was appointed leader of his clan (Nehemiah 12:14); the earthly father of Jesus (Matthew 1:18-25; 13:55; Luke 2); and the man who offered his tomb for Jesus' burial (Matthew 27:57-60).

✦**Mary.** Jesus' mother's name was Mary (Matthew 1:18; Luke 1:26-38; 2:5-7; John 19:25-27). Jesus also had a friend named Mary, who was the sister of Martha and Lazarus (Luke 10:38-42; John 11:1-44; 12:1-8). Jesus cast seven demons out of a woman named Mary Magdalene (Luke 8:2), who was the first to see the risen Lord (John 20:1-18).

✦**Nathan.** There are two Nathans in the Old Testament. One was the prophet who delivered a message from God to King David (2 Samuel 7:1-16) and pointed out David's sinful act with Bathsheba (2 Samuel 12:1-15); and the other was the son of David and Bathsheba (1 Chronicles 3:5).

Bible Names Popular Today

Names found in the Bible are still popular choices today. Here are some of the most popular.

Name	Meaning	Read About It
Anna (a form of the Hebrew "Hannah")	Grace, gracious	Luke 2:36-38
Benjamin	Son of my right hand; son at my right side	Genesis 35:16-22
Daniel	God is my judge	Daniel 1–12
Deborah	Bee	Judges 4–5
Elizabeth	God is my oath; God's promise	Luke 1:5-25
Ethan	Strong; firm; steadfast	1 Kings 4:30-31
Hannah	Grace of God	1 Samuel 1–2
Jared (a form of the name "Jordan")	He who descends	Genesis 5:15-20
Jonathan	God has given	1 Samuel 20
Matthew	Gift of Yahweh	Matthew 9:9-13
Rebekah	To tie or to bind; to secure	Genesis 24
Samuel	God hears	1 Samuel 1:19-20

YOUR NAME MEANS WHAT?!

• **Huldah** was a prophet who sent a message to King Josiah (2 Kings 22:14-20). Her name means "a weasel or mole."

• **Barak**, who along with Deborah, led an army that defeated a powerful opponent of Israel (Judges 4–5), has a fitting name. It means "flash of lightning."

• **Nabal**, a foolish man who refused to give food to David and his fighting men (1 Samuel 25:2-40), also has an appropriate name. Nabal means "fool."

DID YOU KNOW?

Today when we hear the name Judas, we may instantly think of Judas Iscariot, the man who betrayed Jesus (Matthew 26:14-16). For this reason, not many babies are named Judas! But in Bible times, Judas was a popular name. Jesus had another disciple named Judas (sometimes known as Jude), who also was called Thaddeus (Matthew 10:3; Luke 6:16; Acts 1:13). Jesus also had a half-brother named Judas (Mark 6:3).

Photos.com

NATIONS

If you were reading a travel guide, what would you expect to find? Only stuff about places where it's easy to travel? A travel guide usually includes something about every place in a region, including places that are hard to visit. The Bible does the same. It mentions the nations surrounding Israel, many of whom were Israel's enemies at the time.

iStock.com

A Traveler's Guide to the Ancient Near East

Aram/Syria

Where	The Arameans (Syrians) lived northeast of Palestine. The Arameans were tribes of nomadic herdsmen.
Capital & Key Cities	Damascus; Ebla and Mari
Friend?	Friends of the northern kingdom (Israel), and enemies of the southern kingdom (Judah)
Known for?	Jacob, the grandson of Abraham and one of the ancestors of the people of Israel, was born in Aram. Naaman, a commander of the army of Aram was healed of leprosy (2 Kings 5). (See Health and Body, p. 100.) They spoke Aramaic. Some portions of the Old Testament were written in Aramaic, and Jesus often spoke it when addressing crowds.
Mentioned in the Bible	"When news reached the royal palace that Syria had joined forces with Israel, King Ahaz and everyone in Judah were so terrified that they shook like trees in a windstorm" (Isaiah 7:2).

Basalt funeral stele bearing an Aramaic inscription (ca. 7th century B.C.), photo by Marie-Lan Nguyen

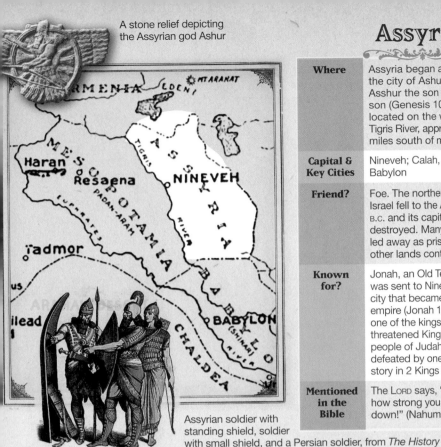

A stone relief depicting the Assyrian god Ashur

Assyria

Where	Assyria began as the area around the city of Ashur, founded by Asshur the son of Shem, Noah's son (Genesis 10:22). The city was located on the west bank of the Tigris River, approximately sixty-two miles south of modern-day Iraq.
Capital & Key Cities	Nineveh; Calah, Ashur, Arbela, Babylon
Friend?	Foe. The northern kingdom of Israel fell to the Assyrians in 722 B.C. and its capital, Samaria, was destroyed. Many of its people were led away as prisoners to live in other lands controlled by Assyria.
Known for?	Jonah, an Old Testament prophet, was sent to Nineveh, an Assyrian city that became the capital of the empire (Jonah 1:1-2). Sennacherib, one of the kings of Assyria, threatened King Hezekiah and the people of Judah. But his army was defeated by one angel. (Read the story in 2 Kings 18:13—20:37.)
Mentioned in the Bible	The LORD says, "Assyria, no matter how strong you are, you will be cut down!" (Nahum 1:12).

Assyrian soldier with standing shield, soldier with small shield, and a Persian soldier, from *The History of Costume*, Braun & Schneider (c. 1861-1880)

Babylonia

Where	Babylonia was in Mesopotamia (Iraq) between the Tigris and Euphrates Rivers.
Capital & Key Cities	Babylon, Ur (Genesis 11:26-28)
Friend?	During the time of Israel's King Solomon (970–931 B.C.), Babylonia was not a military threat. But in three centuries, it became one of the toughest nations in the ancient world. The Babylonians conquered Jerusalem in 587 B.C., destroying the temple and taking many of its people into exile in Babylonia (2 Kings 24:10—25:21).
Known for?	Babylon was famous in the ancient world as a center for writing and scholarly study. They worshiped a god called Marduk.
Mentioned in the Bible	"Then Isaiah told Hezekiah: I have a message for you from the LORD. One day everything you and your ancestors have stored up will be taken to Babylonia. The LORD has promised that nothing will be left" (2 Kings 20:16-17).

The god Marduk with his dragon, from a Babylonian cylinder seal.

179

Cush/Ethiopia

Where	The area of northeast Africa (south of Egypt) was called Cush or Nubia in the Old Testament and Ethiopia (by the Greeks) in the New Testament. But the conquering nation of Egypt controlled it for hundreds of years (beginning around 2575 B.C.)
Capital & Key Cities	Karmah, Meroe
Friend?	Mainly an enemy of Egypt; recorded as an ally of King Hezekiah in Isaiah 37:9
Known for?	Notable people from the area include Moses' wife (Numbers 12:1) and the treasurer of Ethiopia, whom the apostle Philip met on a desert road (Acts 8:26-40). God told the prophet Isaiah to warn King Hezekiah about trusting Cush, rather than him.
Mentioned in the Bible	"Egypt sends messengers up the Nile River on ships made of reeds. Send them fast to Ethiopia, whose people are tall and have smooth skin. Their land is divided by rivers; they are strong and brutal, feared all over the world" (Isaiah 18:2).

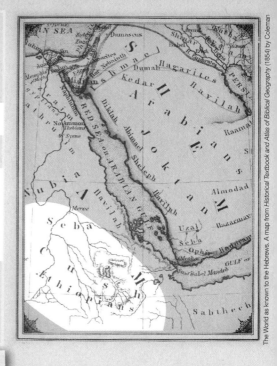

The World as known to the Hebrews. A map from *Historical Textbook and Atlas of Biblical Geography* (1854) by Coleman

Egypt

Where	Egypt developed along the banks of the northern portion of the Nile River. The country is divided into two regions: lower Egypt—the northern part of the country, where the Nile meets the Mediterranean Sea; upper Egypt—the southern region of the Nile.
Capital & Key Cities	Memphis (Cairo); Thebes, Alexandria
Friend?	Friend and foe. In times of famine, Abraham and later Isaac lived in Egypt (Genesis 12:10-20; 26:1-11). Joseph's family was welcomed with open arms after Joseph successfully interpreted the pharaoh's dream (Genesis 41–46). Generations after Joseph died, the Hebrew people were enslaved for over four hundred years. The pharaoh during Moses' time was reluctant to part with this large work force. (See Disasters and Catastrophes, p. 64, for what happened.)
Known for?	Egypt was one of the great civilizations in the world from as early as 4500 B.C. Egyptians believed in many gods, but the main one was the pharaoh, the god-king, who was thought to live in the world of the gods after he died.
Mentioned in the Bible	"Soldiers from the Egyptian towns of Memphis and Tahpanhes have cracked your skulls. It's all your own fault! You stopped following me, the LORD your God" (Jeremiah 2:16-17).

180

Egyptian court official, Egyptian king, fanbearer, from *The History of Costume*, Braun & Schneider (c. 1861-1880)

Macedonia

Greek silver tetradrachm from Alexander the Great

Where	Located north of Greece, Macedonia was a large nation whose history and culture were closely tied to their neighbors to the south.
Capital & Key Cities	Thessalonica (Acts 17:1-9), Philippi (Acts 16), Ephesus (Acts 19)
Friend?	Enemy after Alexander the Great died, and ruling families tried to impose the Greek way of life over the Jewish people in Palestine. The Jewish people finally revolted in 168 B.C. (See Government, p. 94, for more.)
Known for?	In the fourth century B.C., King Philip II conquered much of the land to the south to form the most powerful state of Greece. Later, his son, Alexander III, ("the Great"), used this base to form a vast empire stretching from Egypt to India. Paul traveled to this region on his second missionary journey. (See Paul, p. 186, for more information.)
Mentioned in the Bible	During the night, Paul had a vision of someone from Macedonia who was standing there and begging him, "Come over to Macedonia and help us!" (Acts 16:9).

Olympic victor, priest of Bacchus, Greek king, from *The History of Costume*, Braun & Schneider (c. 1861-1880)

Medes and Persians

Gold plaque of a Mede involved in a religious ritual (5th -4th century B.C.), from the British Museum

Where	Persia became a world power under Cyrus the Great, who united the Medes and the Persians in 549 B.C. From 550–330 B.C., the Persians ruled over a vast empire. Ancient Persia was similar in size and location to modern-day Iran.
Capital & Key Cities	Persepolis; Susa, Ecbatana
Friend?	Foe, but during the rule of Darius I, the temple in Jerusalem was rebuilt (Ezra 3–6). Later, Artaxerxes I permitted two other groups of Jewish exiles to return to Palestine during the time of Ezra and Nehemiah.
Known for?	The Persian Empire introduced better roads, a good postal system, and a universal system of weights and measures. Their religion came from teachings of Zoroaster, one of their prophets. Their belief in angels, Satan, paradise, and the struggle between good and evil forces influenced Judaism and Christianity.
Mentioned in the Bible	"In the first year that Cyrus was king of Persia, the LORD had Cyrus send a message to all parts of his kingdom. This happened just as Jeremiah the LORD's prophet had promised" (2 Chronicles 36:22).

Mede nobleman, Persian nobleman, and Persian, from *The History* of Costume, Braun & Schneider (c.1861-1880)

Midian

Where	The Midianites were a wealthy nation who lived in the northern regio of what is now Saudi Arabia.
Capital & Key Cities	Modiana; Madiana
Friend?	Friends turned enemies. The Midianites became enemies of Israel and repeatedly attacked the land, until Gideon and his army of three hundred defeated them (Judges 6–8).
Known for?	They were the descendants of Midian, the son of Abraham by Keturah (Genesis 25:1-2). Most were farmers and traders. Moses fled to this land after he killed an Egyptian guard who was beating a Hebrew slave (Exodus 2:11-25). He married the daughter of Jethro, a priest in this area.
Mentioned in the Bible	"Then once again the Israelites started disobeying the LORD, so he let the nation of Midian control Israel for seven years. The Midianites were so cruel that many Israelites ran to the mountains and hid in caves" (Judges 6:1-2).

Moab

Where	The Moabites were descendants of Lot's daughter (Genesis 19:36-37) and occupied the mountainous region of modern Jordan on the eastern side of the Dead Sea.
Capital & Key Cities	Heshbon; Elealeh
Friend?	Mostly hostile. See Numbers 21:24; Judges 3:12-50; 1 Samuel 14:47; 2 Samuel 8:2.
Known for?	The Moabites were traders in a region rich in natural resources. They worshiped the god Chemosh, whom King Solomon built a temple to in the later years of his life (1 Kings 11:7). Ruth, the great-grandmother of King David, was from Moab. (Check out the book of Ruth for her story.) Ehud, one of the judges of Israel, killed the bullying king of Moab, King Eglon (Judges 3:12-26).
Mentioned in Bible	"We have heard of Moab's pride. Its people strut and boast, but without reason" (Isaiah 16:6).

A stele describing King Mesha of Moab's wars against the Israelites, photographed c. 1891

DID YOU KNOW? The name *Canaan* means "land of purple."

Philistia

Where	Philistia, the home of the Philistines, was a narrow plain along the eastern coast of the Mediterranean. It was north of Egypt and south of Israel, which also wrapped around its eastern border.
Capital & Key Cities	Ashdod: Ashkelon, Ekron, Gaza, Gath
Friend?	Enemies. The Philistines attacked Israel as they moved into Canaan. Throughout the time of the judges, the Philistines continued to harass the Israelites, until Saul and then David defeated them in a series of battles. By the time King David's son Solomon came to power, Philistia was fully under the control of Israel.
Known for?	Perhaps the most famous Philistine was Goliath, the giant who defeated numerous warriors, only to be killed by a teenager with a sling shot (1 Samuel 17). They worshiped a god called Dagon (Judges 16:23) as well as other gods. (See Idols and Foreign Gods, p. 126.)
Mentioned in Bible	"Once again the Israelites started disobeying the LORD. So he let the Philistines take control of Israel for 40 years" (Judges 13:1).

Roman Empire

iStock.com

Where	Rome was a small city-state in Italy that grew into a gigantic empire. By the time of Jesus, the Roman Empire controlled all the countries around the Mediterranean Sea.
Capital & Key Cities	Rome, Constantinople
Friend?	Conquerors. In 63 B.C., Roman troops led by the general Pompey took over Palestine.
Known for?	Romans became known for their military power, engineering, city planning, legal system, and literature.
Mentioned in the Bible	When Jesus was born, the Roman Emperor Augustus had a firm control of the land (Luke 2:1-20). The apostle Paul lived under house arrest in Rome and there wrote some of the letters found in the New Testament (Romans 1:7).

Roman soliders, from *The History of Costume*, Braun & Schneider (c. 1861-1880)

Other Nations

God promised to give the land of Canaan to the nation of Israel (Genesis 15:18-21)—land in which the following nations lived.

NATION	TERRITORY	READ ABOUT IT HERE
AMALEKITES	Negev, south of Judah	Exodus 17:8-16; Numbers 13:29; 1 Samuel 15
AMORITES	In the mountains of Canaan	Joshua 3:10; 12:8; Judges 1:34-36
GIBEONITES/ HIVITES	Five miles northwest of Jerusalem	Joshua 9
GIRGASHITES	Near the Sea of Galilee	Genesis 10:16; Deuteronomy 7:1
HITTITES	Hattush, in what is now modern-day Turkey	Exodus 23:28; Joshua 12:8
HIVITES	Mizpah (those not living in Gibeon); now Syria	Joshua 11:1-3; 12:8
JEBUSITES	Jerusalem	Joshua 12:8; 15:8 (See also Jerusalem, p. 130.)
PERIZZITES	Central Palestine	Joshua 3:10; 12:8

NUMBERS

In the Bible, you'll find some of the same numbers over and over. Wonder why? Many of these numbers had special meaning to the people of ancient times.

The number one shows uniqueness or unity.
• Many times, God or his prophets proclaim that God is one God. In Deuteronomy 6:4, Moses declares, "Listen, Israel! The LORD our God is the only true God!"
• In Ephesians 4:4-6, the apostle Paul declares: "All of you are part of the same body. There is only one Spirit of God, just as you were given one hope when you were chosen to be God's people. We have only one Lord, one faith, and one baptism. There is one God who is the Father of all people."

iStock.com

Three represents completeness.
• After being swallowed by a fish, the prophet Jonah remained inside of it for three days and three nights (Jonah 1:17—2:10). Jesus later referred to Jonah's time in the fish when speaking of his own death and burial (Matthew 12:40).
• Three days after his death, Jesus was raised to life (Matthew 28:1-10; Mark 16:1-8; Luke 24:1-12; John 20:1-10; 1 Corinthians 15:4).
• The disciple Peter denied knowing Jesus three times (Matthew 26:69-75; Mark 14:66-72; Luke 22:54-62; John 18:15-18, 25-27).
• After he was raised to life, Jesus asked Peter three times if he loved him (John 21:15-19).
• The three virtues that are at the heart of Christian life are faith, hope, and love (1 Corinthians 13:13).

Four indicates the totality of the created world, with four winds and four seasons of the year. Here are some examples:
• The river flowing out of the Garden of Eden was divided into four rivers: Pishon, Gihon, Tigris, and the Euphrates (Genesis 2:10-14).
• The Old Testament prophet Ezekiel had a vision of four "living creatures" (Ezekiel 1:4-14).
• In the New Testament, the apostle John had a vision of four "living creatures" similar to those seen by Ezekiel (Revelation 4:6-8). These four-winged creatures have come to be associated with the four Gospel writers—Matthew, Mark, Luke, and John.

Photos.com

Seven also represents completeness as well as perfection. Some cultures considered this number to be sacred.
• After creating the world in six days, God rested on the seventh day (Genesis 2:2-3).
• Based on the Creation story, seven is the number of days in a week (Genesis 1:1—2:4).
• Seven days before the flood, Noah was told to bring seven pairs of animals that could be used as a sacrifice, as well as seven pairs of every kind of bird (Genesis 7:2-3).
• The king of Egypt had two dreams. In one, he saw seven healthy cows followed by seven thin, sickly cows. In the second dream, he saw a stalk with seven heads of grain, followed by seven wind-scorched heads of grain. The dream represented seven years of plenty, followed by seven years of famine (Genesis 41:1-36).
• When questioned by Peter about forgiveness, Jesus told him to forgive "not just 7 times, but 77 times!" (Matthew 18:22).
• In the book of Revelation, letters were written to the seven churches in Asia (Revelation 1:4).

Photos.com

Rebekah Sells

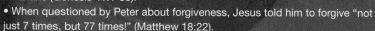

DID YOU KNOW?

Perhaps you think the book of Numbers is just a book of numbers. Although it is much more than that, it mentions significant numbers. For example, in the first chapter you can find out how Moses counted the people of Israel.

Ten sometimes represents completion. After all, 3 + 7 = 10!
- In the Hebrew text of the Creation story, the words "God said" are repeated ten times (Genesis 1:1-31).
- God gave Moses the Ten Commandments at Mount Sinai (Exodus 20:1-17; Deuteronomy 5:1-22).

Twelve represents completeness and perfection.
- God promised that Ishmael (Abraham's son with Hagar) would be the father of twelve princes (Genesis 17:20).
- Jacob had twelve sons whose descendants became the twelve tribes of Israel (Genesis 35:23-26; 49:1-28).
- Jesus chose twelve disciples (Matthew 10:1-4; Mark 3:13-19; Luke 6:12-16).
- Ezekiel's vision of Jerusalem included twelve gates named after the twelve tribes of Israel (Ezekiel 48:30-34). In the apostle John's vision of the new Jerusalem, the city was built on twelve foundations of twelve precious stones, and there were twelve gates of pearl (Revelation 21:11-21).

Forty represents a long period of time with a definite ending. It also represents significant days and years.
- During the great flood, it rained forty days and forty nights (Genesis 7:4, 17-18).
- Moses stayed forty days and forty nights on Mount Sinai (Exodus 24:17-18).
- The Israelites wandered in the desert for forty years (Numbers 14:33-34).
- King David and his son Solomon both ruled Israel for forty years (2 Samuel 5:4-5; 1 Kings 11:42-43).
- Jesus fasted forty days and forty nights in the desert (Matthew 4:1-11).

Moses forbids the people to follow him, James Tissot (19th century)

A Wrong Number?

The number of the beast described in Revelation 13:18 is 666. Some biblical scholars believe 666 refers to Nero, the Roman emperor who persecuted Christians. In the ancient world, significance was given to the numerical value of all letters, so every name had a numerical sum. In Hebrew, the number 666 is the sum of the numerical value of the name "Nero Caesar."

DID YOU KNOW?

Hexakosioihexekontahexaphobia is the fear of the number 666.
(Try saying that six times in a row!)

Paul

A PHARISEE BEGINS

Saul lived his early years in a province of Rome called Tarsus, a major center of education, commerce, and culture. There the young Saul received an excellent early education. He studied under a famous teacher—the Pharisee Gamaliel (Acts 22:3). He became a member of a religious group called the Pharisees, who believed in the strict following of the Law of Moses. Before fulfilling his early plans to be a rabbi, he studied a trade— making tents.

FROM ENEMY TO FRIEND

Imagine an enemy becoming not just a friend, but a best friend. In the first century, a man named Saul hated Christians so much that he held the coats of those who killed the apostle Stephen. (See Heroes, p. 106 for more about Stephen.) Then, to think that Saul not only became an apostle for Jesus but also wrote many of the New Testament letters and started many churches! What changed this man from enemy to follower?

ON THE ROAD TO CHANGE

On his way to Damascus, something amazing happened that completely changed Saul's life. A bright light appeared from heaven, and Saul fell to the ground. He heard the voice of Jesus say, "Saul, Saul. Why are you so cruel to me?" Immediately, Saul lost his eyesight for three days and three nights. His traveling companions led him to Damascus, where a man named Ananias had received a vision telling him to go to Saul (Acts 9:10-16). A reluctant Ananias healed Saul's eyes with God's power.

Much to the shock of the Jesus' followers in Damascus and Jerusalem, Saul became a follower, too. He also became known as Paul, and was chosen by the Holy Spirit (Acts 13:1-3) to bring the gospel message to Jews and Gentiles (non-Jewish people). But this task came with hardships. (See "The Perils of Paul" section, p. 187.)

Toward the end of his life, Paul was arrested in Jerusalem. After several trials before two Roman governors (Felix and later, Festus) and King Agrippa (Herod Agrippa II—see Kings and Queens, p. 146), Paul requested that he be allowed to stand trial in Rome, since he was a Roman citizen. He lived out his final days in Rome while under house arrest and continued to preach about Jesus and God's kingdom (Acts 28:16-31). It is assumed that he was executed as a martyr in Rome around A.D. 64.

iStock.com

For preaching the good news about Jesus, Paul was given thirty-nine lashes five different times, and beaten with sticks three times (2 Corinthians 11:24-25).

THE PERILS OF PAUL

It's not easy being a missionary. Some of the hazards Paul faced as he traveled are described in 2 Corinthians 11:23-27.

Imprisoned (v. 23)

In danger of death (v. 23)

Beaten with whips (v. 24)

Beaten with sticks three times (v. 25)

Stoned (v. 25)

Shipwrecked three times (v. 25)

In danger of falling among robbers or being hurt by his own people (v. 26)

Went without sleep (v. 27)

Suffered hunger and thirst (v. 27)

Lacked warm clothing (v. 27)

Friends Share the Work

Many people joined Paul on his travels to build the early church. Here are just a few of Paul's friends. For more information on Timothy and Silas, other important friends, see Heroes, p. 106.

Lydia

(Acts 16:11-15). Lydia, a Gentile business-woman, is considered the first Christian convert in Europe. She became a Christian when Paul traveled to Philippi. When she heard the news of Christ, Paul baptized Lydia and her family. Paul stayed with Lydia's family for a time.

Priscilla and Aquila

(Acts 18:1-3, 18-19). Paul met this married couple in Corinth. They arrived from Italy because Emperor Claudius had ordered all Jewish people to leave Rome. They taught Apollos, a Jewish man from Alexandria, about the Holy Spirit (Acts 18:24-28).

Titus

(Galatians 2:1-3). After learning about Jesus from Paul, Titus, a Gentile, traveled with Paul to Jerusalem. At Paul's request, Titus traveled to Corinth (2 Corinthians 2:12-13; 7:5-6) and later became a leader of the Christian church at Crete (Titus 1:5).

iStock.com

PACK AND GO!

Paul and John Mark became friends again. In his second letter to Timothy, Paul wrote, "Mark can be very helpful to me, so please find him and bring him with you" (2 Timothy 4:11).

How far would you go to share good news? As a missionary, Paul traveled hundreds of miles throughout Asia Minor (now Turkey) and Greece, and sailed across the Mediterranean Sea to tell people about Jesus. His marching orders from God were:

"I have placed you here as a light for the Gentiles. You are to take the saving power of God to people everywhere on earth" (Acts 13:47).

He lived many years on the go. Put on your walking shoes and travel along with Paul.

Paul's First Missionary Journey (Acts 13-14)

Ever been to Turkey? On his first journey, Paul traveled there with Barnabas and John Mark. They left from the seaport of Antioch in Syria, traveled to the island of Cyprus, then to Perga, the capital of Pamphylia. Although John Mark left them in Perga, Paul and Barnabas continued on to other cities: Iconium, Lystra, Derbe, and finally back to Antioch, before returning to Jerusalem to attend a meeting of church leaders.

Paul's Second Missionary Journey
(ACTS 15:36–18:23)

After quarreling over John Mark (15:36-39), Paul and Barnabas went their separate ways. While Barnabas traveled to Cyprus with John Mark, Paul traveled with Silas to some of the sites visited before: Derbe and Lystra. In Lystra, Timothy joined Paul's missionary team.

Paul had to bypass two Roman provinces—Asia and Bithynia—God told them not to go there (Acts 16:6-7). Macedonia was different, however. One night, Paul saw a vision of a man calling him to "come over to Macedonia to help us" (Acts 16:9). Paul left at once.

Macedonia included important places such as Philippi (a Roman colony), Amphipolis, Apollonia, and Thessalonica. But trouble followed Paul everywhere he went. In Philippi, Paul and Silas were thrown into prison after casting an evil spirit out of a slave girl (Acts 16:16-40). In Thessalonica, a riot began after Paul preached (Acts 17:5).

Traveling to Greece, Paul also visited the great cities of Athens and Corinth. In Athens, Paul debated with philosophers about God (Acts 17:16-34). In Corinth, Paul lived with fellow tentmakers Priscilla and Aquila (Acts 18:1-3; see "Friends Share the Work" section); later, he lived with a man named Titius Justus (Acts 18:7) while preaching every week at the synagogues. After leaving Corinth, Paul traveled back to Antioch.

Paul's Third Missionary Journey
(Acts 18:24—21:16)

Paul left Antioch for Ephesus, where he stayed for approximately three years. During that time he taught new followers and wrote some of the letters that appear in your Bible (see "The Pauline Letters" section). Ephesus was known as the site of the temple of the Greek goddess, Artemis. (See Buildings and Landmarks, p. 26.) While Paul was in Ephesus, he angered a silversmith whose business was making silver models of Artemis, and a riot took place (Acts 19:21—20:1).

Paul traveled to Troas, where he raised from the dead a young man named Eutychus, who had fallen out of a window (Acts 20:7-12). After a sad good-bye to the church leaders of Ephesus, Paul made the long trip back to Jerusalem. At the end of this trip he was accused of bringing a Gentile into the temple and was promptly arrested when rioters threatened his life (Acts 21:27-36).

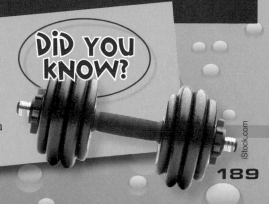

DID YOU KNOW?

Paul begged God three times to remove some type of suffering he was experiencing to keep him humble. While we don't know what the illness was, we know that God replied, "My gift of undeserved grace is all you need. My power is strongest when you are weak" (2 Corinthians 12:7-9).

iStock.com

189

THE PAULINE LETTERS

This chart lists and describes the letters that are part of the New Testament section.

Letter	Place of Writing	Sent to	Theme
Romans	Corinth (during Paul's third missionary journey)	The church at Rome, most of whom were Gentiles	Thought to be Paul's most important letter, he writes about how people can be put right with God by having faith in Jesus.
1 Corinthians	Ephesus	The church at Corinth	Paul teaches them what it means to be a member of the body of Christ and about the gifts of the Holy Spirit.
2 Corinthians	Ephesus	The church at Corinth	Paul argues against false teachers who said Paul's word couldn't be trusted.
Galatians	Ephesus	Churches started on his first missionary journey throughout Galatia in Asia Minor.	Paul defends his right to be called an apostle, warns people against false teaching, and argues that people are put right with God by faith alone.
Ephesians	Possibly while imprisoned in Rome	The church at Ephesus and possibly other churches	A summary of Paul's many teachings with a strong emphasis on the unity that Christ's followers have
Philippians	Possibly while imprisoned in Rome or Ephesus	The prosperous Roman colony of Philippi—citizens of Rome	Paul encourages them to remain faithful and to rejoice in God in every circumstance.
Colossians	Possibly while imprisoned in Rome or Ephesus	The church at Colossae	Paul argues against false teaching and encourages believers to set their hearts on Christ.
1 Thessalonians	Corinth	The church at Thessalonica, a busy seaport city	The oldest document in the New Testament. Paul encourages believers to live in a way that pleases God as they wait for Christ's return.
2 Thessalonians	Corinth	The church at Thessalonica	Similar to 1 Thessalonians, Paul warns believers about false teaching, explains about Christ's return, and encourages believers to continue to do what is right.
1 Timothy	Unknown	Timothy	Instructions to Timothy on how to supervise the affairs of the church
2 Timothy	During a time of imprisonment (location unknown)	Timothy	A very personal letter to Timothy, encouraging him to remain faithful and work hard
Titus	Corinth	Titus	Instructions to Titus on supervising a church and the importance of setting a good example for others
Philemon	During a time of imprisonment (location unknown)	Philemon, a slave-owning Christian in Colossae	A plea for mercy for Philemon's slave, Onesimus, who ran away and later became a Christian

test your knowledge

Quiz time again! Are you up for another three-quiz challenge? Go for it!

There are four possible answers that complete each statement below. Circle your guess.

1. Dropsy (edema) is a disease involving
A. Boils.
B. Swelling.
C. Fainting.
D. Withered limbs.
Hint: See Health and Body, p. 100.

2. Who had a vision of heaven?
A. Micaiah
B. John the Baptist
C. Paul
D. A and C
Hint: See Heaven, p. 104.

3. One of the fruit of the Holy Spirit is
A. Love.
B. Prophecy.
C. Faith.
D. Liveliness.
Hint: See Holy Spirit, p. 124

4. This conqueror established Greek rule throughout Palestine.
A. Cyrus
B. Alexander the Great
C. Pompey
D. Nebuchadnezzar
Hint: See History, p. 114

5. Baal was
A. The Philistines' rain god.
B. The god to which the ancient Phoenicians sacrificed children.
C. The main god of the Phoenicians.
D. The Canaanite storm god.
Hint: See Idols and Foreign Gods, p. 126.

6. This blind man was healed by Jesus.
A. Balaam
B. Barnabas
C. Bartimaeus
D. Barabbas
Hint: See Jesus, p. 136.

7. The name Yeshua (or Joshua) means
A. "Gift of Yahweh"
B. "The Lord saves"
C. "King of justice"
D. "God hears"
Hint: See Names, p. 176.

Answer Key: 1) B 2) D 3) A 4) B 5) D 6) C 7) B

DiD YOU FiND iT?

Use your tracking skills to locate of each of the following. Hint: for answers, check out the Bible passage or section in parentheses.

1. The village where Mary, Martha, and Lazarus lived (John 11:1-3; Holy Land, p. 118)
2. The site of Jesus' baptism (Matthew 3:13-17; Jesus, p. 136).
3. The city around which a wall was rebuilt by Nehemiah and others (Nehemiah 3).
4. The place where Paul was knocked to the ground and blinded (Acts 9:1-9; Paul, p. 186)
5. The Tower of Babel (Genesis 11:1-9; Language, p. 152)

Answer Key: 1) Bethany 2) the Jordan River 3) Jerusalem 4) the road to Damascus 5) Between the Tigris and Euphrates Rivers

Who Am I?

See how quickly you can guess the identity of each person below. Hint: for answers, check out the passage or section in parentheses. You might have to read ahead to find some of the answers.

1. I became the king of Judah at the age of eight and later ordered the temple to be repaired (2 Kings 22: 1-7; Kings and Queens, p. 146).
2. We were both considered wicked queens. (1 Kings 21:25-29; 2 Chronicles 22:2-3; Kings and Queens, p. 146).
3. I was the first high priest of Israel (Exodus 28:29-30; Priests, p. 202).
4. I was a false prophet with a talking donkey (Numbers 22-24; Prophets and Prophecies, p. 212).
5. I led 300 soldiers into battle against the Midianites (Judges 6-7; Weapons and Warfare, p. 228).
6. We lied to Pharaoh to save Hebrew baby boys (Exodus 1:15-22; Women, p. 236).
7. I was the first convert in Europe (Acts 16:13-15; Women, p. 236).

Answer Key: 1) Josiah 2) Jezebel and Athaliah 3) Aaron 4) Balaam 5) Gideon 6) Shiphrah and Puah 7) Lydia

Plants of the Holy Land

iStock.com

Plants That Will Grow on You

Have you ever seen a hyssop plant? How about a broom tree? For such a small country, Israel has an impressive variety of plants and trees. Almost any kind of fruit-bearing tree will grow in the country's fertile soil. Olives, figs, dates, mangos, pistachios, oranges, and lemons are just a few of the trees that grow in this part of the world.

Hyssop

Hyssop is a member of the mint family. It has small leaves and produces bunches of little white or yellow flowers. When a person was healed of leprosy, he was to bring to the priest a hyssop branch, a cedar stick, and two birds (Leviticus 14:4). Mentioned in both the Old and New Testaments, hyssop is sometimes used as a symbol for a person being cleansed from the guilt of sin (Psalm 51:7).

DID YOU KNOW?

The Israelites used hyssop branches as brushes to put sheep's blood above the door and on the doorposts during the Passover (Exodus 12:22).

Lilies

Have you ever picked a bouquet of flowers, perhaps for your mom or for a special friend? The word translated *lilies* in the Bible probably refers to a variety of flowers of different colors, such as the blue hyacinth, the red anemone, and the iris. In the ancient world, lilies were widely regarded as a symbol of beauty (Song of Songs 2:1-2). Several features of the temple were inspired by or shaped like lilies (1 Kings 7:19, 22, 26).

Mandrakes

You've probably seen mandrakes mentioned in the Harry Potter books and movies. But they're in the Bible too. Mandrakes belong to the nightshade family and are related to potatoes and tomatoes. The plant grew well in the lands of the Bible and was often associated with magic. A unique and somewhat eerie characteristic of the plant is that it resembles the human form. Mandrakes have a very distinctive smell and are to this day considered a delicacy in parts of the world. In the ancient world, people believed the roots of the mandrake—also known as love flowers— helped women to have babies. That's why Rachel, who did not have any children, was jealous when Leah's son Reuben gave his mother some mandrakes (Genesis 30:14-16). Leah, at the time, already had given birth to four sons.

DiD YOU KNOW?

Greenhouses and nurseries in North America offer a type of shrub called a "rose of Sharon," which is named after the flower mentioned in the Bible.

Rose of Sharon

No one can say for certain what type of flower the "rose of Sharon" was. It could have been an actual rose, or perhaps a lily, hyacinth, or crocus. It is also possible that the phrase "rose of Sharon" refers to a type of tulip with bright red petals which grows abundantly on the plain between Carmel and Jaffa. In Song of Songs 2:1, the bride compares herself to this common flower that grows abundantly in the Plain of Sharon.

Myrtle

Myrtle is a tall evergreen shrub with shiny leaves and beautiful white blossoms that produce a wonderful fragrance. The ancient Romans and the Greeks valued myrtle greatly. It was even woven into temporary crowns that nobility wore on special occasions. The plant also produces berries which have medicinal value.

Along with olive branches and palm fronds, myrtle was one of the plants Jews were told to use when building their temporary shelters during Succoth, the Festival of the Shelters (Nehemiah 8:15). (See Calendars and Holidays, p. 32.)

DiD YOU KNOW?

When God spoke to Zechariah in a vision, the prophet saw the angel of the LORD standing among the myrtle trees (Zechariah 1:7-10).

The Paper Plant

Have you ever wondered what people in the ancient world used for paper? Papyrus is a type of plant that grew in abundance along the Nile River in Egypt (Job 8:11-12). The stems of this sturdy plant were cut into pieces, split open, and then made into strips. The strips were then laid flat so that a second layer of strips could be laid across them crossways. The sheets were then pressed together to form a smooth and durable writing surface.

Pass the Mustard, Please!

Mustard grows in many parts of the world, but it is particularly valued in Israel. The plant produces yellow flowers and has hairy leaves that can be eaten. The mustard that we have in our refrigerators is made from the seeds of the mustard plant. Mustard seeds were the tiniest seeds that farmers in ancient Palestine knew about. Although the seeds were very small, the plant itself could grow up to ten feet tall! Jesus uses a mustard seed to illustrate how the kingdom of God will grow and expand (Matthew 13:31-32).

Making papyrus paper in ancient Egypt, from 1900.

193

Trees Are Plants Too!

DID YOU KNOW?

The garden where Jesus prayed before the crucifixion was full of olive trees. The word *Gethsemane* means "oil press" (Matthew 26:36-46).

iStock.com

iStock.com

Olive Trees

Olive trees grow in abundance in Israel and are highly valued as a source of oil and wood. When the olives are harvested, they are crushed and squeezed. The oil produced is stored in vats. The oil can be mixed with other ingredients to make delicious foods. In biblical times olive oil was also burned in lamps to give light and was used in ceremonies to anoint kings and priests. When God revealed to Samuel that David would be king, Samuel anointed David with olive oil (1 Samuel 16:12-13).

Almond Trees

In Palestine, almond trees are one of the first trees to bloom in the spring. When the Israelites noticed white and pink blossoms on the almond branches, they knew that winter was over and spring had arrived.

In Hebrew, the words for *watching* and *almond* are very similar—only one letter is different! Perhaps this is why the almond tree was a symbol of *watchfulness* in Israel. God showed Jeremiah a vision of an almond branch as a way of illustrating that God watches for ways to keep his promises (Jeremiah 1:11-12).

iStock.com

iStock.com

DID YOU KNOW?

The two cherubim found within the most holy place of Solomon's temple and its main doors and doorposts were made of olive wood (1 Kings 6:23-36).

DID YOU KNOW?

Jericho was known as "the city of palm trees" (2 Chronicles 28:15).

Cedars

Cedar trees once covered the hillsides of Lebanon (the modern-day country of Lebanon features one on their flag). The wood from these trees was used to construct great palaces and temples. Not only is the wood strong and durable, it also has a pleasing fragrance. In preparation for building the palaces and the temple, first King David and his son Solomon had cedars brought to Jerusalem from Tyre (2 Samuel 5:11; 1 Kings 5:8). Hiram, the king of Tyre, actually made the cedars into rafts and floated them on the Mediterranean Sea from Lebanon to Jerusalem.

Palm Trees

When we hear the word *palm* today, we almost instantly think of a coconut palm. The palms in the Holy Land, however, are extremely tall, sometimes growing one hundred feet high! They produce dates—a very nutritious fruit. When Jesus entered the city of Jerusalem, the crowds waved palm branches as they ran out to meet him (John 12:13).

Broom Trees

The broom tree is a type of desert shrub. The plant's long branches form an upright bush that can grow up to twelve feet high. Broom trees flourish in areas that are too hot and dry for most other plants.

When Elijah ran from the wicked queen Jezebel, the exhausted and terrified prophet rested in the shade of a broom tree (1 Kings 19:1-6).

DID YOU KNOW?

Cedars grow to a height of eighty to one hundred feet. That's about one-quarter the size of a U.S. coast redwood, which grows to around three hundred seventy feet!

iStock.com

Into the Universe . . . and Beyond

Better, faster, clearer communication—and the coverage is unlimited. Does that sound like an ad for the newest cell phone? Guess what! This kind of communication is already available in your service area. In fact, it has been available to everyone since the beginning of the world. It's prayer. Prayer is talking and listening to God. We can pray any time, anywhere, and in any situation. And God promises to listen—always.

iStock.com

Types of Prayers

iStock.com

Type	Purpose
Confession	To admit wrong actions or thoughts
Intercession	To ask for God's help, either on someone's behalf or for yourself
Thanksgiving	To give thanks for what God has given and done
Praise	To acknowledge God's goodness, mercy, love, and holiness
Petition	To make a specific request of God

Psalms as Prayers

All types of prayers are included in the book of Psalms. There are prayers of thanksgiving and praise prayers (Psalms 103; 104). Psalm 119 praises God for his law, and Psalm 136 praises God for what he did for his people. There are also prayers of confession, requests to be freed from the power of enemies, and pleas to God to do what he promised (Psalms 51; 59; 89).

DID YOU KNOW?

Jesus quoted Psalm 22 as a prayer when he was on the cross. Although this psalm describes God's saving love (verse 31: "People not yet born will be told, 'The LORD has saved us!'"), Jesus was only able to utter the opening lines before dying: "My God, my God, why have you deserted me?"

The Bible is full of stories of people who turned to God at crucial points in their lives. As you read about them, see if you can determine which type of prayers they offered.

Famous PRAY-ers from Ancient Israel

Person	Situation	Prayer
Daniel	Taken captive to Babylon, Daniel remained faithful to God even when it meant certain death. When King Darius decreed that he was the only one to whom anyone should pray, Daniel prayed anyway. Read Daniel 6 for the whole story.	Daniel 6:10
David	The shepherd boy who became a king prayed to God throughout his life and in all situations. Even when God turned down his request to build the temple, David gave thanks. Check it out in 1 Chronicles 17.	1 Chronicles 17:18, 20
Ezra	God brought his people back to Jerusalem from captivity in Babylon, but many who returned did not follow God's path. Ezra was so upset that he tore his clothes, pulled out his hair, wept, and prayed.	Ezra 9:5-15
Hannah	When Hannah prayed for a son, she promised to commit him to the service of God. God answered with the birth of Samuel.	1 Samuel 1:10-11
Hezekiah	King Hezekiah reacted to a threatening message from the Assyrian king by praying to God for help. God heard Hezekiah's prayer and saved Jerusalem by wiping out the enemy king and his armies.	2 Kings 19:14-19
Jeremiah	For forty years, the prophet Jeremiah constantly prayed for the people of Judah. He prayed that they would turn from their evil ways and be saved from destruction.	Jeremiah 10:6-16
Jonah	God told Jonah to preach to the sinful people of Nineveh, but instead Jonah took a ship in the opposite direction. After being tossed overboard, Jonah was swallowed by a large fish (Jonah 1). For three days, Jonah prayed from inside a fish's belly!	Jonah 2:1-9
Moses	When spies sent ahead to the promised land gave a scary report, the fearful Israelites rebelled once again. When God announced that he would destroy the people, Moses prayed for them.	Numbers 14:13-19
Nehemiah	While Nehemiah and the Jews returning from Babylon rebuilt the walls of Jerusalem, other people in the area tried to stop them. Nehemiah prayed to God. Check out Nehemiah 4 and 6 for the story and the answer to prayer.	Nehemiah 4:4-5
Solomon	After building the magnificent temple at Jerusalem, King Solomon offered a prayer of praise to God.	1 Kings 8:22-53

The Lord's Prayer

One of the best known of all prayers is the one Jesus taught his disciples. Known as "The Lord's Prayer" or "The Our Father" (because of its opening line), this prayer serves as an ideal model for all prayers. The first part of the prayer relates to God's name, his kingdom, and his will. The rest of the prayer relates to the physical and spiritual needs of the person praying. Here is a modern translation of the prayer as found in Matthew 6.9-13.

Our Father in heaven, help us to honor your name.

Come and set up your kingdom,

so that everyone on earth will obey you, as you are obeyed in heaven.

Give us our food for today.

Forgive us for doing wrong, as we forgive others.

Keep us from being tempted and protect us from evil.

Another account is found in Luke 11:2-4. Some church traditions add a phrase called a doxology (meaning "words of praise") to the end, "The kingdom, the power, and the glory are yours forever. Amen."

Jesus Prays for His Disciples

Photos.com

When Jesus went to the Garden of Gethsemane to pray with his disciples, he knew that he was going to be crucified within twenty-four hours. He didn't try to run away or hide. Instead he prayed to his heavenly Father. In his prayer, Jesus prays for himself and the work he had done on earth. He prays for his disciples that they will remain faithful and that God will protect them. And Jesus also prays for all believers from then until the end of the world. Jesus' prayer is in John 17.

Paul's Prayers

It's clear from Paul's letters that prayer was an extremely important part of this apostle's life. Paul prayed for the people in the churches that he started in various cities. Paul told the Ephesians that he prayed Jesus' followers would grow in their understanding and knowledge of God and God's power (Ephesians 1:15-23). He also prayed that the Ephesians would be strengthened in their faith and love of Christ (Ephesians 3:14-21). Paul prayed that the Colossians would have the knowledge of God's will and live as God's children (Colossians 1:9-14). The apostle considered prayer so important that he encouraged God's people to pray at all times (Colossians 4:2).

The Where, When, How, and Why of Prayer

The Bible . . .	Encourages Us to Pray . . .	Verses
Exodus 23:25	to God alone	"Worship only me, the LORD your God!"
1 Chronicles 17:16-17	humbly yet confidently	"David . . . prayed: LORD God, my family and I don't deserve what you have already done for us, and yet you have promised to do even more for my descendants."
Psalm 50:14-15	thankfully	"I am God Most High! The only sacrifice I want is for you to be thankful and to keep your word. Pray to me in time of trouble."
Matthew 7:7	knowing that God will answer	"Ask, and you will receive. Search, and you will find. Knock, and the door will be opened for you."
John 16:23	in the name of Jesus	[Jesus said,] "I tell you for certain that the Father will give you whatever you ask for in my name."
Philippians 4:6	about everything	"Don't worry about anything, but pray about everything."
1 Thessalonians 5:16-17	at all times	"Always be joyful and never stop praying."
1 Timothy 2:1	for everyone	"First of all, I ask you to pray for everyone. Ask God to help and bless them all, and tell God how thankful you are for each of them."
1 Timothy 2:8	everywhere	"I want everyone everywhere to lift innocent hands toward heaven and pray."

DID YOU KNOW?

God always answers prayer. The answer, however, is not always "Yes." Sometimes it's "No" or "Not yet."

Photos.com

Famous Prayers
Inspired by the Bible

Saint Patrick's Breastplate
(A.D. 365–461)

I arise today
Through a mighty strength,
the invocation of the Trinity,
Through the belief in the threeness,
Through the confession of the oneness
Of the Creator of Creation. . . .

Christ with me, Christ before me, Christ behind me, Christ in me,
Christ beneath me, Christ above me, Christ on my right, Christ on my
left, Christ when I lie down, Christ when I sit down,

Christ when I arise,
Christ in the heart of every man who thinks of me,
Christ in the mouth of everyone who speaks of me,
Christ in every eye that sees me,
Christ in every ear that hears me.

DID YOU KNOW?

Early in his ministry, Billy Graham was very discouraged. He prayed that God would use him "a little bit." One year later, *Newsweek* magazine called him "America's greatest living evangelist."

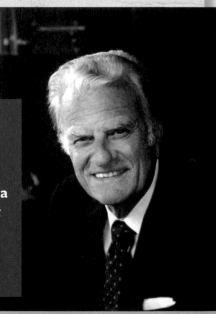

Archives of the Billy Graham Center, Wheaton, Illinois

Prayer of Saint Francis of Assisi
(13th century A.D.)

Lord, make me an instrument of your peace.
Where there is hatred, let me sow love;
where there is injury, pardon;
where there is doubt, faith;
where there is despair, hope;
where there is darkness, light;
and where there is sadness, joy.

O Divine Master, grant that I may not
so much seek to be consoled as to console;
to be understood as to understand;
to be loved as to love.
For it is in giving that we receive;
it is in pardoning that we are pardoned;
and it is in dying that we are born to eternal life.
Amen.

iStock.com

The Serenity Prayer (1943)

The American theologian Reinhold Niebuhr gave a sermon
in 1943 that included a short prayer. When discovered by
members of Alcoholics Anonymous, they quickly made it their
own. It continues to be frequently quoted in "Twelve Step"
literature and recited at meetings. Countless people have
found it helpful. Here is a popular adaptation of the original:

God, grant me the serenity
to accept the things I cannot change,
courage to change the things I can,
and wisdom to know the difference.

PRIESTS

A Nation of Priests

You may notice that Bible is full of references to priests. But have you ever wondered how the role of priest came to be established? At Mount Sinai, God gave his chosen people the law, which instructed them in all religious matters, including the role and conduct of priests.

God told Moses that the people of Israel were to be "my holy nation and serve me as priests" (Exodus 19:6). There were three groups of people, however, who had specific priestly roles to fulfill in service to the people of God: the priests, the high priest, and the Levites.

THE PRIESTS

Of the twelve tribes of Israel, God decided that only men from the tribe of Levi could fulfill the roles of the priesthood. This was one of the most important jobs in ancient Israel. Only descendants of Aaron, Moses' brother, could become priests (Exodus 28:1). In his instructions to Moses, God was very specific about the tasks priests performed, their clothing, and so on. The following were the main duties of the priest. (For other duties, see "Those Hard-working Levites" p. 203.)

Offering the appropriate sacrifices in the tabernacle (sacred tent) or temple (Leviticus 1–7; Deuteronomy 33:10). (For more information on the sacrifices given, see Animals, p. 8.)

Teaching God's law and commandments to the Israelites and declaring God's will to the people (Deuteronomy 33:10).

Checking those with illnesses to determine whether or not the person was fit for worship with the community or should be isolated until declared healed (Leviticus 13–15). (For more information on this role of the priests, see Health and Body, p. 100.)

Illustrations by Guy Wolek

Why was God so specific? Because of the sacred nature of the priests' duties, everything had to be done according to God's law. Neglecting any step or rule could mean death for the priest. See "The Wall of Shame," p. 206, for more information on the consequences of disobedience.)

The LORD said to Moses, "Send for your brother Aaron and his sons Nadab, Abihu, Eleazar, and Ithamar. They are the ones I have chosen from Israel to serve as my priests" (Exodus 28:1).

iStock.com

DID YOU KNOW?

Unlike the other tribes of Israel, the tribe of Levi was not given land to own and cultivate. Instead, they were given small cities throughout Palestine in which to live (Numbers 35:1-8). They were to devote their lives entirely to religious matters and were supported by offerings made by people from the tribes who owned land.

The High Priest

While there were a number of priests serving in the temple at any given time, only one was appointed as high priest. Aaron was Israel's first high priest, serving for nearly forty years. The high priest shared many of the duties of the other priests, but also had responsibilities that only he could fulfill.

• The high priest was in charge of the priests working in the tabernacle or temple.

• The high priest represented the nation before God. On the Day of Atonement (Yom Kippur), the high priest would enter the most holy place in the temple and ask for God's forgiveness on behalf of the nation.

• Only the high priest could enter the most holy place. He was to sacrifice a bull for his own sins then offer two male goats and a ram for the sins of the nation. One of the goats—the scapegoat—was released into the desert (Leviticus 16).

DID YOU KNOW?

John the Baptist's father, Zechariah, was a high priest. Zechariah was one of the temple priests on duty when an angel told him that he and Elizabeth would have a son.

Those Hard-Working Levites

Some of the Levites working in the tabernacle or temple served as assistants to the priests. You might compare these Levites to elders or deacons today. Their tasks:

• Acting as judges in legal decisions (Deuteronomy 17:8-12)

• Taking care of the Book of the Law (Deuteronomy 17:18)

• Taking care of the tabernacle, including transporting it when people moved from one place to another (Exodus 27:20-21; 30:1-10; 40:1-33). They also took care of the meeting tent—the tent Moses used when he met God (Exodus 33:7-11). This tent was placed outside the camp.

• Carrying the sacred chest (the ark of the covenant) (Deuteronomy 10:8-9)

• Cleaning and caring for the special objects of the tabernacle and temple (1 Kings 8: 1-11)

• Collecting gifts and tithes (2 Chronicles 31:2-16)

Families of Levites

Specific families of Levites were assigned certain tasks.

Kohathites (Numbers 4:1-20). They carried the items used in the sacred tent. They were forbidden to touch the objects. After the priests covered them with special cloths, the Kohathites could then move them using poles.

Gershonites (Numbers 4:21-28). They carried the sacred tent, its coverings and curtains, and the tent of meeting. Anyone else who touched them would die.

Merarites (Numbers 4:29-33). They carried the tent frames and other support items.

A Priest's Wardrobe

Make Aaron some beautiful clothes that are worthy of a high priest (Exodus 28:2).

God gave specific instructions concerning the garments that were to be made for Israel's priests (Exodus 28; 39:1-31; Leviticus 8:7-9; 16:4). Some of the high priest's garments were different from those of the other priests.

Illustrations by Guy Wolek

Clothing for the High Priest

• **Ephod:** A ceremonial vest

• **Breastpiece:** a nine-inch square with four rows of beautiful stones and gems, twelve in all (Exodus 28:15-21). Each stone was set in gold filigree and had the name of one of the twelve tribes of Israel engraved on it. The stones were arranged this way:
Row 1: carnelian, chrysolite, emerald
Row 2: turquoise, sapphire, diamond
Row 3: jacinth, agate, amethyst
Row 4: beryl, onyx, jasper

• **Robe**

• **Turban:** A headdress made of linen with a gold strip attached to it. Engraved on this strip were the words "Dedicated to the LORD" (Exodus 28:36).

• **Sash:** A decorative belt

THE EPHOD

The ephod was an elaborate vest made of the finest linen and embroidered with gold, blue, purple, and scarlet yarns. It was worn over the priest's blue robe. Attached to the ephod were two shoulder straps, each with an onyx stone. Upon the stones were engraved the names of the twelve tribes of Israel (Exodus 28:6-14). The breastpiece was joined to the ephod with an intricate series of chains and chords (Exodus 28:22-28). Although the ephod was generally worn only by the high priest, for certain ceremonies it was worn by other priests as well.

Clothing for Other Priests

• **Linen undergarments**

• **A robe**

• **Special caps**

• **A sash**

URIM AND THUMMIM

No one knows exactly what type of objects the Urim and Thummim were. It is possible that they were two stones, each of a different color or with distinguishing marks. The priests used the objects as a means to seek God's guidance. When the people needed to know what to do in a particular situation, the high priest would toss the Urim and the Thummim to see which way the objects fell (Numbers 27:21).

OTHER PRIESTS

Mysterious Melchizedek

Melchizedek is described in Genesis 14:18 as "the king of Salem" and "priest of God Most High." After Abram rescued his nephew Lot and his family by defeating the enemy armies, Melchizedek met Abram and brought him bread and wine, blessing him in the name of "God Most High" (Genesis 14:18-20). In response, Abram gave Melchizedek a tithe, a tenth of everything he had (Genesis 14:20). Although we know very little about Melchizedek's life or origins, the writer of Hebrews compares Jesus to Melchizedek, and says that Jesus is a high priest "just like Melchizedek" (Hebrews 5:5-6).

Eli: The Failed Father Who Mentored Samuel

Eli and his sons, Hophni and Phinehas, were priests at Shiloh (1 Samuel 1:3). Eli is perhaps best known for blessing a childless woman named Hannah, who prayed for and was given a son—Samuel (1 Samuel 1:9-11). Although the Bible indicates that Eli was sincere in his faith and loved God, he was also weak in important areas of his life. This is evidenced by the fact that he allowed his sons to continue behaving wickedly. (See "The Wall of Shame," p. 206.) So God told Samuel that he planned to punish the house of Eli (1 Samuel 3:10-14). Read 1 Samuel 4:11-18 to see what God did.

Proverbs 16:33 refers to the practice of casting lots—stone tokens like the Urim and Thummim—in order to make a decision. The verse makes the point that even if lots are cast, God controls how they will fall: "We make our own decisions, but the Lord alone determines what happens."

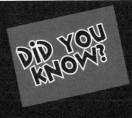

DID YOU KNOW?

THE WALL OF SHAME

Unfortunately, some of the priests mentioned in the Bible were corrupt. Check out this wall of shame.

Nadab and Abihu. These were sons of Aaron and were Israel's first priests (Exodus 28:1). They were also the first priests to die—consumed by fire because they offered "strange" fire to the LORD (Leviticus 10:1-2). Some have suggested that perhaps the priests were drunk, since the same passage teaches that the penalty for priests drinking in the tent of meeting was death (Leviticus 10:8-10).

Hophni and Phinehas. These dishonest sons of Eli served as priests at Shiloh. Although Eli warned them about their behavior, they didn't listen. Because of their sin, Hophni and Phinehas were killed at the hands of the Philistines (1 Samuel 2:12-17 and 4:11-17).

Amaziah. This priest of Bethel refused to listen to the prophet Amos who warned the people of their impending destruction and tried to send him away (Amos 7:10-17).

Pashur. Pashur was the chief officer in the temple during the last years before Jerusalem was defeated by Nebuchadnezzar. Pashur severely abused the prophet Jeremiah by beating him and having him thrown in prison (Jeremiah 20:1-6).

Annas and Caiaphas. Annas served as high priest from A.D. 6 to 15. Although he was eventually overthrown by the Romans, Annas remained an influential figure. Five of his sons later became high priests (Luke 3:2; Acts 4:6). Annas also had a son-in-law, Caiaphas, who became high priest. Caiaphas had Jesus arrested and urged the Roman governor, Pontius Pilate, to have Jesus executed (Matthew 26:57-58; Mark 14:53-54; Luke 22:54).

Illustrations by Guy Wolek

JESUS AS THE HIGH PRIEST OF A NEW COVENANT?

The Levitical high priests were human, so eventually they all died. Jesus, however, is the eternal Son of God, so he lives as our high priest forever (Hebrews 7:23-25).

Because people are sinful, Aaron and his descendants sinned despite their role as priests. Jesus, however, lived a perfect life (Hebrews 4:15). Because Jesus was tempted in the same way that we are, he is able to help us when we face temptation (Hebrews 2:18; 4:14-16).

Animal sacrifices had to be repeated over and over again. Jesus' death on the cross was a sacrifice made only once for all (Hebrews 10:11-14).

JESUS, OUR HIGH PRIEST

The authors of the New Testament understood the Levitical priesthood and the sacrifices offered by the Israelites to be a shadow of the things to come. The role served by Aaron and his descendants pointed to something better—Jesus, the promised Messiah! As the author of Hebrews makes clear, Jesus was both the high priest offering a sacrifice for the sins of the people and the sacrifice itself (Hebrews 8).

Illustrations by Guy Wolek

207

GET TO WORK!

What did people *do* in ancient times?

Whatever needed doing! Starting with hunting and gathering long, long ago, people did what they could to survive. Jobs and professions varied depending on when and where people lived. Some people, called "nomads," lived in small groups, keeping goats and sheep and traveling from place to place to feed their animals. Others lived more settled lives, growing crops, fishing in nearby waters like Lake Galilee, or providing services to those in cities and towns.

Later, as people moved into cities and towns, they became more involved in other types of work. Some became skilled craftsmen. Others worked for the priests or served in the temple. Still others were unskilled laborers who did the most difficult jobs, such as mining, cutting rocks, digging wells, and cleaning streets.

iStock.com

iStock.com

The Word on Work

If you want too much and are too lazy to work, it could be fatal (Proverbs 21:25).

We were meant to enjoy our work, and that's the best thing we can do. We can never know the future (Ecclesiastes 3:22).

But more than anything else, put God's work first and do what he wants. Then the other things will be yours as well (Matthew 6:33).

Do your work willingly, as though you were serving the Lord himself, and not just your earthly master. In fact, the Lord Christ is the one you are really serving, and you know that he will reward you (Colossians 3:23-24).

DID YOU KNOW?

The Bible is against "workaholism." In fact, the concept of "the weekend" has its beginnings in what the Bible has to say about honoring the Sabbath. "Keep the Sabbath holy. You have six days to do your work, but the Sabbath is mine, and it must remain a day of rest" (Exodus 31:14).

Photos.com

Work

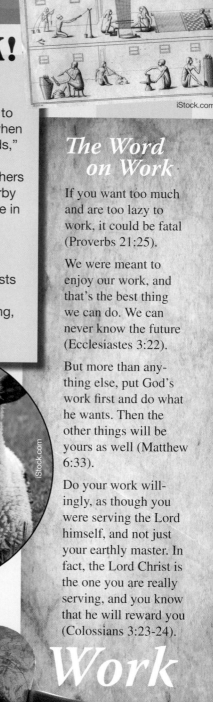

Career Day

PROFESSION	SPECIAL TOOLS	BIBLE REFERENCE
Shepherd, herdsman	Rod, staff	Genesis 4:2 (Abel); 13:1-3 (Abraham & Sarah); Exodus 3:1 (Moses herded goats for father-in-law); 1 Samuel 16:11-13 (boy David)
Farmer, vinedresser	Plow, sickle, basket, threshing sledge, threshing fork, wine and olive presses	Genesis 4:2 (Cain); Ruth; 1 Chronicles 21:18-23; Isaiah 28:23-29
Fisherman	Net, basket	Mark 1:16-20; Matthew 4:19 (Jesus' disciples Peter, Andrew, James, John, Philip)
Potter	Clay, wheel, small sharp tools, tools, paints & glazes, kiln	1 Chronicles 4:23; Jeremiah 18:1-18 (prophet says God is like an all-powerful potter)
Carpenter	Hammer, plane, lathe, chisel, mallet, saw, adze, axe, measuring line	Matthew 13:55 (Joseph)
Weaver	Loom, yarn, fabric	Exodus 35:25-26
Skilled craftsman, esp. in metals (such as silversmith)	Hammer, metal	2 Chronicles 2–4 (workforce for building temple); Acts 19:24 (Demetrius)
Skilled worker or artisan	Chisel, mallet, saw, many more	2 Chronicles 2–4 (builder, stonemason, boat builder, glass workers)
Doctor	Healing oils & beverages, bandages	Luke 4:23; Colossians 4:14 (Luke)
Trader	Scales and baskets for measuring	1 Kings 9:26-28; 1 Kings 5:11; 10:10-13; Ezekiel 27:17
Merchant	Scales and baskets for measuring	Amos 8:5-6; Acts 16:14, 40 (Lydia sold fine purple cloth)
Scribe (writer)	Stylus (pen), ink, papyrus, leather scroll, clay or wax tablets, knife	Ezra 7:1-6,10 (Ezra); Ezekiel 9:2; Jeremiah 36:4 (Baruch)
Tax collector & moneychanger	Tollbooths and tax offices, money-changing tables	Luke 5:27 (Matthew); Mark 11:15-19 (Jesus drives out greedy temple moneychangers)

DID YOU KNOW?

Some people earned money as professional mourners. They were actually paid to cry and wail during funeral processions (Jeremiah 9:17; Matthew 9:23).

A CLOSER LOOK AT . . .

DID YOU KNOW?

Because sheep were so valuable for the wool and meat they provided, they also were used for sacrifices at the temple in Jerusalem. It is likely that some of the sheep in the fields near Bethlehem at the time of Jesus' birth were intended to be offered as temple sacrifices.

Tending Sheep

While watching over a flock of sheep and goats may not seem tough, shepherds in ancient times had a difficult life. They spent most of their time outside watching over their flocks to protect them from robbers or wild animals. At night, shepherds had to count their flock as they gathered them into an enclosed area called a sheepfold, and then again in the morning to make sure they hadn't lost any in the night. Shepherds wandered from place to place or lived in a village where they had the right to feed their flocks in nearby pastures. Sometimes goats would be mixed in with the herd, which made the job even more difficult, since goats tended to climb up rocky hillsides and not stay with the flock.

DID YOU KNOW?

"God called me to this work!" This applies only to full-time religious types, right? Nope. God also needs musicians (like Jubal in Genesis 4:21), government officials (like David's "cabinet" in 1 Chronicles 18:14-17), food-service workers (like Stephen in Acts 6:1-5), clothing-makers (like Dorcas and Simon in Acts 9:36-43), and many more. God calls people to lives of service in *all* kinds of jobs.

Fishing

Since Israel did not border the Mediterranean Sea in Jesus' time, fishing mostly took place on Lake Galilee. The most common fish in Lake Galilee were carp and catfish, but since catfish have no scales, the Jewish people were forbidden by the law of Moses to eat them (Leviticus 11:9-12). Fish were an important part of the local diet and fishing was an important source of jobs and income in Galilee. Several of Jesus' followers were fishermen. (See Disciples, p. 68.)

Merchants and Trading

The dense population of towns was key to creating a strong merchant economy. In biblical times there were great opportunities for mom-and-pop shops and entrepreneurs (Nehemiah 5:15; Acts 16:14, 40). Since Solomon's reign, international trade had gone wild (1 Kings 9–10), encouraged by the temple-building project and the king's rich and famous lifestyle. Exports included farm products (olive oil, wine, grains, dates, dried figs, nuts), perfume, spices, wool, and clothing. Imports consisted of raw materials (tin, lead, silver, copper, iron, gold, timber, linen, purple wool, gems, ivory).

Tax Collecting

Tax collectors in the Roman Empire were known as publicans. Contracts for collecting taxes were often awarded, usually to wealthy foreigners. Contract-holders in turn would hire local men to collect the money (see, for example, Zacchaeus in Luke 19:1-10). The publicans were personally responsible for paying the taxes to the government, but they were also free to collect extra money from the people in order to make a profit. This provided many opportunities for bullying and fraud. Is it any wonder that tax collectors as a group were generally despised? In addition, the Jewish people didn't like tax collectors because they had contact with Gentiles (non-Jewish people), who were considered ritually "unclean." Jesus, however, associated with tax collectors, even making one his disciple (Luke 5:27; Luke 19:1-10).

Who's the Boss?

Did You Know?

Some leaders of the early church also earned money at other jobs. Paul, like his friends Aquila and Priscilla, made tents (Acts 18:3). Today, many Christians work in countries closed to Christianity. While quietly doing their "day jobs" and supporting themselves, they are able to share the good news of Jesus with others. These missionaries are sometimes called tent-makers.

Apprentices

Workers learned their profession as apprentices who helped an experienced craftsman for several years. This system of training eventually developed into guilds (1 Chronicles 2:55; Acts 19:24-27), groups of skilled workers from the same profession. Guilds might include builders, stonemasons (stonecutters), carpenters, woodcarvers, boatbuilders, silversmiths, glass workers, potters, leather workers, weavers, and fullers (people who worked with cleaning and texturing cloth).

In a way, Jesus called his twelve disciples to a three-year "apprenticeship" (Matthew 10:1-14). After Jesus' death and resurrection, many of the people Jesus trained became strong leaders of the early church.

Slaves and Servants

Many people, free and slave, provided personal services as laborers. These servants, typically employed by royalty or other wealthy people, might work as cooks, maids, groundskeepers, tutors, or in child care. In the New Testament the Greek word often translated as *servant* actually means "slave." Slaves were owned by a master, but they weren't necessarily mistreated. Some were field workers, while others were nannies, bookkeepers, and even supervisors or "stewards" (Luke 12:35-48). Many slaves were born to slave parents, some were prisoners of war, and still others had sold themselves into slavery in order to escape poverty.

WOMEN'S WORK

The work women did at home in biblical times was crucial to their families' survival. Women took care of farm animals (some animals actually lived indoors with the family!), assisted with farming and fieldwork, prepared food (including grinding grain into flour and helping with winemaking), and took care of the children. Women had a hand in educating their children. In fact, women in Jesus' day had a hand in almost every profession listed in this chapter.

Prophets and prophecies

The Voice of God to the People

Your message burns in my heart and bones, and I cannot keep silent (Jeremiah 20:9).

Prophets were God's voice to the people of Israel. Sometimes they had visions or dreams or heard God speaking to them. The words God gave the prophets were often strong messages about what the people or their leaders were doing wrong. But just as often they were messages of hope. Either way, prophets did not hold back but boldly proclaimed the messages God gave them.

Because of their special relationship with God and insight into God's message for ancient Israel, prophets would sometimes talk about events that would one day come to pass. Sometimes people tried to use them as fortunetellers even though God told them not to (Deuteronomy 18:10-11).

iStock.com

DID YOU KNOW?

Moses, who led the people out of Egypt, was a special kind of prophet—one that all future prophets would be measured against. God didn't just speak to him in visions, dreams, and riddles. Instead, God spoke to Moses directly (Numbers 12:6-8).

Statue of Moses

False Prophets

God became very angry when people pretended to speak for him. Moses advised the people of Israel to never trust a prophet again if he said something that turned out not to be true (Deuteronomy 18:21-22).

BALAAM
(Numbers 22–24)

This prophet was hired by Balak, the king of Moab, to curse the people of Israel as they camped near Jericho. Although God did speak to Balaam through an angel, Balaam is not counted as one of the true prophets of God. Instead, he is considered to be more of a fortuneteller. He was later killed by the Israelites (Joshua 13:22).

The Prophet Balaam and the Donkey, Rembrandt (1626)

THE PROPHETS OF AHAB
(1 Kings 22:1-28)

When King Ahab of Israel wanted to go to war with Syria, his ally King Jehoshaphat of Judah suggested that Ahab seek God's counsel. Ahab asked some prophets for their advice. Four hundred prophets, including one named Zedekiah, told him to go to war. Only one prophet, Micaiah, a man Ahab disliked, told him not to go. When Micaiah explained that the four hundred prophets lied, Zedekiah slapped Micaiah. But Micaiah was right.

HANANIAH
(Jeremiah 28)

During the reign of King Zedekiah of Judah, the prophet Hananiah delivered a message the people wanted to hear—that God would bring the exiled people out of Babylon within two years. He said, "All this will happen because I will smash the power of the king of Babylonia!" (Jeremiah 28:4). But Jeremiah, a true prophet of the LORD, quickly explained that God did not speak through Hananiah.

NOADIAH
(Nehemiah 6:14)

This woman caused trouble during the rebuilding of Jerusalem's walls. She was probably a false prophet, judging by Nehemiah's prayer that God would punish her.

The Blinding of the Sorcerer, Elymas, Raphael (c. 1517)

BAR-JESUS/ELYMAS
(Acts 13:6-12).

This man who practiced witchcraft tried to keep the governor of the island of Cyprus from listening to the message preached by Paul and Barnabas. Paul rebuked him and predicted that Elymas would go blind, which happened immediately.

The Majors and the Minors:
Profiles of the Poor but Famous

When Israel split into two kingdoms (northern and southern), prophets spoke to the kings and people in both kingdoms. (See Kings and Queens, p. 146, for more information.) So who were the prophets, and who was their audience? The Old Testament contains the writings of sixteen of these prophets. Four are called "major" prophets because their books are long, each one filling a complete scroll. The twelve "minor" prophets spoke just as powerfully, but their collected writings filled only one scroll.

Major Prophets

Prophet	Fun Fact about the Prophet	Key Message	Audience	Time Period B.C.
Isaiah	Named his firstborn son Shear-jashub, which means "a remnant will return" (Isaiah 7:3) and his second son Maher-shalal-hash-baz meaning "swift to plunder, quick to spoil" (Isaiah 8:1-4).	The people rebelled and would be punished. But after they changed their ways, God would restore them.	Judah	736-687
Jeremiah	Took a pair of linen shorts and buried them till they rotted. This was a visual demonstration of what had happened to the people's hearts (Jeremiah 13:1-11).	The people stopped obeying God and would be punished, but God would restore them.	Judah	609- 598
Ezekiel	Ezekiel was carried to a valley filled with dry bones. When he spoke to the bones, they grew flesh and became an army (Ezekiel 37:1-14).	God would judge his people for their sins, but eventually he would restore them.	Jews in captivity in Babylon	598-587
Daniel	Although Daniel was thrown into a den of hungry lions, he was safe because an angel shut the lions' mouths (Daniel 6).	God is all-knowing and all-powerful. He will overcome evil and deliver those who are faithful.	Jews in captivity in Babylon	520

The Prophet Jeremiah Mourning over the Destruction of Jerusalem, Rembrandt (1630)

DID YOU KNOW?

In some translations of the Bible, Joel 1:4 and 2:25 say there will be cutting locusts, swarming locusts, hopping locusts, and stripping locusts. These may sound like different kinds of locusts, but they are more likely descriptions of the stages of growth a locust goes through in its development from a young pupae to a full grown adult capable of stripping the tougher vegetation.

Prophet	Fun fact about the Prophet	Key Message	Audience	Time Period
Hosea	Hosea married an unfaithful woman as an example of God's love toward his people (Hosea 1:2).	Just as the prophet's wife was unfaithful to Hosea, Israel also was unfaithful to God. But God still loved them.	Israel	740-736
Joel	Joel used the word picture of a terrible plague of locusts (grasshoppers) to describe the armies coming in judgment (Joel 1:1–2:11).	God was ready to forgive those who turn away from sin. He would send his Holy Spirit on all people.	Judah	c. 445-443
Amos	Amos shocked the wealthy people by singing a funeral song to them as if they had already been destroyed (Amos 5:1).	Judgment from God would fall on the wealthy people who exploited the needy.	Israel	c. 762-750
Obadiah	Obadiah wrote his prophecy in the form of a song of doom.	Judgment from God was coming to the Edomites who harmed their brothers in Israel.	Edomites and Jews in Judah	520
Jonah	Jonah ran away from his assignment to preach to the Ninevites and was swallowed by a fish (Jonah 1–2).	God's forgiveness is for all people, not just the Jews.	Nineveh, Assyria's captial	783-743
Micah	Micah walked barefoot and naked, howling and mourning for the sin of the people (Micah 1:8-9).	God doesn't want sacrifices, but justice for the poor and true kindness and humility.	Judah and Israel	740-687
Nahum	Nahum was brave enough to prophesy against the Ninevites who were forcing his people to pay money to them (Nahum 2:13).	God's judgment on Nineveh and comfort for Judah	Nineveh and Judah	609
Habakkuk	Habakkuk climbed into a watch-tower to wait for God's answer to his question (Habakkuk 2:1).	"Why are the wicked not being punished?" Because God is all powerful and knows best.	Judah	c. 598
Zephaniah	Zephaniah predicted the destruction of Nineveh ten years before it happened (Zephaniah 1:14-18).	Judgment is at hand. Turn back to God while there is still time.	Judah	640-609
Haggai	His name means "festive," though his message was not.	The people needed to make the task of rebuilding the temple a priority over redecorating their own homes.	Judah	520
Zechariah	Zechariah had a series of visions, including one with the four chariots of heaven pulled by different colored horses (Zechariah 6:1-8).	Though evil is still present, there is hope in the coming of a messiah.	Judah	520-518
Malachi	His name means "my messenger," and he was the last of the Old Testament prophets.	God loves his people enough to confront them about their sins and restore them.	Judah	445-443

DID YOU KNOW? Predicting the destruction of Nineveh was like predicting the destruction of New York City today. Nineveh was known for its great architecture, vast libraries, and a complex irrigation system, which watered the lush gardens throughout the city. Zephaniah's prophecy came true, however, and this ancient capital was so completely demolished that it was not rediscovered until the nineteenth century.

Elijah and the calling down of fire on Mt. Carmel

Prophets without Books

The pronouncements of some prophets were never gathered into books bearing the prophets' names. Yet many of the things they said and did changed Israel and even the world.

Prophet	Fun Fact about the Prophet	Key Message	Audience	Time Period
Elijah	Asked for and received fire from heaven to burn up a water-soaked sacrifice in front of all the people (1 Kings 18).	Warned of judgment from God against the evil and rebellious kings and people	Israel, also Ahab and Jezebel	875-849 B.C.
Elisha	Asked for a double portion of Elijah's power; raised a dead boy to life (2 Kings 4:18-37).	Warned of judgment for evil and reminded the people of God's tenderness, love, and mercy for his people	Israel, also a poor widow	848- 793 B.C.
Nathan	He was a personal prophet to the king (2 Samuel 12:1).	Confronted David about his affair with Bathsheba	King David	1003 B.C.
John the Baptist	Ate locusts and honey, wore camel-hair clothing, lived in the wilderness, and baptized people (Matthew 3:4).	The kingdom of heaven is at hand; turn away from your sins and prepare for the Messiah	People coming to be baptized in the desert of Judea, also the Pharisees	A.D. 26

Reproaches of Nathan to David, Paris psalter.

Women Prophets

The Bible mentions several women who spoke on behalf of the LORD.

Prophet	Fun Fact about the Prophet	Key Message	Audience
Huldah	Huldah was a wife of Shallum, the keeper of the temple wardrobe (2 Chronicles 34:22).	The disaster written on the scroll was going to come true as judgment from God.	Hilkiah the high priest and King Josiah
Deborah	Also a judge, Deborah made decisions for the people who came to her as she sat under a palm tree (Judges 4).	Called Barak to muster an army to fight against the Canaanites.	Israel and specifically Barak
Miriam	Sang a song about Pharaoh's army drowning in the Red Sea (Exodus 15:1-21).	Sent by God as a leader along with Moses and Aaron, praised God for saving Israel.	The Hebrew people as they wandered in the wilderness
Anna	A widow who spent all her time in the temple, Anna was present when Jesus was presented in the temple (Luke 2:36-38).	Praised God for bringing Jesus to those who hoped for the freedom of Israel	Mary and Joseph

Miriam with her brother Moses, from *Heroines of the Bible in Art* (1900)

The Prophecy	Predicted Events	What Happened
Isaiah 11:10-12	Isaiah predicted the return of the Israelites from Assyrian/Babylonian captivity.	Cyrus the Great, the king of Persia, allowed the Israelites to return to Jerusalem (Ezra 1).
Daniel 2	King Nebuchadnezzar's dream of a statue. The gold empire would be taken over by another kingdom, not as strong. The silver empire would be defeated by a bronze one that would rule the world. This would be shattered by the powerful kingdom of iron. One day God would smash this kingdom and set up his kingdom.	The Medes and Persians (silver chest) took Babylon (the gold head) from the Belshazzar, Alexander and the Greeks (bronze) defeated them, and the iron strength of Rome crushed the world and then crumbled and divided while still influencing all that came after it. But the Roman Empire was later destroyed.
Daniel 5:25-28	During a feast, King Belshazzar and his guests saw a mysterious hand writing words on the wall. Daniel told him that the words meant that God was going to take away his kingdom.	That same night the Medes and Persians attacked and split his empire between them. Ever since, the phrase "the writing is on the wall" has been used to describe someone who has realized they're in big trouble.

Daniel telling King Nebuchadnezzar both his dream and the interpretation

Belshazzar's Feast, Rembrandt (1635)

Religion

Who Worshiped What?

The gods worshiped by other nations have never done anything for you or your ancestors. People who ask you to worship other gods are trying to get you to stop worshiping the LORD, who rescued you from slavery in Egypt (Deuteronomy 13:7-9).

iStock.com

Number one on God's ultimate top ten list of commands is *"Do not worship any god except me" (Exodus 20:3)*. The people of Israel needed this reminder. Having been slaves in Egypt for generations, they were influenced by the gods the Egyptians worshiped and would later come under the influence of the gods worshiped by the people living in Canaan—the land God promised to their ancestor Abraham.

• **Sun Worship.** The activity of beach bums and frequent customers of tanning salons? Not quite. Many ancient cultures "worshiped God's creation instead of God" (Romans 1:25). Many people in the ancient world were in awe of the sun's daily return and worshiped it (2 Kings 23:11; Ezekiel 8:16).

Old Egyptian papyrus representing Akhenaten making an offering to Ra (sun).

• **Sumerian Beliefs.** Abraham first lived in Mesopotamia, in what is Iraq today (Genesis 11:26-31; Joshua 24:2). The Sumerians believed in many gods who formed a heavenly council that was led by a chief god, the air-god Enlil.

• **Egyptian Beliefs.** The kings of Egypt, also known as pharaohs, were worshiped as gods. This was in addition to other gods, especially the supreme sun god Amon-Re. In Egyptian art many of these gods are shown having human bodies with animal features

• **Canaanite Religions.** The people of Canaan worshiped many gods and goddesses. Sacrifices (some say even human sacrifices) and idol worship abounded. King Solomon was led astray by some of his wives to worship deities such as Astarte, a goddess of love and war (1 Kings 11:1-5). (For more information on Canaanite gods, see Idols and Foreign Gods, p. 126.)

Ibis-headed god, Temple of Rameses II, Thoth (1198-1167 B.C.)

Photos.com

• **Gnosticism.** Gnostics believed that people could gain salvation by receiving special mystical knowledge. Some Gnostics considered themselves Christians, but they didn't experience their faith or worship in the same way other early followers of Jesus did. These Gnostics may be the false apostles Paul warns against in 2 Corinthians 11. For centuries after Paul's time, Gnostic groups challenged the Christian faith. (See also Galatians 1:6-9; 1 John 2:26-27.)

DID YOU KNOW?

By the first century, Roman emperors were worshiped as gods by some people. The coin Jesus showed his disciples when instructing them about paying taxes was probably a denarius. On one side was a picture of Emperor Tiberius and on the other side the words "Tiberius Caesar Augustus, son of the divine Augustus" (Matthew 22:15-22; Mark 12:13-17).

GODS OF THE GREEKS AND ROMANS

Greek and Roman myths describe many gods and goddesses. Although it was acceptable (and expected) to worship more than one of them, each of these deities was known to have special influence in one aspect of life or another.

God	Worshiped As	Relation to Other Gods	Beliefs About	Bible Reference
Zeus (Greek) **Jupiter** (Roman)	Chief god	Father of many gods/goddesses, brother of Hades (Pluto) and Poseidon (Neptune)	Ruled clouds and rain	During a visit to Lystra, Barnabas was compared to Zeus (Acts 14:8-13).
Apollo (Greek)	God of music, archery, and healing	Son of Zeus	Leader of the Muses	Not mentioned directly. But Paul traveled through Apollonia, which most likely had a temple dedicated to Apollo (Acts 17:1).
Ares (Greek) **Mars** (Roman)	God of war	Son of Zeus and Hera	God of savage war; unpopular with other gods	In Athens, Paul preached at the Areopagus, located on Mars Hill, named for Ares (Acts 17:19).
Artemis (Greek) **Diana** (Roman)	Goddess of animals and hunting	Daughter of Zeus	In charge of nature	While visiting Ephesus, Paul saw the temple of Artemis (Acts 19:23-41)
Athena (Greek) **Minerva** (Roman)	Goddess of war, protector of the city-state	Daughter of Zeus	Helped heroes in battle	Paul likely saw the Parthenon, dedicated to Athena, during his visit to Athens.
Hera (Greek) **Juno** (Roman)	Goddess of marriage and childbirth	Wife of Zeus	Extremely jealous and vengeful	Not mentioned, but Paul and Barnabas might have seen her temple in Olympia.
Hermes (Greek) **Mercury** (Roman)	Messenger of the gods	Son of Zeus, brother of Apollo	Only god who can travel to the underworld and back	During a visit to Lystra, Paul was compared to Hermes (Acts 14:8-13).
Hades (Greek) **Pluto** (Roman)	God of the dead, ruler of the underworld	Brother of Zeus and Poseidon (Neptune), god of the sea	Supervised the trial and punishment of the wicked after death	In some translations of the Bible, death is called "Hades" (Matthew 16:18).

DID YOU KNOW?

Some of the most profound influences in the ancient world (particularly in New Testament times) came from the Greeks. During the third and fourth centuries B.C., Greek philosophers such as Socrates, Plato, and Aristotle tried to understand how people could live a good life in harmony with their city, their culture, and the natural world. Disciples of these great teachers would later form a number of schools of philosophy. By the time of the early Christian church, the teachings of these schools had spread throughout the Mediterranean world. Plato and Aristotle especially had a profound effect on later Christian writers and thinkers.

iStock.com

Satan and demons

WHO IS SATAN?

Satan is the English translation of a Hebrew word that literally means "adversary." In the Old Testament, "the Adversary" or "the Trouble-maker" (called in Hebrew *ha-satan*) is responsible for several acts opposed to God's way. The *ha-satan* is described as:

• the trouble-maker who causes King David to count the people of Israel, something only God was to know, showing that David was trusting in his military might rather than in God's leadership and control (1 Chronicles 21:1-8)

• the one who is allowed to cause suffering for Job (Job 1:6–12; 2:1-7)

• the one who accuses God's chosen servant Joshua, the high priest (Zechariah 3:1-2)

DID YOU KNOW?

In the Old Testament, the snake came to represent evil. The snake who convinced Adam and Eve to eat the fruit from the tree that had the power to let them know the difference between right and wrong is often called "Satan," but his name is never used in that story. (See Genesis 3:1-8.)

THE ADVERSARY

While exiled in Babylon, the Israelites were greatly influenced by Persian thought, particularly the belief that there was a being who was God's chief opponent (Satan) and who had creatures that assisted him in his evil schemes.

During the centuries before Jesus was born, Satan became known as the force of evil that opposed God. In Jesus' time, the powers of evil were known as the "kingdom of Satan." The Gospels describe how Jesus was tempted by Satan, and how he drove out Satan's demons from people on many occasions. Revelation describes a final batt between God and Satan, with G defeating the powers of evil and throwing his adversary into a la of fire (Revelation 20:10).

JESUS IS TEMPTED BY SATAN

(Matthew 4:1-11; Mark 1:12-13; Luke 4:1-13)

According to Matthew 4, Jesus was led into the desert by the Holy Spirit to fast for forty days and nights, and to be tempted and tested by the devil. Satan tempted Jesus in three different ways and Jesus responded by quoting from the Scriptures. Jesus chose to remain faithful to God.

Satan's Temptation	Jesus' Answer
Addressed Jesus' hunger by telling him to turn stones into bread to feed himself	"No one can live on only food. People need every word that God has spoken" (based on Deuteronomy 8:3).
Took Jesus to the top of the temple in Jerusalem and told him to jump, saying angels would catch him (Psalm 91:11-12)	"Don't try to test the LORD your God" (based on Deuteronomy 6:16).
Took Jesus to a high mountain and said all the kingdoms of the world would belong to Jesus if he would worship Satan	"Worship the LORD your God and serve only him" (based on Deuteronomy 6:13).

DEMONS: Who Are They?

Demons are evil spiritual beings that are in rebellion against God. The Bible says that demons:

- have names (Luke 8:30)
- speak (Matthew 8:29; Mark 3:11; 5:12; Luke 4:34; Acts 19:15)
- teach false ideas and beliefs (1 Timothy 4:1)
- experience fear (Luke 8:28; James 2:19)
- know who Jesus is and are afraid of Him (Luke 4:34)
- know their eventual fate (Matthew 8:29)
- possess great strength (Mark 5:2-4; 5:17-26; Acts 19:16; Revelation 9:15-19)

WHAT CAN THEY DO?

A demon's primary purpose is to oppose God (Ephesians 6:12). According to the following examples from the Bible, demons can cause:

Tactic	Reference
False teachings	1 Timothy 4:1
Erratic and harmful behavior	Matthew 8:28; Mark 5:2-5; Luke 8:27-29
Disease	Matthew 10:1; Mark 1:23-26; 3:10-11; Acts 5:16; 8:7
Loss of speech	Matthew 9:32-33
Deafness	Mark 9:25
Blindness	Matthew 12:22
Life-threatening thoughts and actions	Mark 9:22
Seizures	Matthew 17:15; Mark 9:18
Physical defects	Luke 13:11

11 STORIES OF DEMON POSSESSION IN THE BIBLE

DID YOU KNOW?

In the Old Testament there is no word for *demon*.

Man of Capernaum healed by Jesus	Mark 1:21-28; Luke 4:31-37
A man possessed by "Legion" healed by Jesus	Mark 5:1-20; Luke 8:26-39
A man who couldn't talk healed by Jesus	Matthew 9:32-34
A girl from Tyre and Sidon healed by Jesus	Matthew 15:21-28; Mark 7:24-30
A boy at the base of Mount Hermon healed by Jesus	Matthew 17:14-21; Mark 9:14-29; Luke 9:37-43
A blind and deaf man healed by Jesus	Matthew 12:22; Luke 11:14
A woman who suffered for 18 years, healed by Jesus	Luke 13:10-13
Mary Magdalene, healed by Jesus of seven demons	Mark 16:9; Luke 8:1-2
Judas Iscariot, possessed by Satan himself	Luke 22:3; John 6:70-71; 13:27
A slave girl healed by Paul at Philippi	Acts 16:16-18
Sceva's sons tried to use the name of Jesus to drive a demon out of a man, but the man assaulted them.	Acts 19:11-20

iStock.com

TRANSPORTATION

I have been shipwrecked three times, and I even had to spend a night and a day in the sea. During my many travels, I have been in danger from rivers, robbers, my own people, and foreigners (2 Corinthians 11:25-26).

Travel during ancient times was not easy, as you can see from Paul's description of his travels. Washed-out and unlit roads, wild animals, storms, pirates, flooding, thieves, and other obstacles all made travel difficult.

REASONS FOR TRAVEL

So if travel was so hard and dangerous, why did people set out on journeys?

Communication

The Post Office we know today did not exist during ancient times. At first, the only way people were able to communicate was to have messages hand delivered. Messengers traveled by foot and sometimes on horseback to share news or to bring letters written by others (2 Samuel 11:18-24; Esther 8:10; Romans 1:7). Paul asked Christians like Epaphroditus and Titus to visit the church gatherings to encourage the followers there (2 Corinthians 8:16-24; Philippians 2:19-30).

DID YOU KNOW?

The most advanced postal system in the ancient world was the *cursus publicus*, which the Romans developed in the century before the birth of Jesus. By the time of the apostle Paul, the Roman postal system used mail coaches and a relay system, but it was only available to wealthy or powerful people.

iStock.com

iStock.com

DID YOU KNOW?

People often traveled together in big groups called caravans. The camels and donkeys in these caravans often carried valuable cargo, and travelers believed it was safer to travel in groups (Genesis 37:25).

Work

Many people in ancient Israel traveled to find work or to sell their goods. Merchants traveled by ship to sell their products (Ezekiel 27:3-9). When Solomon began work on the temple, he called people from many different areas to bring in materials (1 Kings 5:13-18). (To read more about Solomon's temple, see Buildings and Landmarks, p. 26.)

iStock.com

Festivals and Missionary Journeys

The people of ancient Israel, especially the men, were commanded by the law to attend certain festivals each year: the Passover, the Festival of Shelters, and the Harvest Festival (Exodus 23:14-17). (For more information on festivals, see Calendar and Holidays, p. 32.) They traveled to the places listed on the signpost below.

Jesus sent his disciples throughout Galilee (Matthew 10–11) and later throughout the known world (Matthew 28:19-20; Acts 1:8) to preach about the kingdom of God.

The apostle Paul traveled throughout Asia Minor and Macedonia to tell Gentiles about Jesus (Acts 16:4-5). (You can read more about Paul's journeys in Paul, p. 186.)

DID YOU KNOW?

Groups of people of ancient Israel would travel by foot for several days to attend special festivals at the temple in Jerusalem (Luke 2:41-46).

SHECHEM
(Joshua 24; 2 Kings 12:28-33)

JERUSALEM
(1 Kings 8:1-13)

SHILOH
(Joshua 18:1; Judges 18:30-31; 1 Samuel 1)

Special Worship Places

BETHEL
(Genesis 35:1-15; Judges 20:18; 1 Kings 12:26-30; 2 Kings 12:25)

DAN
(1 Kings 12:29-31)

War

Sadly, one of the main reasons people traveled was to go to war against other countries. The soldiers of Israel traveled to many cities in Canaan in order to gain control of the region (Numbers 31; Joshua 6–11). Later, Judah (the southern kingdom of Israel) was invaded by the Babylonians (2 Kings 24–25). (For more information about the Babylonians, see Nations, p. 178.)

iStock.com

BY LAND

WAYS TO TRAVEL

Some people—like Jesus and his disciples—traveled the old-fashioned way—foot power! (Luke 24:13-17; Acts 10:23-25).

Usually only kings and armies rode horses because they were very expensive. Horses were also used to pull chariots (1 Kings 10:26-29).

Some rode donkeys. The prophet Balaam rode a donkey that later talked to him (Numbers 22:21-35). Jesus rode a donkey into Jerusalem to fulfill a prophecy of the Old Testament prophet Zechariah (Zechariah 9:9; Matthew 21:1-11). People also used donkeys as pack animals to carry heavy loads (Genesis 45:22-24).

Sometimes people rode camels, but they were mostly used as pack animals (Genesis 24:63; 1 Kings 10:2; 2 Kings 8:9). Camels can carry loads of up to one thousand pounds!

DID YOU KNOW?

Camels make good desert travelers because they can eat thorny plants, close their nostrils to blowing sand, and they have long eyelashes to protect their eyes.

BY SEA

Small boats were used for fishing and to travel along bodies of water like the Nile River (Isaiah 18:1-2) or Lake Galilee (Luke 5:1-11).

Travel on the Aegean and Mediterranean Seas required larger ships (Jonah 1:1-5; Acts 16:11; 20:13–16). Large ships were powered and steered by ten to fifty oarsmen and some had sails, too. Sea-going ships were used mostly for moving cargo—passengers had to bring their own food!

Due to unpredictable winter weather, the only "safe" times to travel were between May 26 and September 14 (Acts 28:11-14).

iStock.com

The Phoenicians developed a new way to navigate their ships—by using stars to guide them.

Some ships took a shortcut across land and were pulled on rollers from one sea to another.

ROMAN ROADS

DID YOU KNOW?

The Romans were truly masters when it came to road building. Before the Romans began building their smooth, wide roads, travelers had to worry about the wheels of their carts getting stuck in muddy ruts or getting lost on roads that were nothing more than well-worn paths. Starting about 334 B.C., Roman leaders changed all that by building fifty thousand miles of main roadways. These were no ordinary roads. They were made of layers of sand, stone, and crushed stone, with a layer of smooth stone slabs on top.

Why do you think it was so important for the Romans to build these good roads? They had three main reasons:

(1) Roman soldiers could travel from place to place much more quickly.

(2) Good roads made it easier for the Romans to control and govern distant parts of the empire.

(3) Transporting goods from place to place became much easier, assisting Rome's trade.

Chariots, pulled by one or two horses, were efficient war vehicles since they could move quickly and turn easily (1 Samuel 13:5-6). What a ride!

iStock.com

Tipaza, next to a Roman road, was a military colony under the emperor Claudius.

Perhaps the greatest bonus of the new roads was that it helped the spread of Christianity. When travel became quicker and easier, the Word of God could reach areas as never before!

IMPORTANT ROADWAYS

The King's Highway

If traveling north and south through what is now Jordan, one could travel the King's Highway. Moses and the Israelites traveled this route when they fled from Edom toward Canaan (Numbers 20:14-21).

Great Coastal Highway

Also called the Way of the Sea, this road ran from Egypt to Mesopotamia and was one of the most important routes in Israel. Isaiah mentioned this route in his prophecy (Isaiah 9:1).

Egnatian Way

Paul traveled on this road across Macedonia (northern Greece) during his second missionary journey. He used this road to visit Philippi and Thessalonica (Acts 16:12; 17:1). The Egnatian Way ran east and west through the key cities of Macedonia.

Appian Way

This roadway, sometimes called the "queen of roads," is a famous Italian highway built in the fourth century that ran from Rome to the Adriatic coast. This eighteen-foot-wide highway is about 360 miles long. Sections of it still remain today. Talk about a well-built road!

RATES OF TRAVEL IN THE ANCIENT WORLD

METHOD	DISTANCE TRAVELED
WALKING	20 miles per day
DONKEY	20 miles per day
HORSE	25-30 miles per day
CAMEL	30 miles per day as a pack animal; up to 100 miles a day with a rider
CHARIOT	25 to 35 miles per day
SAILING SHIP	About 5 to 7 miles per hour

iStock.com

FAMOUS JOURNEYS

Figure It!

Pretend that you lived in ancient times. Using the chart, figure out how many miles you would have traveled if you walked on the first two days, rode a fast chariot on the third day, rode a camel on the fourth day and a donkey on the fifth day.

(Correct answer is at the bottom of this page.)

Abraham

The LORD said to Abram: Leave your country, your family, and your relatives and go to the land I will show you. I will bless you and make your descendants into a great nation (Genesis 12:1-2).

At God's command, seventy-five-year-old Abraham (also known as Abram), left the city of Haran with his wife and nephew Lot, and traveled to Canaan. What an amazing trust Abraham had!

Abraham, Jozsef Molnar (1850)

Jacob

Jacob tricked his father into giving the blessing that belonged to his brother Esau. Furious, Esau threatened to kill Jacob. At their mother Rebekah's suggestion, Jacob fled his home in Beersheba to head to his uncle Laban's home in Haran. Along the way, Jacob had a dream in which he saw a ladder or stairway to heaven (Genesis 28:10-15).

Moses

After killing an Egyptian, Moses fled Egypt and headed across the desert to Midian (Exodus 2:11-25). But he later returned to Egypt with his family to lead the people of Israel out of slavery. They began at a place called Succoth and crossed the Red Sea (Exodus 13:17—14:31). After camping in various places in the desert, they arrived at Mount Sinai (Exodus 19).

226

Answer: 125 miles

David

Saul Attempting to Kill David, Guercino (1646)

What would you do if someone started throwing spears at you? You'd probably run, right? That's just what David did. King Saul became jealous of David not long after David killed Goliath. Saul thought David was becoming too popular so he decided he needed to get rid of him. But no matter how hard Saul and his men tried, David, along with God's help, always outsmarted them. After all, it was important for David to stay alive. God had big plans for him—he was going to be king (1 Samuel 18:6-30).

DID YOU KNOW? This long section in Luke that describes Jesus' journey to Jerusalem is known as the "Travel Narrative."

Nehemiah, Ezra, and the Exiles

After being held in Babylon for seventy years, the time had finally come for the Israelites to return to Palestine. Ezra, a scribe, traveled to Jerusalem, bringing with him almost four tons of gold and twenty-five tons of silver for the temple (Ezra 8:24-30). Nehemiah also traveled to Jerusalem, but instead of helping rebuild the temple, he concentrated on rebuilding Jerusalem's walls (Nehemiah 2:1—6:19).

Jesus

When Jesus knew his mission on earth was drawing to a close, he decided to travel to Jerusalem, knowing that he would die there. On his long journey, Jesus spent time blessing children, healing the sick, and teaching people about God's kingdom through parables such as the Good Samaritan. He also sent out seventy-two followers to teach people about the kingdom of God (Luke 9:51—19:28).

Jesus probably never traveled more than eighty-five miles from his hometown of Nazareth.

DID YOU KNOW?

Mary

When Mary, a young woman who lived in Galilee, found out from the angel Gabriel that she would give birth to Jesus, she was confused but excited to be a part of God's plan. Since the angel also told Mary that a relative of hers, Elizabeth, would have a baby as well, Mary traveled to the hill country of Judea to celebrate with Elizabeth (Luke 1:26-56). That was a distance of about seventy miles!

Mary, Joseph, and Jesus

Because the Roman governor demanded a census of the people under his rule, Mary and Joseph traveled to Bethlehem—the ancestral home of Joseph's family line. There, Jesus was born (Luke 2:1-7). But the family did not remain there. Because King Herod wanted to have all male babies killed, the family fled to Egypt, where they remained until Herod died. They then traveled back to Galilee—to the town of Nazareth (Matthew 2:13-23).

Escape to Egypt, Master of the Benedict Passion (c. 1465)

The Conquest
One City at a Time

By the time Joshua led the Israelites into Canaan, the area had faced over five hundred years of control by different nations. Constant fighting weakened the Canaanite city-states, and the small, mobile forces of the Israelites conquered them easily. But when the Israelites reached the plains of Jericho and saw the city locked up tight, they were, literally, stonewalled! But God had a plan.

The commander of the army of God appeared to Joshua and instructed him on how to take Jericho. He told Joshua to gather his men, the priests, the sacred chest (the ark of the covenant), and march around the city, blowing their horns, for seven days. On the seventh day, Joshua commanded the people of Israel to shout because God had already given them the victory over the city (Joshua 6:1-5.) When they shouted and blew their trumpets, the city walls fell flat and the soldiers rushed up and captured the city (Joshua 6:12-25).

A World of Warfare

Ancient Palestine was located on the natural trade and invasion routes between the great empires in Egypt, Asia Minor, Mesopotamia, and the lands around the Mediterranean Sea. Control of the region was a great military advantage to whichever nation could control it. That meant war would be a constant reality for the peoples of the region, and periods of peace would be the exception. The Bible mentions the rare periods of peace under righteous leaders acting with the protection of God (1 Samuel 7:14; 1 Kings 5:4, 12; 2 Kings 20:19; 2 Chronicles 14:1, 6).

Perhaps this prolonged history of warfare is one reason New Testament writers frequently used descriptions of warfare and the implements of war as a way of depicting the Christian life.

"Ai" Think If We Sneak Up Behind Them . . .

Ai was the next city, but the Israelites underestimated the ferocity of the soldiers of Ai and sent only three thousand men to seize the city. The Israelites ended up fleeing the scene, losing thirty-six men in the process. Little did they realize that they lost the war because of the sin of one man—Achan (Joshua 7:6-26). (For more information on Achan see Crime and Punishment, p. 50.)

After dealing with Achan, Joshua came up with a winning strategy. He took thirty thousand of his men and sent them under cover of night to hide behind the city of Ai. He led another force of five thousand men in a direct attack on the city. When the soldiers of Ai came out to fight, Joshua and the five thousand Israelites fled, leading the troops of Ai away from the city.

When the city was empty of its soldiers, Joshua signaled the group of thirty thousand hiding behind the city to rush in and take it. They set the city ablaze. When the men of Ai realized they had been tricked, it was too late. They were trapped between the two groups of Israelite warriors. It was a complete victory.

Israel's Military History

There are three general periods of major military battles in Israel's history:

• Conquest of Canaan 1250 to 1010 B.C.

• Monarchy—1010 to 931 B.C.

• Divided Kingdom—931 to 586 B.C.

# of Canaan

Poor Judgment: Gideon and Samson

The judges described in the book of Judges were military leaders who tried to maintain order in the period before the time of the kings. There were constant disagreements among the tribes and battles with other nations in Canaan. The judges were challenged to find ways to motivate God's people to fight their enemies and stay faithful to God's law. Here are two of the most well known.

An Army of One

Samson's actions (he lit the Philistines' crops on fire with three hundred foxes . . . don't ask—instead read Judges 15:4-5) triggered a war between the Philistine city-states and Samson, one very strong man. The Philistines could never kill Samson or defeat him in battle. The Israelites, however, were afraid of the Philistines and plotted to bind Samson with ropes and bring him to the Philistines. But the Spirit of God came upon Samson, and he broke his ropes.

Seeing the jawbone of a donkey lying on the ground, he picked it up and used it as a weapon. By the time he put down his weapon, one thousand Philistines lay dead (Judges 15:11-17). Later, Delilah tricked him into revealing the source of his strength (his uncut hair). (For more information about Delilah, see Women, p. 236.) Although Samson was captured, God gave him strength. In one final show of strength, he toppled the pillars of the Philistines' temple, killing three thousand Philistines and himself (Judges 16).

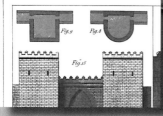

Gideon and His 300 Soldiers

The Midianites were Israel's main enemies in Gideon's day. Gideon was a farmer chosen by God to lead Israel against them. Under God's instructions, Gideon reduced his army of 30,000 to 300 men. Then Gideon was told to take his 300 men by night to the camp of the Midianites where they would surround the camp, each man carrying a torch inside a clay jar and a trumpet.

When Gideon gave the signal, the men broke their jars and started waving their torches, blowing their horns and shouting, "Fight with your swords for the Lord and for Gideon!" (Judges 7:20). The Midianites were so frightened and confused that they actually started attacking one another in the dark, thinking that each was the enemy. When they fled, Gideon's men pursued and destroyed the army. To this day, Gideon's strategy is still seen as one of the best examples of psychological warfare. (For more on Gideon, see Heroes, p. 106.)

Background image by iStock.com

229

Monarchy

DAVID: SHEPHERD, MUSICIAN, GIANT-SLAYER, GUERILLA FIGHTER, KING

Under the rule of King David, Israel was unified. David was another leader God used to lead his people. But long before he became king, he had to deal with a giant problem.

IN THIS CORNER . . .

During the reign of King Saul, the Israelites were continually troubled by the Philistines. But before the armies of both sides could attack one another, the Philistine's champion, Goliath of Gath, proposed an idea: settle matters with a duel. The duel was a form of winner-takes-all combat that was popular in other parts of the ancient Near East. Yet up until the encounter between David and Goliath, it was unknown to the Israelites.

For forty days, Goliath dared the Israelites to send a champion to fight him. But the Israelites were scared. The only one who would step out to meet the challenge was a young shepherd—David—who was only there to deliver food to his older brothers (1 Samuel 17:12-23). When he heard how Goliath mocked God and his people, David became angry and asked King Saul for permission to fight him. Saul granted him permission. With just a sling and a stone, David killed Goliath. The Philistines weren't ready to surrender, so they ran away, breaking the rules of combat (1 Samuel 17:24-54).

CATCH ME IF YOU CAN: THE ADVANTAGE OF MOBILITY

Following David's instant, nationwide fame as a giant-slayer, Saul became jealous of David and sought to kill him. David fled into the countryside and there developed a mobile guerrilla fighting force that frustrated King Saul's efforts at finding him. His small band of fighters could disband and scatter at a moment's notice. David was able to hide from Saul and even conduct guerilla raids on the Philistines. David's ability to actively pursue the Philistines while evading Saul made him a popular man among the people of Israel, so when Saul was defeated by the Philistines at Mount Gilboa, the choice for their new king was obvious. The story of David's years of running from Saul can be found in 1 Samuel 20–30. (For another battle David fought, see Jerusalem, p. 130.)

David with his sling, artist unknown

Sennacherib and His Assyrian Siege Machine

Sennacherib came to power in Assyria in 705 B.C. and immediately had his ability as a military commander put to the test. Rebellion in the eastern and western provinces had erupted, with Babylon and Jerusalem as two participants in the rebellion. Sennacherib sent his armies to subdue Babylon first, and then west to go after Judah and the rebelling towns there. Relying on siege weaponry—like wheeled siege towers with battering rams and archers—Sennacherib's armies easily overwhelmed cities in Judah (2 Kings 18; 2 Chronicles 32). When some cities, like Samaria, could not be breached, they simply waited them out, allowing famine or plague to do its work from the inside the cities. This was what was known as a siege. By the time the Assyrians reached Jerusalem, historical records show that Sennacherib had successfully captured over forty-six different cities and towns and claimed over two hundred thousand slaves.

The Best Offense Is a Good Defense . . .

By the time Sennacherib first crossed into Judah to put down the rebellion, King Hezekiah had already started making plans to build up Jerusalem's defenses (2 Chronicles 32:2-8). Knowing that one key to a successful defense was uninterrupted access to food and water, Hezekiah commissioned the building of an 1800-foot tunnel to the Gihon Spring that connected to the Siloam Pool within the city. However, Hezekiah was worried about how quickly Sennacherib captured other cities, and he tried to make peace by sending Sennacherib a large gift, known as a "tribute."

. . . and an Angel of the LORD

Sennacherib accepted the large sum of gold and silver, but he also sent envoys to Jerusalem to threaten and demoralize its people, telling them that none of the other city's gods saved them, so why should God save them (2 Kings 18:28-35; 2 Chronicles 32:10-15)? Hezekiah asked the prophet Isaiah for advice and also prayed. Isaiah told him not to worry, that Sennacherib would return to his home and to a violent death and that Jerusalem would be spared (2 Kings 19:1-7, 20-34). God's message to Isaiah was fulfilled. When Sennacherib tried to lay siege to Jerusalem, 185,000 of his men were killed by an angel of the LORD. Sennacherib was murdered when he returned home (2 Kings 19:35-37).

Roman soldiers

In order to pay tribute to Sennacherib, Hezekiah had to give all the gold and silver from God's temple and royal treasury. He even had to strip the gold covering the doors and doorposts! Check it out in 2 Kings 18:14-16.

DID YOU KNOW?

Armageddon: The Last Battle?

In the last book of the Bible, Revelation, the apostle John describes a last battle between Jesus and his followers on one side and Satan and his followers on the other. Called Armageddon, it is named after Mount Megiddo, the site of many famous battles in the Old Testament. This fact has led people to wonder if Megiddo was truly the place where the last battle would one day take place, or if John was using this place as a symbol of the ultimate battle between good and evil (Revelation 16:16). Like most of Revelation, the passage about Armageddon is difficult to interpret, but regardless of how literally or figuratively it is taken, it clearly describes a final battle in which Satan is destroyed and Jesus is victorious.

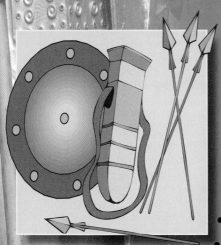

Weapons and Armor in the Bible

- Battering ram (Ezekiel 4:2; 21:22; 26:9)
- Bow and arrow (Genesis 27:3; 2 Samuel 22:35)
- Breastplate, coat of mail (1 Samuel 17:5-6, 38; Isaiah 59:17)
- Girdle, belt (2 Samuel 20:8)
- Greaves, leg protection (1 Samuel 17:5-6)
- Helmet (1 Samuel 17:5-6; Isaiah 59:17)
- Shield (1 Samuel 17:7, 41)
- Sling (1 Samuel 17:48-50)
- Spear, lance, javelin, dart (Joshua 8:18; Judges 5:8; 1 Samuel 18:11; Psalm 35:3)
- Sword (Genesis 27:40; Proverbs 25:18)

Helmet

Breastplate

Sword

Belt

Shield

Shoes

iStock.com

The Armor of God in Ephesians 6

When he wrote about spiritual armor, the apostle Paul was probably inspired by the Roman soldiers who guarded him during his years of being under house arrest. Here is each piece:

- **The belt of truth** (6:14)

- **The breastplate of righteousness— God's justice** (6:14)

- **The shoes of God's good news** (6:15)

- **The shield of faith** (6:16)

- **The helmet of salvation** (6:17)

- **The sword of the Spirit** (6:17)

To Fight a Spiritual Enemy, One Needs Spiritual Armor

In Paul's letter to the Ephesians, he gives them encouragement and instructions on how to fight the spiritual battles of this world by putting on the armor God has given them. Knowing that both Jewish and Greek history were full of warfare, Paul uses images of armor and weapons to make his point, but adds that they are not using these weapons and armor to fight one another, but to fight against the forces of darkness in the spiritual world.

Weights and Measures

An Omer or an Ephah?

While they wandered in the wilderness after escaping from slavery in Egypt, the Israelites were instructed to collect only an *omer* of manna (thin flakes of bread) per person to eat daily (Exodus 16:16). If you were told that an *omer* is about one tenth of an *ephah*, would you understand what that meant? Here's a hint: an omer, also known as a *homer*, is about two quarts.

iStock.com

A Cubit of Ribbon, Please

Here are some of the measurements of the ancient world in comparison to today's measurements. Could you imagine going into your store and asking for an ephah of flour or a cab of cinnamon?

• A **cubit** of ribbon would be roughly 18 inches of ribbon.

• A **span** of rope would be about 9 inches of rope. Several spans of rope would be necessary to tie your donkey to a tree.

• A **log** of milk would probably be equal to a quart of milk. (We envision a different "log of milk," don't we?)

• A **bath** of goat's milk would mean about 6 gallons. That's a lot of goat's milk!

• A **hin** of grape juice would be about four quarts.

DID YOU KNOW?

The Bible refers to "dishonest scales" because silver and gold pieces were weighed and used as coins by merchants (Amos 8:5). A dishonest scale meant merchants cheated their customers.

iStock.com

MEASUREMENTS

LINEAR MEASUREMENTS

Even though measurements in the ancient world differed from place to place, we can get a rough picture of how they compared to today's measurements.

Biblical Unit	Approximate American Equivalent	Scripture Reference
Cubit—the standard measurement of length in the Bible	18 inches—based on the length of an adult's forearm	Genesis 6:15; Revelation 21:17
Span	9 inches	Exodus 28:16
Handbreadth	3 inches—or 3 fingers in width	Exodus 25:24-25

WEIGHTS

In Luke 21:2 we find that one poor widow put two small coins into the temple treasury while the rich gave more coins. Jesus praised the poor woman who gave out of her poverty, while the rich gave from their wealth. Here is a chart showing a system of weighing silver and gold. (For more information on currency, see Currency, p. 54.)

Photos.com

Biblical Unit	Approximate American Equivalent	Scripture Reference
Talents	75.6 pounds	Exodus 25:39
Mina	1¼ pound	Ezra 2:69; Ezekiel 45:12
Shekel	2/5 ounce	Ezekiel 45:12
Pim	1/3 ounce	1 Samuel 13:21

DRY MEASUREMENTS

The *cor* was the standard of measurement for dry goods like wheat and flour. A *cor* represented how much a donkey could carry. The *ephah* was the standard for lesser measurements.

Biblical Unit	Approximate American Equivalent	Scripture Reference
Cor	6 bushels	Ezekiel 45:11-14
Ephah	3/5 bushel	Ruth 2:17
Seah	7 quarts	Genesis 18:6
Omer	2 quarts	Exodus 29:40-41
Cab	1 quart	2 Kings 6:24-25; 7:12-20

LIQUID MEASUREMENTS

A *bath* was the standard liquid measurement in the ancient world. It may have been the amount of liquid in a jar carried by a young girl.

Photos.com

Biblical Unit	Approximate American Equivalent	Scripture Reference
Bath	6 gallons	1 Kings 7:26
Hin	4 quarts	Exodus 29:40-41
Log	1/3 quart	Leviticus 14:10

Women

A Woman's Place

Today, a woman's place in society continues to be a topic of debate in many parts of the world. But in the ancient world, a woman's position in society was pretty much fixed in place. The family household was central to the social structure. In an agricultural society, women were involved in farming, preserving and processing food, making cloth and providing clothing, along with parenting. Proverbs 31:10-31 is a great description of the duties of a woman in biblical times.

Here are some snapshots of several well-known women in the Bible:

Eve: The Beginning of the End

iStock.com

According to Genesis 2:21-23, Eve was the first woman, created from Adam's rib to be the ideal partner. Her name means "life," and all of human life has come from her. But Eve disobeyed God's first command (Genesis 3:1-8). Contrary to what some say, the Bible does not say that Eve tempted or tricked Adam. Instead, the Bible tells us, "Her husband was there with her, so she gave some to him, and he ate it too" (Genesis 3:6). As punishment for their disobedience, God sent them out of the garden (Genesis 3:23) and said that the man would have to work hard to grow food and that the woman would have pain in childbirth.

Sarah: Late to Motherhood

God promised that Abram would have a son (Genesis 15:4). Since Abram (later Abraham) and his wife, Sarai, were both old, having a child seemed impossible. As time passed, Sarai grew impatient and suggested that her Egyptian maidservant, Hagar, bear a child that Sarai could call her own. But when Hagar acted proudly toward Sarai, Sarai treated her harshly (Genesis 16:1-6).

Hagar ran away but returned at the prompting of the angel of the LORD and had a son, Ishmael. When Sarai (now Sarah) did have a son—Isaac—she sent Hagar and Ishmael away (Genesis 21:1-21).

Rebekah:
Playing Favorites

Like Abraham and Sarah, Isaac and Rebekah were unable to have children for many years. After Isaac prayed for children, Rebekah became pregnant with twin sons—Esau and Jacob. While she was pregnant, God told Rebekah that her sons would head different nations and that the older would serve the younger son (Genesis 25:19-26).

Rebekah and Isaac made the big mistake of picking favorites. Isaac favored Esau, the firstborn and a hunter (Genesis 25:28). Rebekah favored Jacob. She helped Jacob trick Isaac into giving him the inheritance and blessing that should have gone to Esau as the firstborn. Afterwards, because she was terrified Esau would kill Jacob for his lie, Rebekah sent Jacob to her brother Laban in Haran (Genesis 27:41-45).

Rachel and Leah:
Sisters of Destiny

It wasn't exactly a fairy-tale wedding. Laban had promised his beautiful daughter, Rachel, to Jacob if Jacob worked for him for seven years. Madly in love with Rachel, Jacob agreed. However, after seven years, Laban instead gave Jacob his older daughter, Leah (Genesis 29:20-27). Jacob made no secret of his disappointment, and Leah soon realized she was unloved.

Jacob openly favored Rachel and, later, her two sons. But Leah had four sons, naming each after the hope that her husband would love her equally (Genesis 29:31-35). Little did either sister know that their children were just the beginning of the great nation of Israel.

DiD YOU KNOW?

Once a woman was married, she was considered a member of her husband's family. If he died without having children, one of his brothers, or the closest male relative, was required to marry the widow. Any children were considered the children of the dead husband. This was known as a "levirate marriage" (Deuteronomy 25:5-10). Boaz's marriage to Ruth was this kind of marriage (Ruth 4:10).

Great Women of the Bible

These women cherished their roles as mothers, caregivers, and faithful friends.

Miriam:
A Protective Big Sister

Miriam is perhaps most well known for protecting her baby brother, Moses, from certain death. (See Kids in the Bible, p. 142 for the full story.) Years later Miriam and Moses were reunited when Moses returned to Egypt to lead the Israelites out of slavery. After the Israelites crossed the Red Sea, Miriam led the women in a song of thanks to God (Exodus 15:19-21).

At one point, Miriam resented that God chose Moses as leader and spoke against him. She was stricken with leprosy as a result. But after Moses prayed, God healed her (Numbers 12:1-16).

iStock.com

DID YOU KNOW?

Miriam was the first woman in the Bible to be called a prophet (Exodus 15:20).

Mary:
Blessed by God

Few women in the New Testament are as easy to recognize as Mary, the mother of Jesus. She was a young girl from Nazareth who was engaged to a carpenter, Joseph. Before they were married, an angel came to her and said that her son would be the Savior and Son of God (Luke 1:26-33). This incredible news nearly ended her engagement to Joseph. But after an angel talked to Joseph in a dream, Mary and Joseph were married (Matthew 1:20-25).

Mary's actions showed her to be a caring mother. She worried about Jesus when he went missing during a trip to Jerusalem (Luke 2:41-50). Mary knew that Jesus was capable of great things (John 2:1-5). She undoubtedly believed that her son was the Lamb of God—the promised sacrifice for the sins of the world—her own included (John 1:29). And during the worst hours of his life—his crucifixion—she was there with him (John 19:25-27).

Elizabeth:
She Knew What Was Coming

Married to the priest Zechariah and a relative of Mary the mother of Jesus, Elizabeth was elderly and without children. An angel told Zechariah that Elizabeth would have a son who would be named John and who would be a "great servant of the Lord" (Luke 1:15).

When Mary visited Elizabeth, the child "moved within her" (Luke 1:41), prompting Elizabeth to say, "God has blessed you more than any other woman." Her son grew up to be John the Baptist, who preached to the crowds about Jesus' coming and baptized them as a sign of their turning to God. He even baptized Jesus (Luke 3:21-22).

Abigail
She Knew What to Do

When David was on the run from Saul (see Heroes, p. 106), Abigail prevented a bloody conflict. Abigail's husband, Nabal, had a name that suited his actions. (Nabal means "fool.") First, he refused to give food to David and his men while they hid near his home. Then Nabal insulted David's messengers. That's when Abigail knew she had to take action. Hoping to keep David from harming her husband and family, she packed up several donkeys with food and brought them to David. David was impressed not only with her beauty but with her gentle words and advice. In fact, he married her after Nabal died. For the story, check out 1 Samuel 25:2-44.

Mary: Apostle to the Apostles

Mary Magdalene, from whom Jesus had forced out seven demons, was a faithful follower of Jesus (Mark 16:9; Luke 8:2). She witnessed Jesus' crucifixion and burial, kept a vigil at his tomb (Matthew 27:45-61; Mark 15:22-41; Luke 23:26—56), and was the first to see the risen Christ (John 20:1-18). Because she told Jesus' apostles that she had seen the Lord, she has become known as the "Apostle to the Apostles."

Famous for All the Wrong Reasons

Jezebel

Wonder why few people name their babies Jezebel? The example of the wife of King Ahab will give you a clue. Jezebel, a Phoenician princess, brought other gods to Israel for idol worship and worked to kill God's prophets (1 Kings 16:29-34; 18:13). Because of her evil actions, she considered the prophet Elijah to be public enemy number one and tried to have him killed (1 Kings 19:1-3). She died a horrible death (2 Kings 9:30-37). (For more about Jezebel, check out Kings and Queens, p. 146.)

Delilah

Delilah was nothing but trouble! She was a Philistine woman who became close to Samson, one of the Israel's judges. Bribed by the Philistine leaders to get the secret of his amazing strength, Delilah tricked Samson into telling her—his hair had never been cut. Delilah told the Philistine rulers, who shaved Samson's head while he slept and then captured, blinded, and imprisoned him. Little did she know that God's power really gave Samson strength. Read all about her in Judges 16:4-23.

Brief Mention, Big Impact

In addition to their more famous "sisters," a number of women are only mentioned briefly in the Bible. Read their stories and see what a difference they made!

The Woman/Women	What She/They Did	Find the Story Here
Shiphrah and Puah	Midwives who helped deliver Israelite babies. When ordered by Pharaoh to let all male babies die, they quietly refused, and God rewarded them with children of their own.	Exodus 1:15-22
The Daughters of Zelophehad	Came forward to challenge the laws regarding inheritance and claimed economic justice for women when there were no male heirs	Numbers 27:1-11
Tabitha (Dorcas)	Christian woman devoted to helping the poor and widows. After prayer, Peter raised her from the dead, and Christianity spread through her town of Joppa.	Acts 9:36-42
Priscilla	Wise Christian woman who helped Apollos understand the truth about the Holy Spirit. Priscilla and her husband, Aquila, were leaders Paul trusted.	Acts 18:18-26
Phoebe	Praised by Paul as a kind and very generous woman as well as a church leader. She delivered one of his letters to a church in Rome.	Romans 16:1-2
Lois (grandmother) **Eunice** (mother)	Both are praised for their wise and loving guidance of Timothy, who later traveled with Paul.	2 Timothy 1:5

DID YOU KNOW?

Paul's first convert in Europe was a woman: Lydia, a businesswoman who later hosted Paul and his companions in Philippi (Acts 16:11-15).

No Shrinking Violets:
A Few Famous Women in Church History

Monica, Mother of Augustine of Hippo
(A.D. 331–387)

Born in North Africa, Monica was a model Christian wife and mother. Her faith led to the conversion of her pagan husband, and she raised her children to know and love Jesus. When her son Augustine rejected the faith, she followed him to Italy, where Augustine accepted Christianity and was baptized in 386, to his mother's great joy. Later, Augustine became the Bishop of Hippo and credited his faith to his mother's prayers. (For more on Augustine, see Literature, p. 156.)

Joan of Arc (1412–1431)

Photos.com

Her nickname was "Maid of Orleans." Born a French peasant, at age sixteen Joan joined the French army against the English, believing that God wanted her to fight. Although she was sent home, she returned dressed as a man and fought with the troops in a number of battles. She was later put on trial, convicted of heresy, and burned at the stake.

Sojourner Truth (1797–1883)

Born into slavery as Isabella Baumfree (after her father's owner) in New York, she was sold from her family at age nine. She escaped from her owner in 1827 and experienced a religious conversion while working for a Christian family. In 1843, she took the name Sojourner Truth based on instructions she believed she received from the Holy Spirit. She became a traveling preacher, an abolitionist, and an outspoken advocate for women's rights and the rights of African American people. Her famous *"Ain't I a Woman?"* speech was given at a Women's Rights Convention in Ohio in 1851.

Gladys Aylward (1902–1970)

Gladys, an English maid, became a Christian and a missionary to China. In Yuncheng, China, she opened an inn. She also worked as a foot inspector to enforce the law banning foot binding. When she was sent to a men's prison to break up a riot, she began prison reform work and later took in Chinese orphans. She was called "Ai-weh-deh" (Virtuous One). When Japan invaded in 1938, orders were sent to capture Gladys, dead or alive. She fled with nearly one hundred orphans to safety. The book *The Small Woman* and movie *The Inn of the Sixth Happiness* were based on her life.

WORSHIP

LET'S START AT THE BEGINNING

Ever wonder how our present-day church practices got started? Or why churches look different from each other? Why do church leaders in some churches wear special robes? The roots of how Christians worship can be traced back to some very early places of worship in the desert of the Sinai peninsula. There God gave Moses a set of rules for how the Israelites were to live and worship. The rules reminded them of God's great love for them and taught them what to do if they sinned by breaking God's laws. Let's look at these early places of worship and what people did there.

the Sacred Tent: Camping Out with God
(Exodus 35–40)

The people of Israel worshiped in a sacred tent (the tabernacle) after they left Egypt and were traveling to the promised land of Canaan. The framework covering for the tent was made from ram skins and woven with goat hair over acacia wood. The curtains of the tent were made from linen and wool dyed blue, red, and purple. The tent could be taken apart and moved to any location.

It was divided into three areas: a rectangular area (called the outer court) for burning sacrifices and a tented sanctuary, which was divided into two areas that were partitioned off by boards and curtains. The front section was called the "holy place" and the partitioned area in the back was called the "holy of holies," where the sacred chest (the ark of the covenant) was kept.

the Temple: A Permanent Resting Place

King David wanted to build a more permanent house for God and even made plans for doing so (2 Samuel 7; 1 Chronicles 22). While God said no to David's request, David's son Solomon later built the temple of David's dreams (1 Kings 5–8). It consisted of several terraces surrounding Mount Moriah, complete with housing for the priests, porters, and singers, as well as rooms for visiting worshipers. The highest terrace housed the great porch and the sanctuary. The builders used lumber shipped from Tyre as well as precious stones, gold, silver, iron, granite, marble, and other treasures. The result was an architectural wonder, massive in design and beautiful to behold.

A TRIP THROUGH THE TEMPLE

When God set up a system of worship, he gave Moses a very specific list of articles to be used in the sacred tent (tabernacle) that would remind the people how to worship properly (Exodus 26–27;

30). There were objects to remind the people of God's presence, as well as objects to remind the people how they could be made clean if they sinned and broke any of God's laws. Years later, when the Jerusalem temple was complete, many of these objects and furnishings were made by Hiram, a bronze worker from Tyre (1 Kings 7:13-47). Here's a list of items that were in the temple and the purpose for each.

Altar of Burnt Offering

This was where animals and offerings were sacrificed. It was 30 feet long, 30 feet wide, and 15 feet high (2 Chronicles 4:1).

the Sea

This large circular tank of bronze measured about 45 feet around, 15 feet across, and 7½ feet high. It was filled with water for the priest to wash in (1 Kings 7:23-26). The Sea rested on twelve bronze bulls—three bulls facing outward in four different directions.

Movable Bronze Stands

These were made of bronze with bases resting on wheels and were used for washing the animals to be sacrificed and for cleansing the court (1 Kings 7:27-39).

the tables for the Sacred Bread

These solid gold tables held twelve loaves of special bread. The loaves were laid out on the Sabbath to be eaten only by the priests after they had been presented to God. Fresh bread was placed on the tables every week (Leviticus 24:5-9; 1 Kings 7:48; 2 Chronicles 4:8, 19).

Altar of Incense

This was where sweet-smelling incense was burned (Exodus 30:1-5; 1 Chronicles 28:18).

ten Golden Lampstands

Each had seven branches holding oil-burning lamps that had to be continuously tended from morning to evening (Leviticus 24:1-4; 1 Kings 7:49).

Sacred Chest

Also known as the ark of the covenant, this chest was made of acacia wood and overlaid with pure gold. Inside the chest were the stone tablets on which were written the Ten Commandments, the laws God gave to Moses and the people at Mount Sinai. The lid of this chest was called the mercy seat where two golden cherubim sat and was the place where God said his Presence would rest (Exodus 25:10-22; 1 Kings 8:1-13).

A LESSON AT THE ALTAR:
Sacrifices and Offerings

So what did they do on that altar for burnt offerings? In Leviticus the words *offering* and *sacrifice* are often used to describe the same thing. People offered a sacrifice to God to be cleansed of sin so that they could worship God with their whole heart. Each sacrifice was meaningful because it related specifically to a situation in life. One of the most important offerings was the sacrifice for sin, which was always a sacrifice of an animal that must be slaughtered as a representation of the person's sin. This helped show the people two things:

1.

That the result of sin was death (Romans 6:23). The animal took the person's place and showed them the consequence of his or her sin (Leviticus 1:4).

2.

Sacrificing an animal showed that because a life was given, a person's life could be saved even though he or she broke God's laws and deserved death. In the New Testament, Jesus is called the "Lamb of God" (John 1:29; 1 Peter 1:19) and is considered the ultimate sacrifice for sin (Hebrews 9:28; 10:10).

There were five types of sacrifices offered on the altar. Some were voluntary (could be given or not), while others were required before a person could worship. Sometimes grain could be offered (Leviticus 2), but most of the time, animals were sacrificed. (For the types of animal sacrifices offered see Animals, p. 8.)

iStock.com

A TOUR OF OTHER PLACES OF WORSHIP IN THE OLD TESTAMENT

The temple was not the only place that worship took place. When God did something important the people often remembered it by building an altar. They had to be careful though not to make those memorials a "sacred place" or worship other gods like the nations around them. Otherwise, like in Leviticus 26:30, God said he would destroy these places and pile their dead bodies on top of them. Here are a few of the places of remembrance—special places where people worshiped and what happened there to make them special.

Place of Worship	Why It Was Special
SHILOH	First permanent place for the sacred tent (Joshua 18:1-2).
GILGAL	God made the water of the Jordan River to stand up like a wall so the Isrealites could cross over to Gilgal. Twelve stones, one for each tribe, were put there to remember it (Joshua 4:19). For a time it became the main religious center where decisions were made.
JERUSALEM	The temple of Solomon was built there (1 Kings 8:1).
SHECHEM	The place where God promised Abraham that he would give the land to his descendants (Genesis 12:6-8).
BETHEL	The place where Jacob had a dream of a stairway to heaven with angels going up and down it and where God renewed his promise to give the land to his descendants (Genesis 28:10-19).

BEYOND THE TEMPLE AND INTO TODAY

Maybe you have seen some connections between the Old Testament worship and the way that Christians worship today. There are many forms of worship and places of worship. Here are some interesting facts about worship since ancient times.

the Synagogue

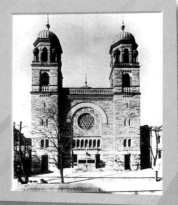

The word *synagogue* is a Greek word meaning "a gathering or assembly of people." Synagogues were small meeting places where Israelites read and discussed the Torah and prayed. Though it is not known when these meeting places began, it is believed that they sprung up after the exile to Babylonia because there was no temple at which to worship. In the New Testament, we often see Jesus and his disciples at the synagogue (Matthew 4:23; Luke 4:16-30).

the House Church

After Jesus was resurrected from the dead, small groups of people began to meet in an upper room to pray (Acts 1:12-13). With the arrival of the Holy Spirit at Pentecost (Acts 2:1-13) and the baptism of about three thousand people on that day (2:41), regular meetings in homes became more widespread (2:42-47). Christians met to encourage one another and recall what Jesus had done for them (Romans 16:5).

Because of their belief in Jesus, many Christians were treated badly by the government leaders. Some were thrown out of the synagogues (John 9:24-34). Meeting in the homes of fellow believers allowed them a place to meet and talk about their faith in Jesus. The missionary journeys of the apostle Paul led to the creation of many house churches.

Churches today

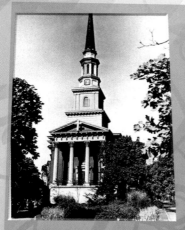

There are many kinds of churches and many ways to worship. Some churches have pastors or priests. Some Christians wear robes, some worship quietly, and some worship with a lot of sound and activity. Some churches have a liturgical format where the same phrases and Scriptures are used each week and the congregation sits and stands or kneels and says prayers of confession in unison. Others have a more spontaneous atmosphere. Many have a band, a particular scriptural message, and distinctive prayers. But whatever the setting, the important thing is an attitude of reverence and awe of God.

WORSHIP PRACTICES

Here are some worship practices Christians follow that you might recognize:

Communion

During the Lord's Supper, Jesus broke bread and passed it and a cup of wine to his disciples. He explained that the bread was his body and the cup of wine was his blood (Matthew 26:26-30; 1 Corinthians 11:17-34). This event is called by a number of names today: Communion, the Lord's Supper, and Holy Eucharist.

iStock.com

Offerings

A basket or plate is passed around or placed in the back of the church where people can offer a portion of their money to God. Giving a portion or a tithe (ten percent) has been a practice in existence since the time of Abraham (Genesis 14:17-20). In the law given to Moses, the people of Israel were required to give a tithe of their harvest to God (Leviticus 27:30).
Traveling preachers like Paul were often supported by the offerings given by others (2 Corinthians 8–9; Philippians 4:14-20). Many Christians today give a tithe of their income as an offering to the local church.

Baptism

In this ceremony a person is either immersed in or sprinkled with water. This is an outward symbol that a follower of Jesus has turned to God and become a member of God's family. This has its roots in the word *tevilah* (or immersion) and comes from the *mikveh* ritual where a person washed to be purified from something unclean (Numbers 19). Another example was the washing part of the ceremony when priests were ordained (Leviticus 8:6-7). Jesus was baptized before he began his ministry (Matthew 3:13-17; Mark 1:9-11; Luke 3:21-23). Before he ascended to heaven, he told his disciples to make disciples and "baptize them in the name of the Father, the Son, and the Holy Spirit" (Matthew 28:19).

DID YOU KNOW?

Labyrinths were discovered in cathedrals of the Middle Ages. In labyrinths, geometrical designs were composed from various pieces of colored marble set in the floors. People walked through the paths and tried to find the center point while thinking about God. Some people think that these may have helped medieval Christians fulfill vows to visit Israel and experience the roots of their beliefs without physically making a trip to the Holy Land.

INDEX

SOURCES

Angels: Kee, Howard Clark, et al., eds. *The Learning Bible*. New York: American Bible Society, 2000.; http://en.wikipedia.org; http://www.inarnia.net/obr-PB.htm
Animals: http://www.americanbirdguide.com/quail.shtml; http://animaldiversity.ummz.umich.edu; http://www.bbc.co.uk/nature/wildfacts/factfiles/415.shtml; http://www.sandiegozoo.org; http://www.factmonster.com; http://www.dailymail.co.uk/pages/live/articles/news/news.html?in_article_id=471121&in_page_id=1770; http://www.mountvernon.org/visit/plan/index.cfm/pid/284/; http://depts.washington.edu/natmap/facts/barn_swallow_712.html; Kee, Howard Clark, et al., eds. *The Learning Bible*. New York: American Bible Society, 2000.
Art: *Great Bible Stories and Master Paintings*. New York: Abradale Press, 1968.; http://198.62.75.5/www1/ofm/sbf/escurs/Giord/04aGiordEn.html (Mosaic floors—Jordan); http://www.ancientworlds.net/aw/Post/125553; http://www.britannica.com/eb/article-9031718/Early-Christian-art; http://www.britannica.com/eb/article-9038593/Gutenberg-Bible; http://www.britannica.com/eb/article-9108722/Michelangelo; http://www.britannica.com/eb/article-9054085/Mozarabic-art; http://www.ecva.org/congregations/features/st_pauls_franklin/st_pauls_franklin_tn.pdf (stained glass); http://www.hunews.huji.ac.il/articles.asp?cat=6&artID=827 (Mosaic floors—Galilee); http://www.le.ac.uk/archaeology/stj/dura.htm (School of Archeological Studies, University of Leicester); http://www.metmuseum.org/explore/Byzantium/byzhome.html ("The Glory of Byzantium," Metropolitan Museum of Art, New York); http://www.mobia.org/index.php; http://www.stjohndivine.org/index.html (stained glass); http://www.stjohndivine.org/documents/CathedralHistory.pdf (stained glass); http://www.turismo-prerromanico.es/arterural/base/MOZARABEING.htm; Kee, Howard Clark, et al., eds. *The Learning Bible*. New York: American Bible Society, 2000.; Van der Meer, F., *Early Christian Art*. Chicago: University of Chicago Press, 1967.
The Bible: Anderson, Ken, *Where to Find It in the Bible*. Nashville: Thomas Nelson, 1996.; Davis, Kenneth C., *Don't Know Much about the Bible*. New York: Eagle Brook, 1998.; Kee, Howard Clark, et al., eds. *The Learning Bible*. New York: American Bible Society, 2000.; *Life Application Bible*. Iowa Falls: World, 1989.
Buildings and Landmarks: *Archaeological Study Bible*. Grand Rapids, MI: Zondervan, 2005.; http://abcnews.go.com/GMA/7Wonders/story?id=2583185&page=1; http://www.bible-history.com/babylonia/BabyloniaThe_Ishtar_Gate.htm; http://www.history.com; http://news.nationalgeographic.com/news/2007/07/photogalleries/seven-wonders/index.html. 2-16-08; http://unmuseum.mus.pa.us/hangg.htm; http://www.new7wonders.com/classic/en/n7w/results/; http://www.history.com/minisite.do?content_type=Minisite_Generic&content_type_id=54819&display_order=2&mini_id=54814. 2-16-08; Joyce, C. Alan, et al. (editors), "The Seven Wonders of the Ancient World," *2008 World Almanac & Book of Facts* (New York: The Rosen Group, 2008).; Kee, Howard Clark, et al., eds. *The Learning Bible*. New York: American Bible Society, 2000.; Miller, Stephen M. *Who's Who and Where's Where in the Bible?* Uhrichsville, OH: Barbour Publishing, 2001.; Schippe, Cullen, Stetson, Chuck, *The Bible and Its Influence*. Fairfax, VA: BLP Publishing, 2006.; Whitehouse, David. "Library of Alexandria Discovered," BBC News Online, 12 May; 2004, http://news.bbc.co.uk/2/hi/science/nature/3707641.stm.;
Calendar and Holidays: Douglas, J.D., et al., eds. *New Bible Dictionary*, 2nd ed. Wheaton, IL: Tyndale House and Intervarsity Press, 1962, 1980.; http://en.wikipedia.org; http://www.bible.org; http://www.christianity.about.com; http://www.crivoice.org/cyeaster.html (The Voice); Kee,

Howard Clark, et al., eds. *The Learning Bible*. New York: American Bible Society, 2000.
Christmas: http://en.wikipedia.org/wiki; http://inventors.about.com/od/cstartinventions/a/Xmas_Lights.htm; http://www.christiananswers.net; http://www.christianitytoday.com/history/newsletter/christmas/cane.html; http://www.factmonster.com; http://www.biography.com/search/article.do?id=9177011; http://goitaly.about.com/od/christmasinitaly/a/nativity_2.htm; http://www.crivoice.org/cy12days.html; http://en.wikipedia.org/wiki; http://inventors.about.com/od/cstartinventions/a/Xmas_Lights.htm; http://www.info4net.com/articles/christmas-gift-giving/index.html; http://www.thehistoryofchristmas.com/trivia/gifts.htm
Clothing and Cosmetics: Elwell, Walter A., Philip W. Comfort, eds., *Tyndale Bible Dictionary*. Wheaton, IL: Tyndale House, 2001.; http://www.biblesociety.com; http://www.biblefragrances.net; http://www.studylight.org/dic/hbd; http://www.womeninthebible.net;
Creation: http://cf.blueletterbible.org/lang/lexicon/lexicon.cfm?Strongs=H0120&Version=kjv); http://www.htmlbible.com/sacrednamebiblecom/kjvstrongs/index2.htm; http://www.perseus.tufts.edu/cgi-bin/ptext?doc=Perseus%3Atext%3A1999.04.0062%3Aid%3Deuphrates2); http://strongsnumbers.com/greek/2096.htm; http://www.windows.ucar.edu/tour/link=/earth/moons_and_rings.html&edu=elem;
Crime and Punishment: *How People Lived in the Bible*. Nashville: Thomas Nelson, Inc., 2002.; http://www.factmonster.com; http://www.geocities.com/TimesSquare/Dungeon/1461/rome28.htm?200825; Kee, Howard Clark, et al., eds. *The Learning Bible*. New York: American Bible Society, 2000.; *Zondervan's Compact Bible Dictionary*. Grand Rapids: Zondervan, 1993.
Currency: Barclay, William, *The Gospel of Luke*. Louisville: Westminster-Jon Knox Press, 2001.; Elwell, Walter A., Philip W. Comfort, eds. *Tyndale Bible Dictionary*. Wheaton, IL: Tyndale House, 2001.; http://en.wikipedia.org/wiki; http://www.projects.ex.ac.uk/RDavies/arian/amser/chrono1.html; http://www.biblegateway.com; http://www.studylight.org/dic/hbd; http://www.studylight.org/grk/vlew.cgi?number=1323; Kee, Howard Clark, et al., eds. *The Learning Bible*. New York: American Bible Society, 2000.; *The Illustrated Bible Dictionary*, vol. 2. Wheaton: Tyndale House/Inter-Varsity Press, 1980.
Customs and Culture: Corswant, W. *A Dictionary of Life in Bible Times*. London: Hodder & Stoughton Ltd., 1960.; Himelstein Rabbi Dr. Shmuel, *The Jewish Primer: Questions and Answers on Jewish Faith and Culture*. New York: Facts on File Publications, 1990.; Kee, Howard Clark, et al., eds. *The Learning Bible*. New York: American Bible Society, 2000.; Keener, Craig S. *The IVP Bible Background Commentary, New Testament*. Downers Grove, IL: InterVarsity Press, 1993.; Ryken, Leland, et al., gen. eds. *A Dictionary of Biblical Imagery*. Intervarsity Press, 1998.; Sherman, Joseph, *Your Travel Guide to Ancient Israel*. Minneapolis: Lerner Publishing, 2004.; Walton, John H, et al. gen. eds. *The IVP Bible Background Commentary, Old Testament*. Downers Grove, IL: InterVarsity Press, 2000.; http://members.aol.com/zimlechem/Ancient_Is.html
Disasters and Catastrophes: Achtemeier, Paul J., gen. ed., *Harper's Bible Dictionary*. San Francisco: Harper & Row, 1985.; Dowley, Tim, Stephen Motyer, eds. *The Crossway Illustrated Bible Handbook*. Wheaton: Crossway Books, 2005.; Kee, Howard Clark, et al., eds. *The Learning Bible*. New York: American Bible Society, 2000.; Metzger, Bruce M. and Coogan, Michael D., eds., *The Oxford Companion to the Bible*. New York: Oxford, 1993.; Ryken, Philip Graham, R. Kent Hughes, ed., *Exodus: Saved For God's Glory*. Wheaton, IL: Crossway, 2005.

Disciples: Achtemeier, Paul J., gen. ed., *Harper's Bible Dictionary*. San Francisco: Harper & Row, 1985.; Kee, Howard Clark, et al., eds. *The Learning Bible*. New York: American Bible Society, 2000.; *Life Application Bible* (NRSV). Iowa Falls: World, 1989.

Easter: Kee, Howard Clark, et al., eds. *The Learning Bible*. New York: American Bible Society, 2000.; http://encarta.msn.com; http://www.factmonster.com; http://www.news.monstersandcritics.com; http://www.lastdaysofchrist.com; http://www.festivals.iloveindia.com/easter/traditions/easter-in-israel.html; http://www.italiaplease.com; http://www.roadsideamerica.com; http://www.whitehouse.gov/easter/history.html; *Zondervan's Compact Bible Dictionary*. Grand Rapids: Zondervan, 1993.

Education: Corswant, W. *A Dictionary of Life in Bible Times*. London: Hodder & Stoughton Ltd., 1960.; Elwell, Walter A., Philip W. Comfort, eds. *Tyndale Bible Dictionary*. Wheaton, IL: Tyndale House, 2001.; Himelstein Rabbi Dr. Shmuel, *The Jewish Primer: Questions and Answers on Jewish Faith and Culture*. New York: Facts on File Publications, 1990.

Food: Kee, Howard Clark, et al., eds. *The Learning Bible*. New York: American Bible Society, 2000.; Packer, J. I., M.C. Tenney, eds., *Illustrated Manners and Customs*. Nashville: Thomas Nelson, 1980.

Geography: *Archaeological Study Bible* (NIV). Grand Rapids, MI: Zondervan, 2005.; David, Leonard, "Satellite Closes in on Noah's Ark Mystery," from *Space.com*. 2006, posted at http://www.cnn.co/2006/TECH/space/03/13/satellite.noahs.ark/index.html.; Kee, Howard Clark, et al., eds. *The Learning Bible*. New York: American Bible Society, 2000.; Miller, Stephen M. *Who's Who and Where's Where in the Bible?* Uhrichsville, OH: Barbour Publishing, 2001.; Rowen, Beth, ed., *Time for Kids Almanac 2008*. New York: Time, Inc., 2007.; http://198.62.75.4/www1/ofm/fai/FAInebo1.html; http://encarta.msn.com/*encyclopedia_761568078/great_rift_valley*.html (Great Rift Valley); http://www.ancientsandals.com/overviews/mount_carmel.htm; http://www.bibleplaces.com/elahvalley.htm; http://www.biblicalheritage.org/Archaeology/eden.htm; http://www.extremescience.com/DeadSea.htm; http://www.factmonster.com; http://www.geographia.com; http://www.mountainsprings.org/userfiles/file/Israel/Outline%20of%20Jezreel%20Valley%201.pdf

God: Kee, Howard Clark, et al., eds. *The Learning Bible*. New York: American Bible Society, 2000.; http://www.bible.org; http://www.preceptaustin.org/attributes_of_god.htm; Lewis, C. S. *The Problem of Pain*. New York: Harper Collins, 2001, page 91 (quote).; Roberts, Rev. Alexander, James Donaldson. "The Five Books Against Marcion," chapter X of in *The Ante-Nicene Fathers: Translations of the Writings of the Fathers Down through A.D. 325*. New York: Charles Scribner & Sons, 1903, page 278, downloaded from http://books.google.com.

Government: Dowley, Dr. Tim, ed. *The History of Christianity*. Oxford, England: Lion Publishing, 1977.; Elwell, Walter A., Philip W. Comfort, eds. *Tyndale Bible Dictionary*. Wheaton, IL: Tyndale House, 2001.; Kee, Howard Clark, et al., eds. The Learning Bible. New York: American Bible Society, 2000.; Smith, William, Sir. *Smith's Bible Dictionary*. New York: Thomas Nelson, 1986.; Willmington, H.L., *Wilmington's Book of Bible Lists*. Wheaton, IL: Tyndale, 1987.

Health and Body: Corswant, W. *A Dictionary of Life in Bible Times*. London: Hodder & Stoughton Ltd., 1960.; http://www.journals.uchicago.edu/doi/pdf/10.1086/313562?cookieSet=1; http://archinte.ama-assn.org/cgi/content/full/159/19/2273?maxtoshow=&HITS=10&hits=10&RESULTFORMAT=&fulltext=prayer&searchid=1&FIRSTINDEX=0&resourcetype=HWCIT; Kee,

Howard Clark, et al., eds. *The Learning Bible*. New York: American Bible Society, 2000.; Packer, J. I., M.C. Tenney, eds., *Illustrated Manners and Customs*. Nashville: Thomas Nelson, 1980.; Rosner, Dr. Fred. *Medicine in the Bible and the Talmud, Selections from Classical Jewish Sources*. New York: Ktav Publishing House, Inc, 1977.

Heaven: Alcorn, Randy. *Heaven*. Carol Stream, IL: Tyndale House, 2004.; Alcorn, Randy with Linda Washington. *Heaven for Kids*. Carol Stream, IL: Tyndale House, 2006, page 180 (quote).; *Zondervan's Compact Bible Dictionary*. Grand Rapids: Zondervan, 1993.; Kee, Howard Clark, et al., eds. *The Learning Bible*. New York: American Bible Society, 2000.; Piper, Don with Cecil Murphey. *90 Minutes in Heaven*. Grand Rapids: Revell, 2004, page 33 (quote).; "Heaven—Where Is It? How Do We Get There? Barbara Walters Explores the Meaning of Heaven and Afterlife," posted at http://abcnew.go.com/2020/Beliefs/story?id=142258http://abcnews.go.com/International/Beliefs/story?id=1374010.

Heroes: Elwell, Walter A., Philip W. Comfort, eds. *Tyndale Bible Dictionary*. Wheaton, IL: Tyndale House, 2001.; http://archive.operainfo.org/broadcast/operaMain.cgi?id=99&language=1; http://www.bibles.com/absport/news/item.php?id=151; http://www.britannica.com/eb/article-9043921/Jonathan; http://www.britannica.com/eb/article-12585/Moses; http://www.britannica.com/eb/article-9065239/Samson; http://www.britannica.com/eb/article-9072539/Saint-Timothy; http://www.studylight.org/dic/hbd/view.cgi?number=T6244; http://www.studylight.org/dic/hbd/view.cgi?word=samson&action=Lookup; http://www.studylight.org/dic/hbd/view.cgi?number=T4372; http://www.studylight.org/dic/ats/view.cgi?word=joseph&action=Lookup; Kee, Howard Clark, et al., eds. *The Learning Bible*. New York: American Bible Society, 2000.

History: Kee, Howard Clark, et al., eds. *The Learning Bible*. New York: American Bible Society, 2000.; http://en.wikipedia.org/wiki/Timeline_of_Christianity; http://www.britannica.com/eb/article-2941; http://www.britannica.com/eb/article-9021816; http://www.churchtimeline.com

Holy Land: Douglas, J.D., et al., eds. *New Bible Dictionary*. 2nd ed. Wheaton, IL: Tyndale House and Intervarsity Press, 1962, 1980.; Kee, Howard Clark, et al, eds. *The Learning Bible*. New York: American Bible Society, 2000.; http://www.britannica.com/eb/article-219421; http://www.britannica.com/eb/article-45058; http://www.jewfaq.org/israel.htm; http://lcweb2.loc.gov/frd/cs/iltoc.html; http://www.palestinefacts.org/pf_independence_recognition_who.php

Holy Spirit: Kee, Howard Clark, et al., eds. *The Learning Bible*. New York: American Bible Society, 2000.; http://en.wikipedia.org/wiki/Baptism_of_Jesus; http://www.britannica.com/bps/topic/134014/Council-of-Constantinople; http://www.britannica.com/bps/topic/269934/Holy-Spirit; http://www.factmonster.com/ce6/society/A0824030.html http://www.factmonster.com/ce6/society/A0838203.html; http://www.bible-knowledge.com/fruits-of-the-holy-spirit.html; http://www.allaboutgod.com/gifts-of-the-spirit.htm

Idols and Foreign Gods: Kuhrt, Amelie. *The Ancient Near East*. London: Routledge, 1995.; Smith, William, Sir, *Smith's Bible Dictionary* (New York: Thomas Nelson Publishers, 1986).; Willmington, H.L., *Wilmington's Book of Bible Lists*. Wheaton, IL: Tyndale, 1987.

Jerusalem: Alexander, T. Desmond, et al., eds. *New Dictionary of Biblical Theology*. Downers Grove: InterVarsity Press, 2000.; Browning, W.R.F., ed. *Dictionary of the Bible*. New York: Oxford University Press, 1996.; Cohen, Shaye J.D. *From the Maccabees to the Mishnah*. Philadelphia: Westminster Press, 1987.; Dowley, Tim, Stephen Motyer, eds. *The Crossway Illustrated Bible Handbook*. Wheaton: Crossway Books, 2005.; Kee, Howard Clark, et al., eds. *The Learning Bible*. New York: American Bible Society, 2000.; Yadin, Yigael, *Jerusalem Revealed*. New Haven: Yale University Press, 1975.

Jesus: Barker, Kenneth, gen. ed. *The NIV Study Bible*. Grand Rapids: Zondervan, 1985.; Kee, Howard Clark, et al., eds. *The Learning Bible*. New York: American Bible Society, 2000.; http://www.christianitytoday.com/history/newsletter/2000/dec08.html

Kids in the Bible: Elwell, Walter A., Philip W. Comfort, eds. *Tyndale Bible Dictionary*. Wheaton, IL: Tyndale House, 2001.; http://www.bbc.co.uk/dna/h2g2/A603776; Kee, Howard Clark, et al., eds. The Learning Bible. New York: American Bible Society, 2000.; Thompson, J.A. *Handbook of Life in Bible Times*. Downers Grove, IL: InterVarsity Press, 1986.

Kings and Queens: Barker, Kenneth, gen. ed. *The NIV Study Bible*. Grand Rapids: Zondervan, 1985.; Kee, Howard Clark, et al., eds. *The Learning Bible*. New York: American Bible Society, 2000.; *The Baker Bible Dictionary for Kids*. Baker Book House, 1997.; *The Eerdmans Bible Dictionary*. Grand Rapids: Eerdmans Publishing, 1987.

Languages: *Holman Bible Dictionary*. Nashville: B&H Publishing, 1991.; Kee, Howard Clark, et al., eds. *The Learning Bible*. New York: American Bible Society, 2000.; Lendering, Jona "Babylonia: country, language, religion, culture," posted at http:///www.livius.org/ba-bd/babylon/babylonia.html; http://en.wikipedia.org; http://www.BibleGateway.com; http://www.britannica.com; http://www.ChristianAnswers.net

Literature: *Bede's Ecclesiastical History*. London: George Bell and Sons, 1907.; Cowan, Louise and Os Guinness, eds. *Invitation to the Classics*. Grand Rapids, MI: Baker Books, 2006.; Gilson , Etienne. *The Christian Philosophy of Saint Augustine*. New York: Random House, 1960.; González, Justo L. *The Story of Christianity*. New York: HarperCollins, 1984.; http://en.wikipedia.org/wiki/C%C3%A6dmon; http://www.britannica.com/eb/article-9018510/Caedmon; http://www.britannica.com/eb/article-9060024/Pilgrims-Progress; http://www.britannica.com/eb/article-24812/Saint-Augustine; http://www.bedfordmuseum.org/johnbunyanmuseum/books.htm; http://www.ccel.org/ccel/bede/history.txt; http://www.fordham.edu/halsall/basis/bede-book1.html; Kee, Howard Clark, et al., eds. *The Learning Bible*. New York: American Bible Society, 2000.

Magic and Fortunetelling: Barker, Kenneth, gen. ed., *The NIV Study Bible*. Grand Rapids: Zondervan, 1985.; *Holman Bible Dictionary*. Nashville: B&H Publishing, 1991.; Kee, Howard Clark, et al., eds. *The Learning Bible*. New York: American Bible Society, 2000.; *Matthew Henry's Commentary on the Whole Bible Complete and Unabridged*. Hendrickson Publishers, Inc. 1991.; Ryken, Leland, et al., gen. eds *A Dictionary of Biblical Imagery*. Intervarsity Press, 1998.; *The American Heritage Dictionary*. New York: Bantam Doubleday Dell Publishing Group, Inc., 1983.; *The Illustrated Bible Dictionary*, vol. 2. Wheaton: Tyndale House/Inter-Varsity Press, 1980.; http://www.BibleGateway.com; http://www.britannica.com

Miracles: Kee, Howard Clark, et al., eds. *The Learning Bible*. New York: American Bible Society, 2000.; Miller, Stephen M., *How to Get Into the Bible*. Nashville, Tennessee: Thomas Nelson Publishers, 1998.; *What Does the Bible Say About . . . The Ultimate A to Z Resource*. Nashville, Tennessee: Thomas Nelson, 2001.; *Zondervan's Compact Bible Dictionary*. Grand Rapids: Zondervan, 1993.

Movies: http://en.wikipedia.org; http://justus.anglican.org/resources/bio/73.html; http://movies.nytimes.com/movie/41635/The-Robe/overview; http://news.bbc.co.uk/cbbcnews/hi/newsid_4070000/newsid_4073600/4073673.stm; http://www.ben-hur.com/meet.html; http://www.factmonster.com; http://www.filmsite.org/aa56.html; http://www.imdb.com; http://www.jesusfilm.org; http://www.newjerusalemcommunity.net/?c=49&a+1951; http://www.rottentomatoes.com; http://www.texasfasola.org/biographies/johnnewton.html; http://www.tcm.com/tcmdb/title.

jsp?scarlettTitleId=79235; http://www.thenativitystory.com/cast.html; http://www.worldnetdaily.com/news/article.asp?ARTICLE_ID=33168

Music: Fleming, William and Macomber, Frank, *Musical Arts & Styles*. Gainesville: University of Florida Press, 1990.; Freedman, David Noel, ed. *The Anchor Bible Dictionary*. New York: Bantam, 1992.; Kee, Howard Clark, et al., eds. *The Learning Bible*. New York: American Bible Society, 2000.; Libbey, Ted, *The NPR Listener's Encyclopedia of Classical Music*. New York: Workman Publishing, 2006.; "Music," *Encyclopædia Britannica 2007 Deluxe Edition*. Chicago: Encyclopædia Britannica, 2008.

Names: Dowley, Tim, Stephen Motyer, eds. *The Crossway Illustrated Bible Handbook*. Wheaton: Crossway Books, 2005.; Koessler, John, *Names of the Believers*. Chicago: Moody Press, 1997.; Peterson, Sarah M., ed., *The Book of Names*. Wheaton, IL: Tyndale House, 1997.; Robinson, George *Essential Judaism*. New York: Pocket Books, 2000.; Rowley, H.H. *Dictionary of Bible Personal Names*. London: Nelson, 1968.; Ryken, Philip Graham, *Exodus: Saved for God's Glory*. Wheaton, IL: Crossway, 2005.; Tabb, Mark A., *Names of Heroes of the Faith*. Chicago: Moody Press, 1997.

Nations: http://creationwiki/index.php/Arvadites; http://net.bible.org/dictionary.php?dict=dictionaries&word=hamath; http://net.bible.org/dictionary.php?word=Zemarites; http://www.bible-history.com/map-israel-joshua/map-israel-joshua_the_girgashites_encyclopedia.html; http://www.britannica.com/EBchecked/topic/376237/Meroe; http://www.studylight.org/dic/hbd/view.cgi?number=T6566; Kee, Howard Clark, et al., eds. *The Learning Bible*. New York: American Bible Society, 2000.; Kuhrt, Amelie, *The Ancient Near East*. London: Routledge, 1995.; Smith, William, Sir., *Smith's Bible Dictionary*. New York: Thomas Nelson, 1986.; Starr, Chester G, *A History of the Ancient World*. Oxford: Oxford University Press, 1983.

Numbers: Kee, Howard Clark, et al., eds. *The Learning Bible*. New York: American Bible Society, 2000.; http://news.bbc.co.uk/1/hi/world/americas/7163767.stm; http://www.biblestudy.org/bibleref/meaning-of-numbers-in-bible/introduction.html; http://www.studylight.org/dic/hbd/; http://www.usatoday.com/news/nation/2006-06-05-sixes-devil_x.htm

Paul: Barker, Kenneth, gen. ed., *The NIV Study Bible*. Grand Rapids: Zondervan, 1985.; Kee, Howard Clark, et al., eds. *The Learning Bible*. New York: American Bible Society, 2000.; *New American Revised Standard Bible*. Philadelphia and New York: A.J. Holman Company, 1973.; http://www.biblemap.org; http://www.biblequestions.org; http://www.britannica.com/EBchecked/topic/447019/Saint-Paul-the-Apostle#default; http://www.christiananswers.net/dictionary/paul.html

Plants of the Holy Land: Barker, Kenneth, gen. ed., *The NIV Study Bible*. Grand Rapids: Zondervan, 1985.; "Bible Wood Spotlight: Broom," http://www.inspiredwoods.com/newsletters_broom.php.; Browning, W.R. F. *A Dictionary of the Bible*. New York: Oxford University Press, 1996.; Dowley, Tim, Stephen Motyer, eds. *The Crossway Illustrated Bible Handbook*. Wheaton: Crossway Books, 2005.; Kee, Howard Clark, et al., eds. *The Learning Bible*. New York: American Bible Society, 2000.; Ryken, Philip Graham, *Jeremiah and Lamentations: From Sorrow to Hope*. Wheaton, IL: Crossway, 2001.; Metzger, Bruce M., Michael D. coogan, *The Oxford Guide to Ideas & Issues of the Bible*. Oxford University Press, 2001.; Walker, Winifred, *All the Plants of the Bible*. New York: Doubleday & Company, Inc., 1979.; Willmington, H.L., *Wilmington's Book of Bible Lists*. Wheaton, IL: Tyndale, 1987.; http://www.christusrex.org/www1/ofm/mag/HolyLnA4.html.

Prayers: Kee, Howard Clark, et al., eds. *The Learning Bible*. New York: American Bible Society, 2000.; http://skdesigns.com/internet/articles/prose/niebuhr/serenity_prayer; http://www.britannica.com/eb/article-9024975; http://www.christnotes.org/-/_100-amazing-answers-to-prayer_0800758315.asp; http://www.prayerfoundation.org/st_patricks_breastplate_prayer.htm; http://www.the-serenity-prayer.com/home.php

Priests: Achtemeier, Paul J., gen. ed., *Harper's Bible Dictionary*. San Francisco: Harper & Row, 1985.; Browning, W.R.F., ed., *Dictionary of the Bible*. New York: Oxford University Press, 1996.; Dever, Mark, *The Message of the New Testament*. Wheaton, IL: Crossway, 2005.; Dowley, Tim, Stephen Motyer, eds. *The Crossway Illustrated Bible Handbook*. Wheaton: Crossway Books, 2005.; Elwell, Walter A., Philip W. Comfort, eds., *Tyndale Bible Dictionary*. Wheaton, IL: Tyndale House, 2001.; *Holman Concise Bible Dictionary*. Nashville: B&H Publishing, 1997.; Kee, Howard Clark, et al., eds. *The Learning Bible*. New York: American Bible Society, 2000.; Willmington, H.L., *Wilmington's Book of Bible Lists*. Wheaton, IL: Tyndale, 1987.

Professions and Tools: Douglas, J.D., et al., eds. *New Bible Dictionary*, 2nd ed. Wheaton, IL: Tyndale House and Intervarsity Press, 1962, 1980.; Gordon, Cyrus H., and Gary A. Rendsburg, *The Bible and the Ancient Near East*. New York: W.W. Norton & Company, 1997.; Hinnells, John R., Editor, *A Handbook of Ancient Religions*. New York: Cambridge University Press, 2007.; http://www.www.britannica.com/eb/article-9008087; Kee, Howard Clark, et al., eds. *The Learning Bible*. New York: American Bible Society, 2000.; Thompson, J. A. *Handbook of Life in Bible Times*. Downers Grove, IL: InterVarsity Press, 1986.

Prophets and Prophecies: http://instruct1.cit.cornell.edu/courses/nes263/spring06/dri6/plagueinjoel.html; http://www.britannica.com/eb/article-23085/Israel; http://www.britannica.com/dictionary?va=feet%20of%20clay; http://www.britannica.com/eb/article-32935/international-relations; http//www.learnthebible.org//Prophets.htm; Kee, Howard Clark, et al., eds. *The Learning Bible*. New York: American Bible Society, 2000.; *Life Application Study Bible* (Wheaton: IL, Tyndale House, 2004).; *The New Scofield Reference Bible*. New York: Oxford University Press, 1967.

Religion: Gordon, Cyrus H., and Gary A. Rendsburg, *The Bible and the Ancient Near East*. New York: W.W. Norton & Company, 1997.; Hinnells, John R., ed. *A Handbook of Ancient Religions*. New York: Cambridge University Press, 2007.; http://www.geocities.com/albaland/apollonia3; http://www.theoi.com/Olympios/Ares.html; Kee, Howard Clark, et al., eds. *The Learning Bible*. New York: American Bible Society, 2000.; Thompson, J.A. *Handbook of Life in Bible Times*. Downers Grove, IL: InterVarsity Press, 1986.

Satan and Demons: Gordon, Cyrus H., Gary A. Rendsburg. *The Bible and the Ancient Near East*. New York: W.W. Norton & Company, 1997.; Hinnells, John R., ed. *A Handbook of Ancient Religions*. New York: Cambridge University Press, 2007.; Kee, Howard Clark, et al., eds. *The Learning Bible*. New York: American Bible Society, 2000.

Transportation: Coleman, William L, *Today's Handbook of Bible Times & Customs*. Minneapolis: Bethany House, 1984.; Gower, Ralph. *The New Manners and Customs of Bible Times*. Chicago: Moody Press, 1987.; Kee, Howard Clark, et al., eds. *The Learning Bible*. New York: American Bible Society, 2000.; Miller, Stephen M. *Who's Who and Where's Where in the Bible?* Uhrichsville, OH: Barbour Publishing, 2001.

Weapons and Warfare: Elwell, Walter A., Philip W. Comfort, eds., *Tyndale Bible Dictionary*. Wheaton, IL: Tyndale House, 2001.; http://www.britannica.com; Kee, Howard Clark, et al., eds. *The Learning Bible*. New York: American Bible Society, 2000.; Willmington, H.L., *Wilmington's Book of Bible Lists*. Wheaton, IL: Tyndale, 1987.

Weights and Measures: Barker, Kenneth, gen. ed., *The NIV Study Bible*. Grand Rapids: Zondervan, 1985.; http://www.bibles.com/brcpages/WeightsandMeasures; Kee, Howard Clark, et al., eds. *The Learning Bible*. New York: American Bible Society, 2000.

Women: Barker, Kenneth, gen. ed., *The NIV Study Bible*. Grand Rapids: Zondervan, 1985.; *Holman Bible Dictionary*. Nashville: B&H Publishing, 1991.; http://sonrisecenter.org/m_gladys.html; http://www.BibleGateway.com; http://www.Britannica.com; http://www.cnn.com/WORLD/9709/mother.teresa/profile/index.html; Kee, Howard Clark, et al., eds. *The Learning Bible*. New York: American Bible Society, 2000.; Kiefer, James E., "Gladys Aylward, Missionary to China," posted at http://justus.anglican.org/resources/bio/73.html; *Matthew Henry's Commentary on the Whole Bible Complete and Unabridged*. Hendrickson Publishers, Inc. 1991.; *The Illustrated Bible Dictionary*. Wheaton: Tyndale House/Inter-Varsity Press, 1980.; Ryken, Leland, et al., gen. eds. *A Dictionary of Biblical Imagery*. Intervarsity Press, 1998.

Worship: Achtemeier, Paul J. gen. ed., *Harper's Bible Dictionary*. San Francisco: Harper & Row, 1985.; "Baptism—Pagan or Jewish? by Ceil Rosen," July 1, 1983, posted at http://jewsforjesus.org/publications/issues/2_10/baptism; Gordon, Cyrus H., and Gary A. Rendsburg, *The Bible and the Ancient Near East*. New York: W.W. Norton & Company, 1997.; Hinnells, John R., ed.. *A Handbook of Ancient Religions*. New York: Cambridge University Press, 2007.; http://www.britannica.com/eb/article-9046731/labyrinth; Kee, Howard Clark, et al., eds. *The Learning Bible*. New York: American Bible Society, 2000.; *Life Application Study Bible*. Wheaton: IL, Tyndale House, 2004.; Weber, Robert E., *Twenty Centuries of Christian Worship*. Nashville: Hendrickson Publishers, 1994.

IMAGE CREDITS